Evelyn Sharp

The making of a prig

Evelyn Sharp

The making of a prig

ISBN/EAN: 9783743322332

Manufactured in Europe, USA, Canada, Australia, Japa

Cover: Foto ©ninafisch / pixelio.de

Manufactured and distributed by brebook publishing software (www.brebook.com)

Evelyn Sharp

The making of a prig

THE
MAKING OF A PRIG

BY
EVELYN SHARP

JOHN LANE: THE BODLEY HEAD
NEW YORK AND LONDON
1897

Copyright, 1897,
BY JOHN LANE.
All rights reserved.

University Press:
JOHN WILSON AND SON, CAMBRIDGE, U.S.A.

The Making of a Prig

CHAPTER I

It was supper time at the Rectory, and the Rector had not come in. There were two conflicting elements at the Rectory, the Rector's disregard of details and his sister's sense of their importance. There was only one will, however, and that was his sister's. So the meals were always punctual, and the Rector was always late; a fact that by its very recurrence would have long ceased to be important, had not Miss Esther loved to accentuate it by a certain formula of complaint that varied as little as the offence itself. This evening, however, he was later than usual; and Miss Esther did not attempt to conceal her impatience as she glanced from the old clock in the corner down to the fireplace, where another familiar grievance awaited her.

"Katharine, how often have I told you not to lie on the rug like a great boy?" she said

The Making of a Prig

querulously, in the tone of one who has not the courage or the character to be really angry. She added immediately, "I want you to ring the bell for the soup."

The girl on the floor rolled over lazily, and shut her book with a bang.

"Daddy hasn't come in yet," she said, sitting up on her heels and shaking the hair out of her eyes. A latent spirit of revolt was in her tone, although she spoke half absently, as if her thoughts were still with her book. Miss Esther tapped her foot on the ground impatiently.

"It is exactly two minutes to eight," she said sharply. "I asked you to ring the bell, Katharine."

The girl walked across the room in a leisurely manner, and did as she was told with a great assumption of doing as she wished. Then she sat on the arm of the nearest chair, and the rebellious look returned to her face.

"How do you know it is daddy's fault, Aunt Esther? The Stoke road is awfully bad, and it's blowing hard from the northwest. He may have been kept, and cold soup's beastly. I think it's a shame."

"I really wish," complained Miss Esther, "that you would try and control your expres-

The Making of a Prig

sions, Katharine. It all comes of your romping so much with young Morton. Of course I am a mere cipher in my own house; but some day your father will be sorry that he did not listen to me in time. Can you never remember that you are not a boy?"

"I am not likely to forget," muttered Katharine. "I should not be sticking in this stupid old place if I were. I should be working hard for daddy, so that he could live with his books and be happy, instead of grinding his life away for people who only want to get all they can out of him. What's the use of being a girl? Things are so stupidly arranged, it seems to me!"

"My dear," said Miss Esther, who had only caught the end of her speech, "it is difficult to believe that your father is one of God's chosen ministers."

"But he isn't," objected Katharine. "That's just it. They made him go into the church because there was a family living; so how on earth could he have been chosen? Why, you told me so yourself, Aunt Esther! It's all rubbish about being chosen, isn't it?"

"Don't chatter so much," said Miss Esther, who was counting her stitches; and Katharine sighed petulantly.

The Making of a Prig

"I can't think," she went on to herself, "how he was ever weak enough to give in. He must have been absent-minded when they ordained him, and never discovered it until afterwards! Don't you think so, Dorcas?"

But Dorcas, who had only just brought in the soup, was hardly in a position to make the necessary reply; and Katharine had to content herself with laughing softly at her own joke. The meal passed almost in silence, and they had nearly finished before they heard the sound of wheels on the wet gravel outside. Miss Esther looked up, and listened with her chronic air of disapproval.

"Dear me," she sighed, "your father has driven round to the stable again by mistake. What are you doing, Katharine? I was just going to say grace."

But Katharine had already dispensed with the ceremony by vanishing through the door that led into the kitchen; and Miss Esther hurried over it alone, and managed to be seated in her chair near the reading-lamp, upright and occupied, by the time her brother came into the room. There was something pathetic in the way she elaborated her little methods of reproach for the sake of one on whom the

The Making of a Prig

small things in life made no impression at all. And when the Rector entered, smiling happily, with Katharine hanging on his arm and whispering eager questions into his ear, it was easy to see that his mind was occupied by something far more engrossing than the fact that he was late for supper. But Miss Esther preserved her look of injury, and the Rector, who was making futile efforts to produce a paper parcel from the pocket in his coat tails, suddenly gave up the attempt as he caught sight of her, and began to smooth his sleek white hair with a nervous hand.

"Yes, Esther," he said, although she had not spoken a word.

"We have sent away the soup, but there is some cold meat on the side, I believe. Katharine, do be seated instead of romping round the room like that! Your father can see to himself," was all that Miss Esther said.

"Yes, Esther," said the Rector submissively; and he helped himself to some apple pie, and sat thoughtfully with the knife in his hand until Katharine came and replaced it with a fork. "It is a windy night," he continued, as no one seemed inclined to say anything. Miss Esther was waiting for her

The Making of a Prig

opportunity, and Katharine had caught the infection of her mood, and was again absorbed in her book on the hearthrug.

"Tom Eldridge came up about his dying wife, and Jones's baby is no better," said Miss Esther, presently.

"Dear, dear! how very unfortunate!" observed the Rector, smiling.

"I said you must have been detained unexpectedly," continued Miss Esther, with more emphasis. "They seemed very much in want of a little counsel."

"I'm certain they weren't," said Katharine audibly. "Eldridge wanted some more port wine, and Mrs. Jones came to see what she could get. And I don't fancy either of them got it."

"Very unfortunate!" said the Rector again. "I was certainly detained, Esther, as you cleverly divined,—unavoidably detained."

"People," said Miss Esther, very distinctly, "who have spiritual brothers and sisters depending upon them, have no right to be detained."

"I never can think," put in Katharine, "how any one has the courage to be a clergyman. It simply means having crowds of relations, dull, sordid, grasping relations, who

The Making of a Prig

come and rob you systematically in the name of the Lord."

"A spiritual man," continued Miss Esther, without heeding the interruption, "is not —"

"Oh, auntie," implored Katharine, "do let daddy eat his supper in peace."

"My child," interposed the Rector gently, "I have finished my supper. Does Eldridge expect me to do anything to-night, Esther? Or Mrs. Jones?"

"My dear Cyril," said Miss Esther sternly, "if your own instincts do not prompt you to do anything, I should say they had better go untended."

The Rector sighed, and played with his knife. He was looking like a schoolboy in disgrace. Katharine gave a scornful little laugh.

"What *is* the good of making all that fuss over a trifle? Just as though the cough of Jones's baby were half as important as the genuine rat-tail daddy has picked up at Walker's!"

The murder was out, and Miss Esther put down her knitting and prepared for a characteristic outburst. But the Rector had already unwrapped his treasure and placed it on the table before him, and her bitterest reproaches fell unheeded on his ears.

The Making of a Prig

"Genuine sixteenth century," he murmured, as he stroked it reverently with his long, thin fingers.

"Only yesterday," said the strident voice of his sister, "you were telling me you had no money for a soup kitchen. It was a poor living, you said; and now— How can you set such an example,— you with a mission in life?"

"I vow I'll never have a mission in life," said Katharine, "if it means giving up everything that makes one happy. Poor daddy!"

"One of Christ's elect," continued Miss Esther, "to be turned aside for a bit of tawdry pewter! For what you can see in a tarnished, old-fashioned thing like that, is more than I can understand."

The Rector looked up for the first time.

"Indeed, Esther," he said in a hurt tone, "it is a fine piece of sixteenth century silver." Katharine cast a wrathful look at the stern figure near the reading-lamp, and came over to her father's side. The rebellious note had gone from her voice altogether as she spoke to him.

"Let me look, daddy, may I?" she asked. Cyril Austen pulled her on to his knee, and they bent together over the old spoon. Miss Esther knitted silently.

The Making of a Prig

"Let me see," said the Rector presently, turning an unruffled countenance towards his sister, "what were we saying? About some parishioners, wasn't it?"

"Parishioners? How can you talk of parishioners, when the first trivial temptation draws you from the right path and — and makes you late for meals? Isn't it enough to neglect your sacred duty, without upsetting the household as well? Coming in at this time of — what is it now, Cyril?"

For a worried look had suddenly crossed the Rector's face. He pulled out his watch, and consulted it with the nervous haste of a man who is constantly haunted by having forgotten something.

"Let me see, — how very stupid of me," he said, laughing slightly. "I fancy there was something else, now; whatever could it have been, I wonder? It was not the spoon, Esther, that made me late. Kitty, my child, what did I say to you when I came in, just now?"

"You said, 'I have picked up a genuine rat-tail at Walker's;' and then you gave your hat to Jim, and hung up the whip on the hat peg!"

"Bad child!" said the Rector, still looking

The Making of a Prig

uneasily about him. "I wonder if Jim would know?"

But here a light was thrown on the matter by the entrance of Dorcas, who brought the ambiguous message from Jim that the pony was ready to start again, if the Rector was "going to do anything about the poor creature down agin the chalk pit."

"Bless my soul!" exclaimed the Rector. "To be sure, that was it. Esther, brandy and blankets, my dear,—anything you've got! We must bring him home at once, of course. I knew there was something. Esther, will you—? Ah, she always understands."

For, to do her credit, Miss Esther never wasted her time in reproaches when there was really something to be done; and in the bustle that followed, while the pony carriage was being filled with everything that could be of use in case of an accident, Katharine found herself left in the hall, with the intolerable feeling of being neglected, and burning with curiosity as to the cause of it all.

"Daddy, daddy, what is it? Is any one hurt? May n't I come too?" she pleaded, as the Rector came out to look for his coat.

"Eh, what? Oh, a poor fellow broken his leg in the chalk pit. Doctor's with him now.

The Making of a Prig

What is he like? Kind of tourist, I should fancy; evidently did n't see his way in the dark. There, run off to bed, Kitty; you 'll hear all about it in the morning."

"But I want to hear *now*," said the child, quivering with impatience. "What sort of man is he, daddy? Shall I like him, do you think? Oh, do tell, daddy!"

"My child, I hardly noticed. My hat — ah, thanks! He had a black beard, I fancy, — quite young though, I should say, — and a sallow face —"

"How unhealthy it sounds; and I hate unhealthy people! I don't think I want to go now," said Katharine, in an altered tone.

Nevertheless, when the unwilling pony was being urged again into the storm and the darkness, some one slipped through the little group in the porch, and sprang into the carriage beside the Rector. And the Rector, who was incapable of a decided action himself and never disputed one on the part of others, threw the rug over her knees, and they drove off together to the scene of the accident. It was a wild, black night; and the Rector shivered as he bent his head to the furious gusts of wind, and allowed the pony to struggle on feebly at its

The Making of a Prig

own pace. But Katharine sat upright with her head thrown back, and would have liked to laugh aloud as the wind caught her long loose hair and lashed it, wet with rain, across her face.

The chalk pit was situated at the further end of the village; on a fine day, it might have been reached in a ten minutes' drive, but to-night it was nearly half an hour before the pony managed to bring its load to a standstill beside the group of men who had been waiting there since dusk. Katharine recognised all the village familiars who came forward at their approach,—the doctor, who had tended her childish maladies; the schoolmaster, who had taught her to read; the churchwarden, who still loved to tell her stories that she had long ago learnt to know by heart. But she had no eyes for any of these to-night; she looked beyond them all, as she jumped lightly out of the carriage, at the man who lay on the ground with his eyes closed. A lantern hung from the branch above, and swung to and fro in the wind, casting intermittent gleams of light across his face.

He opened his eyes wearily as the Rector came forward, and they rested at once upon Katharine, who stood bending over him with

The Making of a Prig

the rather heartless curiosity of a very young girl.

"Kitty, move out of the way, my child," the Rector's voice was saying.

"I don't think he looks unhealthy at all," said Katharine dreamily.

CHAPTER II

The sun rose, the following morning, on a scene of devastation. The storm of the previous night had come at the end of a month's hard frost, and everything was in a state of partial thaw. Glistening pools of water lay in the fields on the top of the still frozen ground, looking like patches of snow in the pale sunshine; and a curious phenomenon was discernible in the brooks and the ditches, where a layer of calm water covered the ice that still bound the flowing stream below. The only trace of last night's gale was a distant moaning in the tree-tops; while above was a deepening blueness of sky and a growing warmth in the sunshine. There was winter still on the ground, and the beginning of spring in the air.

Two women had met under the beech-trees at the edge of the chalk pit. Early as it was they had already collected large bundles of sticks; for the beauty of the morning was nothing to them, and the storm, as far as they

The Making of a Prig

were concerned, merely meant the acquisition of firewood. They had matter for conversation enough, however; and it was this that was making them loiter so early in the morning near the scene of yesterday's accident.

"Is it the poor thing what fell down yonder, you be a-talkin' of, Mrs. Jones? 'Cause I see Jim hisself this blessed morning, I did, and you can't tell me nothing I doan't know already, you can't, Mrs. Jones," said Widow Priest with fine scorn.

There was a jealousy of long standing between the two neighbours. Mrs. Jones was the sturdy wife of the sexton, and her family was both large and increasing,—a fact which she attributed entirely to Providence; though, when three of them succumbed to insufficient food and care, she put down their loss to the same convenient cause, and extracted as much consolation as she could out of three visits to the churchyard. Widow Priest, on the other hand, had buried no one in the little churchyard on the hill. For her husband had committed suicide, and they had laid him to an uneasy rest without the sedative of a religious ceremony; and his widow was thus robbed even of the triumph of alluding to his funeral. So her widowhood did not bring her its usual

The Making of a Prig

compensations; and she felt bitter towards the wife of the sexton, who had buried her three and kept five others, and would probably replace the lost ones in time.

"I bain't so fond o' gossiping nor what you be, Widow Priest," returned Mrs. Jones in loud, hearty tones. "I got no time for talking wi' strangers here an' strangers there, wi' my man an' five little 'uns to do for. An' then there's always the three graves of a Saturday to tidy up, which you ain't got, poor thing; not but what I'm saying it be your fault, in course, Widow Priest."

Widow Priest gave a contemptuous sniff as she sat down to tie up her fagots, and Mrs. Jones remained standing in front of her, with one arm thrown round her bundle of sticks, and the other placed akimbo, an effective picture of triumphant woman.

"Touching the poor thing what broke his back yonder," she continued cheerfully: "I was putting the baby to bed at the time, I was, and I see the whole thing happen from my top window, I did. He jumped the fence, all careless like, jest as though he did n't know the pit were there for sure. An' straightway he tripped up, he did, an' down he went. God help him, I says! An' I puts the baby down,

The Making of a Prig

an' I says to our Liz, 'Here, my child,' I says, 'stand by your precious brother while I goes across to the pit,' I says. An' jest as I says that, up comes the Rector an' the doctor with him, driving friendly like together they was. So I says to our Liz, 'It's Providence,' I says, 'what sent they two blessed creatures here this day,' I says. An' I caught up my shawl, I did, an' went hollerin' after them. 'What is it, Mrs. Jones?' says the Rector, 'is it the baby again?'—'Baby?' I says, 'no, sir; not but what it racks me to hear that child cough, it do. There be a man yonder,' I says, 'jest broke his neck down agin the chalk pit.' Lord! it were a sight to see they two men turn that pony round! An' the rain were that bad, it give me lumbago all down my back, that did. Not but what I soon got back to baby again, poor little angel, with a cough that makes my heart ache, to hear it going jest like the others did afore they died. But ye didn't see him fall in, now; did ye, Widow Priest?"

The widow shouldered her fagots grimly, and stalked off with dignity. When she reached the bend of the road, she turned round and shouted a parting word in a tone of unmitigated contempt.

The Making of a Prig

"It bain't his neck, *nor* his back, Mrs. Jones. It be both his legs, an' he be at the Rectory now, in the best bedroom, he be; an' there he'll likely stop a month or two, Jim says, he do. But Jim didn't give ye a call perhaps, Mrs. Jones?"

"Bless ye, Widow Priest, I ain't told ye half what I know," cried Mrs. Jones. "You be a poor thing, you be, if ye can't stand to hear a body's tale; an' you that's so lonesome too, an' got no one to do for, like I have. Lord, what a hurry some folk do be in, for sure! Eh, but that be Miss Katharine yonder, blest if it ain't; an' Widow Priest be out o' sight, too! I reckon as Miss Katharine knows more nor Jim, an' I be going —"

But a wail from the cottage opposite awakened the mother's sense of duty, and she hastened across the road and forgot all about the accident in an immediate necessity for castigation.

Katharine came over the brow of the hill that sloped down towards the chalk pit, scaled the wooden fence at the bottom, and skirted the edge of the little chasm until she came to the line of beech-trees. Here she paused for a moment, pecked a hole in the soft ground with her heel, and peered thoughtfully down

The Making of a Prig

into the pit. Then she turned abruptly away again, and struck across the fields to the further side of the village, where she sped down a grassy lane that was for the most part under water, and stopped at last before a gap in the hedge that was hardly large enough to be noticeable. She squeezed adroitly through it, however, and came in view of an ugly modern house standing in a neglected looking garden, with an untidy farmyard and some stable buildings at the back. Here she was careful to keep a clump of box-trees between herself and the front of the house, until she could come out with safety into the open and approach the iron fence that separated the paddock from the lawn. This she vaulted easily, dropping lightly on the grass beyond, and managed to arrive at last unnoticed, under a small oriel window at the corner of the house. She picked up a handful of small stones, and swung them with a sure aim at the little glass panes, and called, " Coo-ey," as loudly as she dared.

" Lazy toad! " she muttered impatiently. " On a morning like this, too! And just when I had got a real adventure to tell him, that he knows absolutely nothing about, not anything at all! "

The Making of a Prig

She did not throw up any more stones, but mounted the iron railings instead, and sat there with her feet dangling and her eyes fixed on the oriel window.

"It's the biggest score I've ever had over him," she chuckled to herself. "I think I shall *explode* soon, if he doesn't wake up. I'm getting so awfully hungry, too; it must be eight o'clock."

She called again presently, without changing her position; and this time there was a sign of life behind the oriel window, and the curtains were drawn aside. Katharine forgot all her previous caution, and gave a loud "whoop" of satisfaction. The lattice flew open, and some one with rumpled hair and flushed cheeks looked out and yawned.

"Don't make such a shindy, Kit; you'll wake the mother," he grumbled. "Why the dickens have you come so beastly early?"

"Because Aunt Esther was asleep, of course," answered Katharine promptly. "Hurry up, Ted, and have your bath; it'll make you feel piles better. And you'll have to get me some food; I could eat my boots."

"Don't do that," said Ted. "Last night's steak will do just as well."

"How is *she?*" asked Katharine, with a

The Making of a Prig

jerk of her head towards the front of the house.

"Awful. She's getting worse. She docks the pudding course at supper now. Don't go, Kitty; I'll be down directly."

He was not long, but she was full of impatient reproaches by the time he joined her at the fence.

"I believe you'd like to give the world a shove to make it go round quicker," he retorted, swinging himself up beside her.

"Well, you surely don't think it moves very fast now, do you?" she said. "At all events, Ivingdon doesn't," she added emphatically.

"Well, what did you come for, old chum?" he asked, smiting her shoulder with rough friendliness. "Not to complain of this slow old hole, I bet?"

"Get me something to eat, and I'll tell you."

"Oh, hang, Kitty! I can't. Cook will swear, or go to the mother, or something. Can't you wait till you get home?"

"No, I can't. And I didn't tell you to go to cook, or to *her*; did I, stupid? Isn't there a pantry window, and isn't the larder next to the pantry, and aren't the servants having

The Making of a Prig

breakfast in the kitchen, out of the way? Eh?"

"Well, I'm bothered! But I can't get up to that window, anyhow."

"There's a loose brick just below, and you *know* it, you lazy boy! What's the use of being exactly six foot, if you can't climb into a window on the ground floor? *I* can, and I'm only five foot four. Oh, you need n't bother, if you're afraid! I can keep my news, for that matter."

"I don't believe there is any news. Why, I only saw you yesterday afternoon. And nothing ever happens in Ivingdon. You are only rotting, are n't you, Kit?"

"All right; I don't want to tell you, I'm sure. Good-bye," said Katharine, without moving a step.

He called himself a fool, and told her she was a beastly nuisance, and that of course there was n't any news, and he did n't want to hear it if there was. And he finally strolled round to the pantry window, as she knew he would, and returned with a medley of provisions in his hands. They laughed together at the odd selection he had made,—at the cold pie he was balancing on a slice of bread, and the jam tart that crowned the jug of milk; and they fought

The Making of a Prig

over everything like two young animals, and drank out of the same jug and spilled half its contents, and ended in chasing one another round the paddock for no reason whatever.

"Walk home with me, and I'll tell you the news. Come on, Ted!" she cried.

"Guess I will, and chance it. If she does n't like my being late for breakfast she'll have to do the other thing. Through with you, Kitty, and don't make the hole any larger! There's always the chance that she might have it mended, in a spasm of extravagance, and that would be so bally awkward for us."

She told her news as they went swinging along side by side over the wet fields, leaping the pools of standing water, and switching the wet twigs in each other's face. But they grew quieter as the interest of the tale deepened; and by the time Katharine had reached the episode of the chalk pit, Ted was walking gloomily along with his hands in his pockets and his eyes bent on the ground.

"You always have all the luck, Kitty," he said mournfully. "Why was n't I there? Think of the use I should have been in helping him into the carriage; only think of it, Kitty!"

The Making of a Prig

"You wouldn't have been a bit of good," she returned cruelly. "You're much too clumsy. They wouldn't even let Jim or daddy help. *I* held his head, so there!"

"Well, I suppose I could have held his beastly head, too, couldn't I?" roared Ted.

"It wasn't a beastly head; it was awfully nice,—hair all silky, not baby's curls like yours," said Katharine scornfully. "And wasn't he plucky, too! His leg must have hurt frightfully, but he just didn't say a word or utter a sound. All the way home, whenever the thing jolted him, he just screwed up his mouth and looked at me, and that was all. It was the finest thing I've ever seen."

"But you haven't seen much," said Ted.

"No, I haven't. But I've seen you squirm when you had toothache. And you're not fit to speak to if you have an ordinary headache," laughed Katharine.

They walked the rest of the way in silence.

"That is where he lies now," said Katharine, with a dramatic gesture towards the spare-room window. Her cheeks were red with excitement, and she never noticed the look on Ted's face as he shrugged his shoulders and made a great pretence of whistling carelessly.

"What sort of a chap is he? Some tourist

The Making of a Prig

bounder, I suppose," he condescended to say.

"He isn't a bounder. He has awfully nice hands,—white, and thin, and soft. He's rather pale, with a lot of black hair and a curly beard."

"What a played-out chap to make such a fuss about!" said Ted, turning away contemptuously. "Sounds more like a monkey than anything else. Good-bye. I wish you joy of him!"

"I suppose I'll see you again some time?" she called after him.

"Oh, yes; I suppose so."

"And it *was* news, wasn't it, Ted?"

"You seem to think so, anyway."

"Poor Ted!" She laughed, and ran indoors. But he had hardly crossed the first field before she had caught him up again, breathless and penitent.

"I didn't mean it, Ted; I didn't, *really*, old boy. It wasn't news, and he *is* a monkey, and I'm a horrid pig. Come up after lunch, won't you, Ted? I promise not to talk about him once, and I want to show you something. You will come, Ted, won't you?"

She flung her arms round him in her impulsive way, and gave him one of her rough,

The Making of a Prig

playful hugs. But for the first time in his life, Ted shook her off stiffly, and hastened on.

"What's the matter?" asked Katharine, more perplexed than annoyed.

"Oh, all right; I'll come. Don't be a fool, Kitty!" he jerked over his shoulder; and she turned away, only half satisfied, and went slowly into the house. It was characteristic of her that the smallest lack of response from some one else would change her mood immediately; and when she entered the dining-room a few minutes later, her vivacity was all gone, and the first words she caught of the conversation at the breakfast-table only helped to irritate her still further.

"Oh, bother Mr. Wilton!" she said crossly. "The whole house seems to have gone mad over Mr. Wilton. I am tired of hearing his name."

The Rector seemed unconscious of her remark, and only pulled her hair softly as she slipped into the chair beside him. But Miss Esther stopped abruptly in the middle of a sentence, and cast a meaning glance towards Katharine which her father did not see, though she of course did.

"My dear," said Mr. Austen, in reply to his sister, "I am sure you are quite compe-

The Making of a Prig

tent to do it. Nancy always said you were a born nurse; and Nancy knew, bless her! Besides, the poor young man has been sent to us in his affliction, and there is nothing else to be done, is there? My child, it will not interest you; we were only saying that Mr. — Wilton, is it? — would require careful nursing; and your aunt —"

"Really, Katharine, there is no necessity for you to interfere. You know too much as it is, and this question is not one that concerns you at all. Perhaps you will keep to the matter in hand until it is settled, Cyril!"

"My dear, I thought it was settled," said the old man mildly. "The poor young fellow has to be nursed, and you are the best person to do it. So there is nothing else, is there, Esther, that need detain me? I am rather anxious — that is, I would like to finish my paper on the antiquities of the county, and it is already ten minutes past —"

"It is a most extraordinary thing," interrupted Miss Esther irritably, "that you never will give your attention to anything that really matters. You totally misunderstand my meaning, Cyril. How can I, your sister and a single woman, with due propriety — Katharine, you can go and feed the chickens."

The Making of a Prig

Katharine did not move, and the Rector got up from his chair.

"My dear," he remonstrated, "I think you over-estimate the difficulty. It is the duty of the woman to look after the sufferer, is it not? I really think there is nothing more to be said about it. Meanwhile—"

"I don't know why you are in such a hurry, Cyril; it is the day for the library to be cleaned, so you cannot use it yet. The whole business is most inopportune; why should he break his leg in Ivingdon, when he might have done it quite conveniently in the county town, and been taken to the infirmary like any one else?"

The Rector wondered vaguely why his room was cleaned more than once a week; but he sat down again and folded his hands, and said that he was of the same opinion as before and saw no reason why the unfortunate young man should not be nursed by Miss Esther.

"No more do I," said Katharine. "What's the difference between nursing Shepherd Horne through bronchitis and nursing Mr. Wilton with a broken leg, except that Mr. Wilton is presumably not so unwashed? I never can see why the poor people should have the monopoly of impropriety, as well as of the Scriptures. Besides, you can easily reduce him to the level of a villager by reading the Psalms to him every day. That would make you feel quite proper, wouldn't it, auntie? And I dare say he wouldn't mind it much, when he got used to it."

"Your profanity," said her aunt severely, "is becoming perfectly outrageous. If you were sometimes to say a few words of reproof to your own daughter, Cyril, instead of dreaming your life away—but there, I must go and look after poor Mr. Wilton! I wonder whether he likes his eggs boiled or scrambled?" she added doubtfully. For Miss Esther was one of those women who reserve the best side of their nature for the people who have no real claim upon them; and she took little interest in any one who was neither poor nor afflicted. The unpractical temperament of the Rector both astonished and chafed her, and she had nothing but a fretful endurance for her high-spirited niece, in whom a natural longing for action and an inordinate sense of humour were fast producing a spirit of revolt and cynicism. But an invalid, who was thus thrown suddenly into her power, appealed strongly to the Rector's sister; and her diffidence had entirely disappeared by the time

The Making of a Prig

she had gone through all the objections that propriety impelled her to raise.

"I feel quite thankful," she said, smiling blandly, "that the poor fellow has fallen into such good hands."

"So do I," remarked Katharine, as the door closed. "It will be all the better for your paper on the local antiquities, won't it, daddy? Daddy *dear*, just think of all the time we shall have to ourselves, now that she's got Mr. Wilton on her hands! Poor Mr. Wilton! Let's come and clear Dorcas out of the library and look at what you've done, shall we? Come along, daddy, *quick!*"

The Rector stroked her long hair, with a doubtful look on his face.

"I am afraid, Kitty, I do not look after you as I should," he said. "I am a bad old sinner, eh?"

"That's why I love you so. You are a brick!" exclaimed Katharine.

And she dragged him impetuously out of the room.

CHAPTER III

MEANWHILE, Paul Wilton lay wearily in the old-fashioned guest-room over the porch. The pain of his broken limb had kept him awake most of the night; and now that the suffering was less the discomfort remained, and he felt no more inclined to sleep than before. With a kind of mechanical interest he had watched the pale light on his striped blind grow deep and red, and then again pale and bright, as the sun came up over the hills. His restlessness increased as the time wore on; the sensation of being unable to move began to grate on his nerves, and he wished impatiently that something would break the stillness of the house, and awaken the people in it who were sleeping so unreasonably. He raised himself on his elbow as a light step came along the passage outside, and sank back again with a feeling of disappointment when it passed his door, and went downstairs into the garden. In reality it was much earlier than he thought; and it was still some time longer before the

The Making of a Prig

usual early morning sounds testified to the existence of a maid. He heard the stairs being swept, and suffered silently as the broom was struck clumsily against his wall in its downward course. Then the front door was unbolted with a good deal of noise, and a few mats were banged together in the open air, and something was done with the door scraper. A conversation, held across the lawn with Jim, had the effect of an altercation, though it was in reality only an inquiry on the subject of milk, shouted shrilly in broad dialect. Later on, came the welcome crackle of a fire and the clatter of teacups; and a smell of hot bacon began to pervade the air.

"At all events, that means breakfast," muttered Paul. "It is not to be hoped that it will be worth eating, but at least it will bring a human being into the room. I wonder why ordinary people never have any ideas for breakfast beyond hot bacon! It is sure to be in thick chunks, too, and salt, oh, very salt! Don't I know it? It recalls my childhood. There will be eggs, too,—there always were eggs when we had visitors; and bad coffee made by unaccustomed hands, also because there is a visitor. I know that coffee too. On the whole, it is wiser to keep to tea in strange

The Making of a Prig

places of this sort, although one knows beforehand that it will be thick, and black, and flavourless. I know the tea, best of all. In quite decent houses, one gets that tea."

Nobody came to him, although there were other voices about the house now; and he turned from his dissertation on food to a study of the pictures on the wall. They were of the class that had also been known to him in his childhood; and he smiled sardonically as he glanced at the two texts hidden in a maze of illumination, and the German print of John the Baptist standing in layers of solid water, and the faded photograph of a baby girl with tangled curls and a saucy mouth. Something in the shape of that mouth suggested the shadowy events of last night to his mind, and brought with them the vague recollection of a girl's face looking curiously down at him, and the pleasurable sensation of being supported by two firm, soft hands. He rather liked dwelling on that part of last night's adventures, until a real twinge of pain in his leg recalled also the less pleasant episodes, and he shuddered as he remembered the horrors of his transit from the chalk pit to the Rectory.

"I hate being in pain; it is so vulgar," he muttered distastefully; and a dread crossed his mind lest his suffering should become more than he could bear with dignity.

A timid knock came outside the door, and the maid entered to draw up the blind. She looked clumsy, and Paul sighed. She sidled along the wall to the door again as soon as she could, and asked shyly when he would have his breakfast.

"As soon as you like; and — er — Mary, would you kindly give me that coat? What's the time? And is it a fine day?" asked Paul hurriedly. He was almost childish in his anxiety to keep her in the room for another moment. But to be called by the cook's name so far confused her that she vanished precipitately; and Paul smiled, a little more cynically than before, and returned to his observations of the pictures. Just then he heard the end of the conversation between the boy and girl, under his window, and was amused at his own share in their quarrel.

"Anyhow, if that young woman is going to be about, it may not be so bad, after all," he reflected.

He was reduced to despondency again, however, by the arrival of the breakfast, which fully realised his expectations. For one who professed to have a wide grasp of life, Paul

The Making of a Prig

Wilton was singularly affected by trifles. His spirits were not raised when he found who his nurse was to be; and, competent as Miss Esther soon proved herself, he remained convinced that the child with the joyous laugh who made so much merriment about the house, would have suited him far better. And again, he was amused at his interest in some one whom he had hardly seen, and who would probably turn out to be an undeveloped schoolgirl, some one who would ride roughshod over his susceptibilities, and even fail to understand his feelings about things. It seemed impossible to him that he should be able to endure any one who did not understand his feelings about things. She might be plain, too; women with fascinating voices were often extremely plain. And if she were neither mature nor attractive, there could be no object in giving her another thought; for woman, to Paul Wilton, was merely an interesting necessity,—like his food; something to fill up the gaps that were not occupied by work, or art, or any of the real things of life; and something, therefore, to be taken in as delicate a manner as possible. He liked to talk to beautiful women in picturesque surroundings,—to play on their emotions, and

The Making of a Prig

to dally with their wit; but the women had to be beautiful, and their setting had to be appropriate.

"Please do not trouble to wait," he said to Miss Esther in the afternoon, when he found her preparing to sit with him. "I shall be quite happy if you will have the goodness to give me the paper and the cigarette case. Thanks."

When she had gone, having lacked the courage to tell him that tobacco smoke had never yet polluted the sacred mustiness of the best spare room, Paul lay back with a sense of relief, and began to review his situation gloomily.

"How I could have made such an ass of myself, I don't know," he murmured. "Foisting myself on complete strangers for six or seven weeks at least! And such strangers, too! Good Lord, how shocked the dear lady looked when I said I hadn't a relation left who cared a hang whether I was alive or dead. I must tell her, as an antidote, that my father was a parson; I have known that to take effect in the most ungodly circles. Perhaps, if I could swear I should feel better. But I am not a swearing man; besides, she might leave me to that painfully dull maid if I did. And

The Making of a Prig

that would be a pity," he added reflectively; "for, at least, she does know how to make a fellow as comfortable as a fractured leg will let him be."

A sudden shoot of pain made him turn his head wearily on one side. He had told the doctor, only that morning, that it was nothing, and that he did not suffer much; and then had been unreasonably disappointed at the professional verdict that it was a simple fracture, and presented no complications. He would have liked to be an interesting case, at least.

"I wonder if I am likely to get a glimpse of that jolly little girl," he went on, looking idly at the faded photograph opposite. "It is probably the one who steadied my head in the dark, last night; the one who laughs, too. A Philistine place like this could never produce two of them. However, I shall never find out as long as I am nursed by that dragon. And after all, why trouble about it? It shows what a baleful effect idleness can have upon a man, when an unsophisticated parson's daughter with a jolly laugh can — hullo!"

He heard voices on the landing, and listened eagerly. There was the sound of a scuffle and a stifled laugh, and some one shook the door by falling clumsily against it.

The Making of a Prig

"Come in, do!" shouted Paul desperately, and the door opened with a jerk.

"I say, did we disturb you, or anything? I'm beastly sorry; but Kitty would rot so, and I couldn't help it, really. And, I say, I'm awfully sorry you're so hit up."

It was Ted, apologetic and self-conscious. Paul smiled encouragingly; it was at least some one to talk to, even if it was a boy under twenty, for whose kind he had as a rule little sympathy. He could see there was some one else too, on the landing outside; so he smiled a little more. It pleased him to have his curiosity satisfied, though perhaps he would not have liked it to be called curiosity.

"You see, Kitty will play so poorly," pursued Ted, plunging his hands in his pockets to give himself more confidence. "I shouldn't have dreamt of bothering you like this, if it hadn't been for Kitty."

"I am quite content to believe that it was the fault of Miss Kitty, whose acquaintance I have not the honour of possessing," said Paul gravely. "But won't you come in a little further, and explain matters?"

Ted came in a good deal further, just then, assisted by an unexpected push between his shoulders.

The Making of a Prig

"It's so poor of Kitty; and it isn't my fault, I swear it isn't!" said Ted, in an injured tone. "You see, she wants me to say — Oh, hang, Kit, do let a fellow explain! Well, she says that — that — well, she wants to come in too, don't you see? She doesn't see why she should have to go and talk to horrid old men in the village, when they won't let her come in and talk to you; at least, that's what she says. And she says it's all rotten humbug — Well, you know you did! But Miss Esther will about kill me when she finds it out. Kitty never thinks of that, she's so poor."

Paul smiled again, partly at himself for being young enough to appreciate the childishness of the situation.

"Where is Miss Esther?" he asked, like a man, wisely.

"Oh, she's out right enough; but still —"

"Yes," said Paul reflectively, "I recognise that there are still difficulties in the way. But don't you think, as I am decidedly as much afflicted as the other horrid old men you mentioned, and as Miss Esther is out, that — we might all agree to vote it rotten humbug? Just for a few minutes, you know!"

And Katharine, who had been listening

The Making of a Prig

anxiously to every word, slipped into the room at this point of the negotiations, and closed the door; nodded cheerfully to Paul as though she had known him all her life, and dropped sideways on the chair at the end of his bed.

"I knew you wouldn't mind," she said. "Ted declared you would; but Ted's so awfully dense sometimes, isn't he?"

Paul was willing to admit that, on this occasion, Ted had been remarkably dense; but he only murmured some commonplace about the correctness of her judgment, and the honour he felt at her discrimination.

"Oh, I *knew!*" said Katharine confidently. "I am never wrong about people. Ted is. He makes fearful hashes about people; I always have to tell him who is to be trusted, and who isn't."

"I should like to know," observed Paul, "how you manage to know so much about people whom you have never seen before,—myself, for instance!"

"But I have seen you before! Oh, I forgot; of course, you didn't know. I was with daddy last night when he came to fetch you. Don't you remember? I suppose you were too bad to notice much."

The Making of a Prig

"That must have been it," assented Paul. "I just remember some one supporting my head, or it may have been my shoulders —"

"It was your head. That was me!" cried Katharine, with animation. "Was n't Ted jealous when I told him, — that's all!"

"I was n't," said Ted. "But it was just like Kitty. Girls always do have all the luck."

"I am glad," said Paul drily, "that at least one of you was fortunate enough to view my discomfiture."

Ted laughed, but Katharine became suddenly thoughtful.

"I was very sorry for you, I was really," she said.

"Oh, no, excuse me, — merely interested," said Paul.

Katharine reflected again.

"Perhaps I was; how caddish of me!" she said, and looked at him doubtfully. Paul raised his eyebrows; to be taken seriously by a woman, at such an early stage of her acquaintance, was a new experience to him.

"Oh, please," he exclaimed, laughing, "don't be truthful whatever you are! It's much more charming to think that you *were* sorry for me."

The Making of a Prig

Katharine still seemed puzzled. She turned to Ted instinctively, and he came to her rescue.

"She thought you were awfully plucky and all that; she told me so. I was rather sick about it, of course; but, after all, it wasn't really worth minding because you were hit up so completely, you see."

"You are a singularly brutal pair of young people," observed Paul, glancing from one to the other. "I should like you to have the feel of my leg for half an hour. I fancy you would find yourselves 'hit up,' as you are pleased to call it."

"Oh, but we're not a bit brutal," objected Katharine. "Ted never can help saying what he thinks at the moment,—that's how it is. It's because he shows all his feelings, don't you see?"

"You mustn't think Kitty is unfeeling because she doesn't say things," continued Ted. "She hates spoofing people, and she never says things she doesn't mean. She doesn't always say them when she does mean them; it's rather rough on a fellow sometimes, I think," he added feelingly.

The garden gate swung to, and they sprang to their feet simultaneously.

The Making of a Prig

"Shall we scoot?" asked Ted, who seemed the more apprehensive of the two.

"I suppose so. Bother!" said Katharine regretfully. Ted was already gone, but she still lingered. The flying visit to Paul, instead of satisfying her curiosity about him, had only roused it still more; and she sauntered half absently towards him, without the least pretence of being in a hurry to go.

"Good-bye," she said, and put her hand into his. It was the first time she had shown any signs of shyness, and Paul began to like her better.

"Not good-bye," he said lightly. "You will come in again, won't you? We shall have a good lot to tell each other."

"Shall we?"

"Well, don't you think so?" He dropped her hand and laughed. It seemed absurd that this child, who behaved generally like a charming tomboy, should persist in taking him seriously when he merely wanted to frivol.

"I'll come if it won't bore you," said Katharine shortly. She was wondering what there was to laugh at.

"Can you write a tolerable hand?" he asked.

"I write all daddy's things for him."

The Making of a Prig

"Then we'll see if something can't be arranged," he began. He congratulated himself on his tact in helping to gratify her evident wish to see him again; but she baffled him once more by suddenly brightening up, and seizing upon his suggestion before he had half formed it.

"Could I be your secretary, do you mean? Why, of course I could. What fun! Aunt Esther? Oh, that's nothing. *I* will manage Aunt Esther. Good-bye."

She managed Aunt Esther very effectually at supper time, by calmly announcing her intention of becoming Mr. Wilton's secretary. And the Rector's sister, who was a curious compound of conventional dogma and worldly ignorance, and knew into the bargain that it was of no use to withstand her headstrong niece, gave in to her newest whim with a bad grace.

"Do as you like; I am no longer the head of the house, I suppose," she observed fretfully.

"Oh, yes, you are, Aunt Esther!" retorted Katharine with provoking cheerfulness. "*I* only want to be Mr. Wilton's secretary."

Paul was not so elated as she had expected to find him, when she walked into his room in

The Making of a Prig

Miss Esther's wake on the following day, and told him that she had gained her point and was ready to become his secretary. Being such a responsive creature herself, she always expected every one else to share her emotions.

"Are n't you glad?" she asked him anxiously.

Not being able to explain that what he wanted was not so much a secretary as a pretty girl to amuse him, he said with his usual smile that he was delighted, and proceeded to dictate various uninteresting letters of a business-like character.

"So you live in the Temple," she observed, as she folded up a letter to his housekeeper. "Is n't it a gloriously romantic place to live in?"

"It is convenient," said Paul briefly. And that was all the conversation they had that day.

He wanted no letters written the next day, and she read the paper to him instead. But Miss Esther stayed in the room all the time, with her knitting, and there was no conversation that day either. On the third day, however, her aunt was wanted in the parish; and she deputed the Rector to take her place in the sick room. She might have known that he would forget all about it, directly she was

The Making of a Prig

gone; but Miss Esther always acted on the assumption that her brother possessed all the excellent qualities she wished him to have, and it never occurred to her that he would spend the afternoon in finishing his paper on the antiquities of the county.

"Aunt Esther has gone to see a poor woman who has lost her baby. I never can imagine why a woman who has lost her baby should be visited just because she is poor. Can you?" said Katharine, as she settled herself on the spare-room window-seat with her writing materials.

"No," said Paul, concealing his satisfaction that Miss Esther was of a different opinion. "You needn't bother about writing any letters to-day, thanks," he continued carelessly; "and I don't think I want to hear the paper, either."

"Don't you? oh!" said Katharine, looking disappointed. "Then there's nothing I can do for you?"

"Oh, yes. You can talk, if you will," said Paul, smiling. "Come and sit on the chair at the end of the bed, where you sat the first day you came in. I can see you, then."

"It is ever so much nicer to see the person you are talking to, isn't it?" observed Katharine, as she obeyed his suggestion.

The Making of a Prig

"Much nicer," assented Paul, though it had never occurred to him to suggest that Miss Esther should occupy that particular chair. "Now then, talk, please!"

Katharine made a sign of dismay.

"I can't," she said. "You begin."

"Who is your favourite poet?" asked Paul solemnly. She disconcerted him by taking his question seriously, and he had to listen to her enthusiastic eulogies of several favourite poets, before he had an opportunity of explaining himself.

She detected him in the act of suppressing a yawn, and she stopped suddenly, in the middle of a sentence.

"I believe I am boring you dreadfully. Shall I go?" she asked. The colour had come into her cheeks, and her voice had a note of distress in it.

"I want you to tell me something, first," was his unexpected reply. "Do you talk about poetry to young Morton?"

"Ted? Why, no, of course not. What an awful reflection! Ted isn't a bit poetic, not a little bit; and he would scoff like anything. I have never talked about the things I really like to anybody before; not even to daddy, much."

The Making of a Prig

This was a little dangerous, and the tomboy daughter of the parson was not the kind of personality that was likely to make the danger fascinating. And Paul's first impulse was to wince at the unstudied frankness of her remark; but four days of seclusion had been exceedingly chastening, and the flattery that underlay her words was not unpleasing to him.

"Then what made you suppose *I* cared about poetry, eh?" he asked deliberately.

"Why," said Katharine, staring at him, "you began it, don't you remember? I thought you wanted me to tell you what I thought."

"Yes, yes; I am aware of that. But don't you think we have talked enough about poetry for one day?" said Paul, half closing his eyes. He was already regretting his stupidity in expecting her to understand him.

"How awfully funny you are! First you say—"

"Yes," said Paul, as patiently as he could, "I know. Don't let us say any more about it. Supposing you were to talk to me now as you would talk to young Morton, for instance!"

Katharine shook her head doubtfully.

"I don't think I could. You're not like

The Making of a Prig

Ted; you don't like the same sort of things. You're not like me, either."

Paul smiled grimly.

"We're both the same in reality, Miss Kitty. Only, you are focussing it from one end, and I from another. I mean, you are too abominably young and I am too abominably old, for conversation. We shall have to keep to the favourite poets, after all."

Katharine had come round to the side of the bed, and was regarding him critically, with a very serious look on her face.

"What is the matter?" she asked abruptly. "I hate people to say they are old — when they are nice people. It makes me feel horrid; I don't like it. I never let daddy talk about growing old; it gives me a sort of cold feel, don't you know? I wish you wouldn't. Besides, I am not young, either; I am nearly nineteen. I know I look much younger, because I won't put my hair up; but my skirts are nearly to the ground. What makes you say I am too young to be talked to?"

"I said you were too young for conversation. It is not quite the same thing, is it?"

"Isn't it?" said Katharine, and she looked away out of the window for a full minute. What she saw there she could not have told,

The Making of a Prig

but it was something that had never been there before. When she brought her eyes round again to his face, the serious look had gone out of them, and they were twinkling with fun. "I know!" she laughed. "Let's talk without any conversation."

"She's the same woman, after all," was Paul's reflection.

They did not mention the favourite poets again; but they had no difficulty for the rest of the afternoon in finding something to talk about. It was getting late when the garden gate gave its usual warning, and Katharine got up with a sigh.

"When shall I see you again?" he asked. They had not gone through the formality of shaking hands, this time.

"When Aunt Esther has *not* gone to see a poor woman who has lost her baby," said Katharine, laughing.

"Nonsense! we will keep the letters and the newspaper for that kind of visit. Won't some one else die, don't you think, so that we can have another talk?"

"I'll see," said Katharine, which could not strictly be called an answer to his question. But it fully satisfied Paul.

CHAPTER IV

THE weeks crept on; and Paul Wilton, from being merely an object of interest and pity, gradually became the greatest mystery in the neighbourhood. Such a reputation was entirely unsought on his part, although, had he been aware of it, the probability is that it would not have been wholly unpleasing to him. For it had been his pose through life to mystify people,— not by deliberately assuming to be what he was not, but by strenuously avoiding any appearance of what he was; and his indifference, which was what people first noticed in him, was entirely feigned for the purpose of concealing that his real attitude towards life was a critical one. It was not unreasonable that a man of this calibre, suddenly placed in a quiet country parish, should end in making some sort of a sensation there. Miss Esther from the beginning had suffered much, and silently; but a man who had a father in Crockford and a mother in Debrett,

The Making of a Prig

was to be forgiven a good deal, and she felt compelled to overlook even the ash of his cigarettes, and his French novels, when she found them both on the chaste counterpane of the best spare-room bed. But there were others in Ivingdon who, not having much of a pedigree themselves, were inclined to undervalue the importance of one; and some of these, the doctor, for instance, and Peter Bunce the churchwarden, came to the Rector for enlightenment.

"Eh, but he doan't give hisself away much, do he, now?" said the churchwarden, jerking his thumb in the direction of the lame man, who had just swung himself past the window on his crutches. "He be proper close, I reckon, eh?"

"He is a very intelligent young man," said the Rector vaguely. "He has quite an appreciation of Oriental china."

It was Sunday afternoon, and the Rector was dispensing whiskey and cigars to his guests, with a prodigality that might have been attributed to Miss Esther's absence at the Sunday school. There was an ease, too, about their manners and their conversation, which was to be traced to the same cause.

"I suppose he's beastly clever, and all that,

The Making of a Prig

isn't he?" asked Ted morosely. He was sitting on the window ledge, a convenient position which allowed him to shout occasional answers to the questions that came from Katharine on the other side of the lawn. Just then, however, she was joined by Paul; and Ted knew instinctively that he would have no more questions to answer after that.

"It is difficult to say what he is," observed the doctor. "You can't get him to talk; at least, not much. Generally, when I've done all the professional business, he relapses into total silence, and I just have to go; but sometimes he is inclined to be chatty, and then he makes a delightful companion. But the odd thing is, that I know no more about the man himself at the end of a conversation than I did at the beginning. A barrister, did you say he was? That accounts for the judicial manner, then; but the question is, what is there behind it all?"

No one seemed to have an answer ready to the doctor's question; but Peter Bunce took a long pull at the whiskey, and brushed the cigar ash from his capacious waistcoat, and attacked the subject with fresh vigour.

"There ain't no finding out anything about no one, without you take a bit o' trouble," he

The Making of a Prig

remarked wisely. "Mayhap Mr. Austen, yonder, might know a something more than us folk. Hasn't he got never a father, now? There's a won'erful lot to be gathered from knowing of a man's father, there is. Like enough he's one o' they London folk, as daren't speak aloud for fear of its getting into the newspapers. London folk is mighty well watched, so I've heard; there's never a moment's peace or safety in London, some say. Mayhap Mr. Wilton's father is a London gen'leman, now!"

"His father?" said the Rector, with sudden enthusiasm. "His father was something short of a genius, sir! He is the best authority we have on the numismatics of his neighbourhood. Have you never heard of Wilton's 'Copper Tokens'?"

"Guess we have, sir, pretty often," laughed Ted.

The Rector looked pathetic, and handed him another cigar, with an apprehension that arose from the distant clang of the garden gate.

"They all laugh at me," he said in a cheery tone that evoked no one's pity. "I'm an old fool; oh, yes, we know all about that. But if you had read Wilton's 'Copper Tokens,' you wouldn't want to know who this man's father

The Making of a Prig

was. Let me see,—what did I do with my Crockford?"

"I expect you thought it was a hymn-book and carted it up to church this morning," said Ted, in a tone of forced merriment. He still had one eye on the lawn, and what he saw there did not raise his spirits.

"Died at the age of fifty-eight, when his son was a lad of eighteen, he tells me," continued the Rector. "That was the same date that the fifth edition of the 'Copper Tokens' was issued, some ten or fifteen years ago now. Bless me, how time flies when we're not growing any younger!"

For the space of a moment or two, everybody present was occupied with a mental calculation. The churchwarden was the first to give up the attempt, and he returned doggedly to the original topic.

"Age ain't got nothing to do with it," he began, heaving a sigh of relief as he substituted his pipe for the unusual cigar. "'Cause why? Some folk's old when they're young, and other folk's young when they're old; that's where it lays, you see."

Nobody did see; but Ted threw in a vicious comment.

"The Lord only knows how old he is,

but he's as played out as they make them," he said.

The churchwarden smiled, without understanding, and Cyril Austen was too deep in his Crockford to hear what was passing; but the doctor had been young himself, not so long ago, and he understood.

"Does he talk about leaving? he asked in a casual manner, directing his remark to the boy on the window ledge. "There's nothing to keep him here now, as far as I can see."

"Don't know anything about him," said Ted, with a studied indifference. "I should have thought, from the way Kitty speaks of him, that London couldn't do without him for another moment. What they all see in him, I don't know. I suppose it's because I'm such a rotten ass, but he seems just like anybody else to me as far as brains are concerned. And he can't talk for nuts. But Miss Esther says his family is all square; and that's enough for the women, I suppose."

The doctor nodded sympathetically, and Ted laughed as if he were a little ashamed of taking himself so seriously.

"He's going to make himself scarce on Wednesday," he continued, rather more cor-

The Making of a Prig

dially. "He's got a pal of his coming down on business to-morrow, and they're going off together. Good thing, too, eh? Don't know anything about the pal — he's not any great shakes, I expect; but Wilton swears he knows a lot about coins, and of course that will fetch the Rector. Fact is, this place is getting too clever for me. There's Kitty, who rots about poetry and things till it makes you sick. She never used to; and it's no good her trying to spoof you that she isn't altered, because she is, — and all for the sake of a chap like Wilton, who hardly ever opens his mouth! It's so poor, isn't it?"

But here the arrival of Miss Esther postponed any further discussion of the Rectory guest. The doctor suddenly remembered that he had a patient to visit, and took an abrupt departure; and the churchwarden refused a curt invitation to tea, and went hastily after him. Ted lingered a moment or two, without being noticed at all; and Miss Esther, having successfully routed her brother's guests, went into the garden to disturb the conversation on the other side of the lawn.

Some two days later, Paul Wilton and his friend from London were pacing up and down the narrow strip of gravel path that skirted the

The Making of a Prig

house on the south side. In the absence of Katharine, who had induced him to prolong the period of helplessness, as he would have wished to prolong any other pleasurable sensation, Paul had no reason to play the invalid; and, except for an occasional limp, there was nothing in his walk to indicate lameness. There was the usual inexplicable smile on his face, however, as he listened to the bantering conversation of the man at his side, and occasionally interrupted it with one of his dry, terse remarks. His companion was a little elderly man, with small features and a fresh complexion, whose geniality was the result of temperament rather than of principle, and whose conversation was toned with a personal refrain that made it naïvely amusing.

"That's a pretty child, by the way," he was saying, with the air of a connoisseur. Katharine had just left them, and they could hear her laughing with her father indoors. Paul murmured an assent, and went on smoking. His companion glanced at him sideways, and smiled gently.

"Very pretty," he repeated, "but ridiculously young. And who is the charming boy who is so gone on her? She does n't see it a bit, and he has n't the pluck to tell her. I'm

The Making of a Prig

quite sorry for that boy; I've been in his shoes many a time, and I know what it feels like. He's got a lot to teach her, that's certain, eh? Doesn't interest you, I suppose! If it had been me, now, chained here with a broken leg and nothing to do, with an idyllic love story going on under my eyes — ah, well! you are not made that way, and I am too old, I suppose. Besides, in spite of her charm, she isn't exactly my style."

"No," said Paul; "she is not your style."

"All the same, she's remarkably pretty, and I'm not too old to admire a pretty woman," chuckled his companion. "'Pon my word, I'm quite inclined to envy that boy. Just imagine a veritable woman, still thinking herself a child, with a delightful boy for her only companion, and no one to stand between them! I'd have given worlds for such a chance when I was his age."

"But, you see, you are not his age; so it is no use trying to cut him out. Besides, you ought to know better, Heaton, at your time of life," said Paul, in a jesting manner that was a little strained. Heaton took his remark rather as a compliment than otherwise.

"You won't alter me, my boy; you'll find me the same to the end of the chapter, — so

The Making of a Prig

make up your mind to that. I'm not ashamed of it either, not I! Seriously, though, I'm quite interested in our little love story yonder. I should like to help that boy. Silly ass! why doesn't he make a plunge for it? He isn't likely to have a rival."

"Perhaps that is why he doesn't," observed Paul. "But I don't see why we should trouble ourselves about it."

"That's where you're so cynical," complained Heaton. "These little affairs always interest me intensely; they bring back my youth to me, and remind me of my lost happiness. Oh, life! what you once held for me! And now it is all gone, buried with my two sweet wives, and I am left alone with no one to care what becomes of me."

His eyes were moist as he finished speaking, and Paul walked along at his side without offering any consolation. He would have found it difficult to explain why he had chosen Laurence Heaton for a friend. It would be more correct to say, perhaps, that Heaton had chosen him, and that he had lacked the energy or the power to shake him off. It was generally true that his sentimental egotism bored Paul excessively, and yet he found something to like in a nature that was so unlike his own;

and he was so secretive himself that the artless confidences of Heaton, if a little wearisome, at least relieved him of the necessity of adding to the conversation. Besides this, he was a man who never willingly sought the friendship of others, and the obvious preference that the good-natured idler, who was so many years his elder, had shown for him when they first met at a public dinner, had secretly flattered him not a little, and their acquaintance had grown after that as a matter of course.

"All the same," resumed Heaton in his ordinary manner, "an outsider never can do much in these cases. Perhaps it would be better to leave them alone; and yet, if the boy were to come to me for the benefit of my larger experience—"

"Don't you think," interrupted Paul, "that we have talked about a couple of children as much as we need? It's all very well for an old reprobate like yourself to spend your time in reviving your lost youth, but I have n't so much leisure as you have, and I want to hear about those shares you mentioned in your letter last week."

Heaton laughed good-humouredly.

"You don't realise, my dear fellow, how anything like that always interests me. But

The Making of a Prig

you wait until your time comes; at present you are too cynical to understand what I mean."

"Or too romantic," suggested Paul.

"Oh, no!" said Heaton. "Romance is only an equivalent for inexperience; I think you're a cold-hearted beggar who lets the best things in life go by, but I shouldn't call you inexperienced. You've got a finished way with women that always appeals to them; women love a little humbug, if it's well done. I'm too obvious for them, too simple-minded, and that always frightens them off."

"Does it?" smiled Paul.

"Now, you ought to marry," continued Heaton briskly. "I believe in marriage, hanged if I don't! and it's been the making of me. Everything that is good in me I owe to my married life."

"Did it really take two marriages?" murmured Paul. His companion smiled at the joke against himself, and they stood for a moment in silence, looking over the lawn that had just acquired its fresh bloom of green. Katharine's voice came out to them again through the open window, this time raised in indignant dispute with her aunt.

"She is a curious mixture of hardness and sentiment," said Paul involuntarily, "and her

The Making of a Prig

surroundings have made her a prig; but she interests me rather."

"Ah," said Heaton, "I quite agree with you. There *is* a touch of the prig about her. But can you wonder? She is the only bit of life and prettiness about the place, and she never meets her equal. They think a good lot of her, too. And the parson's daughter generally thinks a good lot of herself."

"She does it rather charmingly," said Paul, in a dispassionate tone, "and she is fairly well read, and knows how to express herself. For a woman, she has quite a sense of criticism."

"That's bad," said Heaton decidedly, "very bad. A woman should have no sense of criticism. That is what makes her a prig. In fact, as I have often said to you before, a prig is made in three ways. First of all, she is made by her own people, if she happens to be clever; and secondly, by the world, if she happens to be successful; and thirdly, by her lover, if she is'nt in love with him. But of course if she *is* in love with him he may be the cause of her unmaking."

Some one in a light-coloured print frock jumped out of a side window and disappeared in the direction of the summer-house. The

The Making of a Prig

two men stood and looked after her without being noticed.

"As you say," remarked Heaton blandly, "she does it rather charmingly."

Paul roused himself with an effort.

"Half-past three," he said, looking at his watch. "Didn't you promise to go and look at the Rector's coins some time this afternoon?"

And in another five minutes he had joined Katharine in the summer-house.

CHAPTER V

The summer house was set far back in the shrubbery, and although hidden from the house by laurels and box-trees, was open at the front to a stretch of brightly coloured flower beds and trimly cut grass. It was a glorious day in May, and spring in its fulness was come. The white fruit blossoms had given place to crumpled green leaves, and the early summer flowers were in bud. Paul Wilton lay on a low basket chair, where he had flung himself down after making his escape from his garrulous friend; and at his feet, with an open book on her lap, sat Katharine. Obviously, a great many poor women had lost a great many babies, since the day she had sat on the chair at the end of his bed and talked about her favourite poets, for the book on her lap was only a pretence to which neither of them paid the least attention, and their conversation was of a purely personal nature, the kind of conversation that has no subject and no epigrams, and is carried on in half-finished sentences.

The Making of a Prig

"I am beginning to understand why you don't paint or write or do things, although you know such a lot about them," observed Katharine, half closing her eyes and making a picture of the square of sunlit garden as she saw it framed in the woodwork of the summer-house door.

Paul smiled. It was very pleasant to be told by this child of Nature that he knew "such a lot about things."

"Tell me why," was all he said, however.

"I think it is because it puts you in a position to criticise every one else. It makes you so superior, in a sort of way. Oh, bother! I never can explain things. But don't you see, if you were a painter yourself, you couldn't say that there was only one painter living, as you do now. Could you?"

"Perhaps I could," said Paul, and laughed gently at her look of surprise.

"Of course I know you are only laughing at me," she said in an injured tone. "You never think I am serious about anything."

"My dear Miss Katharine," he assured her, "on the contrary, I think you are most terribly serious about everything. I have never had so much serious conversation since I was nineteen myself. You will have to

The Making of a Prig

grow older, before you learn to be young and frivolous."

"But *you* are not frivolous," she protested. "You know you are not. You only say that to tease me."

"I only say it to convince you. It is not my fault if you do not understand, is it?"

"I do understand, I am certain I do. At least"—she paused suddenly, and looked at him with one of her long critical looks. "Perhaps you are right, and I don't understand you a bit. How queer! I don't think I like the feel of it." She ended with a little gesture of distaste.

"I shouldn't bother about it, if I were you," said Paul calmly. "You will understand better when you are older—and younger. Meanwhile, it is very pleasant, don't you think?"

She was leaning forward with her hands folded under her chin, and did not answer him.

"What made you choose to be a barrister?" she asked suddenly.

He shrugged his shoulders.

"Merely because it presented greater opportunities for idleness than any other profession, I suppose."

The Making of a Prig

Katharine swung herself round on her low stool, and looked at him incredulously.

"But don't you ever want to *do* anything,— you with all your brains and your talents?" she cried impatiently. "Surely you must have some ambition?"

"Oh, no," replied Paul, arranging the cushions at the back of his head and sinking down on them again. "I hope I shall always be comfortable, that's all; and I have enough money for that, thank the Lord!"

"Supposing you had been poor?"

"Don't suppose it," rejoined Paul; and her puzzled features relaxed into a smile.

"I can't think why you have a face like that, then," she said reflectively.

"What's the matter with my face? Does it suggest possibilities? To think that I might have been a minor poet all these years, without knowing it!"

Katharine returned to her examination of the flower beds; and Paul lay back, and blew rings of smoke into the air, and watched her through them with an amused look on his face. He recalled some casual words of Heaton's which had annoyed him very much at the time,—"If I'm not in love with a woman, I don't want to give her another thought;" and he glanced at her slim waist as she sat there, and tried lazily to analyse his own feelings towards her.

"What are you thinking about?" she asked, turning round again.

"About you," he said, and brought his feet lightly to the ground and sat up and stretched himself.

"What about me?" she asked curiously.

"I am wondering if you will miss me very much when I am gone," he said, and slid slowly along the chair until he sat behind her, where he could just see her rounded profile as she turned her face away from him.

"Oh, yes, awfully! I wish, I do wish you were not going!" She was looking very hard at the flower beds now.

"So do I, Miss Katharine. It has been quite delightful; I shall never forget your sweet care of me. But you will soon forget all about me. And besides, there is Ted."

"What has that got to do with it?" she asked swiftly.

"Oh, nothing, surely! It was merely an inconsequent reflection on my part."

There was a pause for a few moments.

"Talk," he said suddenly, and put his hand gently against her cheek. It warmed under

The Making of a Prig

his touch, and he heard the tremor in her voice as she spoke.

"I — I can't talk. Oh, please don't!"

"Can't you? Try."

She put her hand up to his, and he caught hold of her fingers, and dropped a light kiss on them as they lay crumpled up on his palm. Then he pressed them slightly, and let them go, and walked away to the house without looking at her again. His countenance was as unmoved as if he had just been talking archæology to the Rector; but his reflections seemed absorbing, and he hardly roused himself to move aside when Ted came lounging out of the house and ran against him in the porch.

"Hullo!" said Ted. "I'm awfully sorry; I didn't see you, really."

"Oh, no matter!" said Paul, who, never being guilty of a clumsy action himself, could afford to remain undisturbed. "Miss Katharine's in the summer house," he added, in answer to Ted's disconsolate look. "We've been reading Browning. At least, Miss Katharine out of her goodness has been trying to make a convert of me. I am afraid I was an unappreciative listener."

Ted glanced inquiringly at him. Somehow,

The Making of a Prig

it was not so easy to disapprove of Paul to his face as it was behind his back.

"How poor!" he said sympathetically. "Kitty does play so cheap, sometimes, does n't she? Browning is enough to give you the hump, I should think. But she never does that to me."

"Probably," said Paul, disengaging a cigarette paper; "she would not feel the same necessity in your case. You would have greater facilities for conversation, I mean. Won't you have a cigarette?"

Ted looked towards the shrubbery, but lingered as though the invitation commended itself to him.

"I think I 'll have a pipe, if it 's all the same to you. May I try that 'baccy of yours? Thanks, awfully!"

They sat down on opposite sides of the little porch, and puffed away in silence.

"You have n't been over much, lately," observed Paul presently.

Ted glanced at him again, but was disarmed by his tone of friendliness.

"No," he said. "At least, I was over once or twice last week, but I never got a look in with Kitty. I mean," he added hastily, "she was out, or something."

The Making of a Prig

"Ah!" said Paul indifferently; "that was unfortunate."

"It was a howling nuisance," said Ted, his troubled look returning. "The truth is," he went on, feeling a desire for a confidant to be stronger than his distrust of Paul, "there's something I've been trying to tell Kit for a whole week, and for the life of me I can't get it out."

"Going to make a fool of himself at the very start," thought Paul.

"You see," continued Ted with an effort, "*she* has been playing up so, lately."

"Your mother?" questioned Paul.

Ted nodded.

"And now she's got me a confounded berth in some place in the city,—candles, or grocery, or something beastly. It's the poorest thing I ever heard. And I've got to start on Thursday, so I must leave home tomorrow. And Kitty doesn't know; that's the devil, you see."

"I'm sorry," said Paul gravely.

"Got it through some cousin of my father's," Ted went on in his aggrieved voice. "No one but a cousin of one's father ever hears of such rotten jobs. Said it would be the making of me, or some rot. I've heard that before; the

The Making of a Prig

men who never did a stroke of work themselves always talk that sort of cheapness. Have to be there at half-past eight in the morning, too, blow it!"

"I'm sorry," said Paul again. He began to feel a vague interest in the boy as he sat opposite and stretched his long legs out to their full length, and jerked out his complaints with the brier between his teeth.

"*She* thinks it such great shakes, too; just because she won't have to keep me any longer. She ought never to have had a son like me; I wasn't meant for such beastly work. Why was I born? Why was I?"

"The parents of the human animal are never selected," said Paul, for the sake of saying something.

"I know I'm a fool, — *she's* told me that often enough; so I don't expect to get anything awfully decent. But why did they educate me as a gentleman? They should have sent me to a board school, and then I should have been a bounder myself, and nothing would have mattered. What's the use of being a gentleman and a fool? That's what I am; and Kit's the only person in the world who doesn't make me feel it, bless her!"

Paul threw away his cigarette, and made a

The Making of a Prig

sudden resolve. He was amused, in spite of himself, at the very youthful pessimism in Ted's remarks; and for a moment he felt almost anxious that the boy should not spoil his career by a false start. There was something novel, too, in his playing the part of counsellor, and Paul Wilton was never averse to a new sensation. So he leaned forward and tapped his companion on the knee with his long, pointed forefinger.

"You may send me to the devil, if you like," he said with his placid smile, "but I should like to give you a word of advice first. May I?"

Ted looked more depressed than before, but he did not seem surprised.

"Fire ahead!" he said sadly. "I can stand an awful lot. People have always given me advice, ever since I was a kid; it's the only thing they ever have given me."

"I don't suppose it is my business at all," said Paul, making another cigarette with the elaborate precision he always spent on trifles; "but I've seen so many nice chaps ruined through a mistake in early life, and I know one or two things, and I'm older than you, too. Now, how do you mean to tell that child over there that you are going away?"

The Making of a Prig

Ted started.

"What do you mean?" he asked. But his lower lip was twitching nervously, and his colour had deepened.

"Well, this is what I mean. Given an emotional creature like that, who has never seen any man but you, and a young, impetuous fellow like yourself, going to say good-bye to her for an indefinite period,—well, you are both extremely likely to arrive at one conclusion; and my advice to you is,— Don't."

Ted said nothing, but continued to stare at the tesselated floor. The elder man rose to his feet, and restored the match box to his pocket.

"I nearly did it myself once," he said; "but I didn't."

Ted looked him thoughtfully up and down.

"I shouldn't think you did," he said, with unconscious sarcasm. Then he too rose slowly to his feet, and stood on the doorstep for a moment, with his hands in his pockets. "I think you're a confounded cynical brute," he said rather breathlessly, "but I believe you're right, and I won't."

And he walked across the lawn to the shrubbery with the air of a man on whose decision depends the fate of nations.

Paul frowned slightly, as he always did when

he was thinking deeply, and then threw off his preoccupation with a laugh. Even when he was alone, he liked to preserve his attitude of nonchalance.

"How have I contrived to fall among such an appallingly serious set of infants?" he muttered. "Hey-day! here's for London and life!" And he turned indoors to look for a time-table.

Ted stalked straight into the summer house, with his head in the air and his mind filled with high-souled resolutions. Any one less occupied with his own reflections would have seen that Katharine was sitting with an absent look in her eyes, while the book she held in her hand was open at the index-page. But Ted only saw in her the woman he had just sworn within him to respect; and he took the book reverently out of her hand, and sat down, also just behind her, on the end of the basket chair. It was the same basket chair.

"Kitty, I say," he began, clearing his throat, "I've come to tell you something."

Katharine glanced at his solemn face, and looked away again. She wished he had not sat just there.

"It must have something to do with a funeral, then," she said, with a flippancy that

The Making of a Prig

would have aroused the suspicions of a more observant person. But Ted was still absorbed in his high-souled resolutions, and her abstraction failed to make any impression on him.

"No, it has n't," he rejoined gloomily. "I wish it had! I should n't mind being dead, not I! It would cure this hump, anyhow. Perhaps some one would be sorry, then; don't know who would, though! *She*'d only complain of the expense of burying me."

"Poor old man, who has been bullying you now?" asked Katharine, in a dreamy voice that she strove to make interested. "Has *she* been doing anything fresh?"

"Has she, that's all! She's been doing something to some purpose, this time. Got me a beastly job, in a beastly city place; a pound a week; soap, or wholesale clothing, or something poor. Says I ought to be thankful to get anything. Thankful indeed! *She* never shows a spark of gratitude for her bally seven hundred a year, I know."

"Oh, Ted! every one is going away. What shall I do?" The words escaped her involuntarily. But he was still too full of his own troubles to notice anything except that she seemed distressed; and this, of course, was only natural.

The Making of a Prig

"I knew you'd be cut up," he said, kicking savagely at the leg of the chair. "You're the only chap who cares; and you'll forget when I've been gone a week. Oh, yes, you will! I ought never to have been born. They're sure to be rank outsiders, too; and I can stand anything sooner than bounders. It's too beastly caddish for words, and I'd like to kill him for his rotten advice. What does he know about anything, a played-out chap like that?"

Ted's conversation was apt to become involved when he was agitated; but on this occasion Katharine made no attempt to unravel it.

"Poor Ted," she murmured tonelessly, and continued to think about something else.

"I don't know why you are so cut up about it. I'm such a rotten ass, and you're so infernally smart! I haven't any right to expect you to care a hang about me; I won't even ask you to write to me, when I'm gone," cried Ted, making desperate efforts to keep his high-souled resolutions. "It's a rotten, caddish world, and I'm the rottenest fool in it."

He waited for the contradiction that always came from Katharine at this point of his self-

The Making of a Prig

abasement; but when she said nothing, and only went on staring in the opposite direction, he felt that there was something unusually wrong, and came hastily round to the front of her chair and repeated his last remark with emphasis.

"You may say what you like, but I am. All the same, I would sooner chuck the whole show than make you unhappy. I'll be hanged if I don't go away to-morrow without a single —" He stopped abruptly; for she was looking up at him piteously, and his high-souled resolutions suddenly melted into oblivion. "Kitty, old chum, don't cry! I'm not worth it,— on my soul I'm not; blowed if I've ever seen you cry before! Good old Kit, I say, don't. Oh, the devil! Do you really mind so much?"

"Please, Ted, go away; you don't understand; go away; it isn't that at all! Don't, Ted, don't! Oh, dear, whatever made me cry?" gasped Katharine. But Ted would take no denial: a woman's tears would have disarmed him, even if he had not been in love with her; and Katharine, the tomboyish companion of years, appeared to him in a strangely lovable light as she sobbed into her hands and made the feeblest efforts to keep him away.

The Making of a Prig

His arms were round her in a moment, and her head was pulled down on his shoulder, and he poured a medley of broken sentences into her ear.

"How was I to know you cared, old chum? Of course I have always cared; but I never thought about it until that played-out London chap turned up and put it into my head. Dear old Kitty! Why, do you know, I was half afraid you were going to like him, one time; wasn't I a rotten ass? But, you see, you're so bally clever, and all that; and I supposed he was, too, and so I thought,— don't you see? And all the while, it was me! Buck up, Kit! I won't split that you cried, on my honour I won't. Oh, I say, I'm the most confoundedly lucky chap— But, oh, that infernal office in the city!"

Katharine disengaged herself at last. His kisses seemed to burn into her cheeks. She pushed back the basket chair into the corner of the summer-house, and put her fingers over her eyes to shut out the flower beds and the sunlight.

"Stop, Ted! I don't know what you mean. You must not think those things of me; they are simply not true. I can't let you kiss me like that. Has the world gone suddenly mad,

The Making of a Prig

this afternoon? I don't understand what has happened to every one. I don't understand anything. Will you go, please, Ted? If you won't, I — I must."

She forced out the disjointed sentences in hard, passionless tones. Ted stood absolutely still where she left him, and watched her stumble through the doorway and disappear among the laurel bushes and the old box-trees. Then he rumpled up his thick hair with both his hands, and laughed aloud.

"I ought never to have been born," he said, and his voice broke.

CHAPTER VI

ON a foggy morning in the beginning of the following January, Ted Morton strolled out of his bedroom shortly before eight o'clock, and rang the bell for breakfast. He yawned as though he were only half awake, and swore gently at the weather as he stirred up the fire to make a blaze.

"What an infernal day!" he muttered, and pulled down the blind and lighted the gas. The housekeeper brought in his breakfast and his letters, and wisely withdrew without saying anything. Ted took the lid off the teapot, and examined the three envelopes in turn. His face brightened a little as he came to the third, and he buttered some toast and ate it standing.

"Well, I'm hanged! Not a single bill, and one from Kit, good old Kit! That'll wait, and that. Well, I can stand hers; it's sure to be funny, at all events."

He put on one boot, and then stood up

The Making of a Prig

again and read her letter, with a large cup of tea in his right hand. The smile on his face faded gradually as he read, and he looked almost thoughtful when he folded it up again and placed it in his breast-pocket. He was staunch in his belief that Katharine could do no wrong, but her latest idea went far to shake his conviction.

"You see, it is like this," her letter ran.

"There is plenty of money, really, but we have to behave as though there were none; so the effect is the same, it seems to me. I never thought about it before; I only found it out by accident, when I overheard Aunt Esther abusing daddy for buying some old architectural books. It seems as though he really does spend a good lot, without knowing it; but then, why shouldn't he? I won't have daddy bullied, so that I should have enough bread and butter to eat; it is sordid and horrible. They don't say a word about my earning my own living, but that is what they are driving me to do; it seems ridiculous that I should make other people uncomfortable by being here, when there is plenty of money in the world waiting to be earned by some one. Don't you think so? But when I said I would come up to London and give lessons, Aunt Esther had heroics, and said I should kill her. She didn't say how, and I'm sure I did not feel particularly murderous; I only wanted to laugh, while she lay on the sofa and said I was undutiful for trying to save her anxiety! I don't understand pa-

The Making of a Prig

rents. They hide everything from you, and behave as if they were wealthy; then they abuse you for costing so much to keep; and then, when you say you will keep yourself, they call you undutiful. There is no doubt that if we were to send away one of the servants, I should be able to stay at home; but Aunt Esther would have a fit at the idea. It seems to me that we spend half our income in trying to persuade people of the existence of the other half. Anyhow, I am coming up at once to look for work. I haven't told daddy yet, and don't know how I am going to; he will be so dreadfully cut up at losing me. But I am sure he will understand; he is the one person who always has understood. And won't it be glorious when I have earned enough money to give him everything he wants? About rooms: I saw an advertisement of some, a few doors from you. Do you know them? I thought it would be rather nice to be near you," etc., etc.

Ted answered her letter the same evening. Writing letters was always a labour to him, but he toiled over this one more than usual.

"Of course you know what you are playing at," he wrote, "but I believe it is awfully hard to get anything to do. London is packed with people trying to find work; and most of them don't find it. As to the rooms, it would be beastly jolly to have you so close, but I don't advise your coming here; this street pals on to Regent Street, you know, and it

The Making of a Prig

is n't supposed to be pleasant for a girl. I will explain more fully when I see you. Let me know if I can do anything for you. I'm a rotten ass at expressing myself, as you know; but it will be awfully decent to have you to take about. Only I don't like the idea of your grinding away alone; it's rotten enough for a man, but it's miles worse for a woman. Write again soon. It *is* a life, is n't it?"

It was nearly a fortnight before he heard from her again, and he felt guiltily conscious of not having encouraged her as much as she expected. Then came another letter, in her small, firm handwriting; and he tore it open anxiously.

"I am coming up by the 4.55 on Wednesday," she wrote. "Will you meet me? I thought perhaps you might, as it is a late train. Oh, Ted, I feel so old and different somehow; I don't believe I *could* climb into that pantry window now! Daddy took it so strangely; he hardly said anything at all. Do you think it is possible that he really does not love me as much as I love him? And I mind leaving him so much that it quite hurts every time he asks me to do anything for him. Why was I made to like people more than they like me? Why, I believe daddy was rather relieved than otherwise. And I thought he would never be able to do without me! Am I very conceited, I wonder? But indeed, I do believe he will miss me dreadfully when I am

The Making of a Prig

gone. Aunt Esther won't speak to me at all; I feel in disgrace, without having done anything wrong. Parents are inexplicable; they seem to grow tired of us as we grow up, just like birds! And they persist in treating us like children, while they are forcing us to behave as if we were grown up; I can't understand them, or anything. Things seem to be going all wrong, everywhere. I have heard of a sort of home for working gentlewomen, near Edgware Road; it seems respectable, and it is certainly cheap. They have left me to arrange everything, just as though I were going to do something wicked. And I thought all the while I was doing something so splendid and heroic! You will meet me, won't you? I feel so forlorn and miserable."

Ted wrote back immediately:—

"It is a beastly rotten world. Neither of us ought to have been born. I will cut the office and meet you. Buck up."

And the following Wednesday saw him on the platform at Euston, trying to find Katharine in the crowd of passengers who were pouring out of the 4.55 train. It was not long before he discovered her, looking very unlike her surroundings, and pointing out her luggage, half apologetically, to a porter who seemed inclined to patronise her. There was an exaggerated air of self-possession in her bearing,

The Making of a Prig

which did not conceal her provincial look and rather showed that she felt less composed than she wished to appear. Ted examined her for a moment doubtfully, and then made his way towards her. He had not seen her once since she left him in the summer-house, eight months ago; and he was amazed at himself for not feeling more disturbed at meeting her again now. Perhaps her prosaic winter clothing helped to rob the occasion of romance; for, in his mind, he had vaguely expected to find her wearing the garden hat and print frock in which he had last seen her. But when she turned round and saw him, the frank pleasure in her face was the same as it had always been, and the episode that had been enacted in the summer-house seemed all at once to be blotted out of their past.

"You dear old boy, I knew you'd come! I feel so awfully out of it, in this noise! Do make that porter understand I want to get across to Gower Street, will you? He seems confused. I don't speak a different language, do I? Just look at that glorious pair of bays; but, oh, what a shame to give them bearing-reins! Why, Ted, what a swell you are in that frock coat; you look just like the vet. at Stoke on Sundays! Oh, I'm so sorry; I

The Making of a Prig

forgot! I want to get to Edgware Road, you see, and I thought—"

"Oh, we'll cab it, then! Nonsense! it isn't a bit cheaper, only nastier. Girls never understand these things. Hadn't you better get in, instead of examining the points of the horse? It won't stand any quieter than that, if that's your idea."

The porter went off with a handsome gratuity, and Katharine settled herself in her corner of the cab, and began to examine her companion.

"You've altered a little bit, Ted," she observed. "You're not so afraid of unimportant people as you used to be. I believe you would go into the post office at Stoke for your own stamps, now, instead of sending me because the girl laughed at you. Do you remember? You are such a swell, too; how you must be getting on at that place!"

"Oh, I don't think so. I don't want to get on there; no decent chap would," said Ted, and Katharine changed the conversation.

"The streets seem very full," she said, as they came to a block in the traffic.

"Up to the brim," said Ted laconically. "I always wonder the horses don't tread on one another's toes, don't you?"

The Making of a Prig

She laughed in her old joyous manner, and he leaned back contentedly and looked at her.

"At all events, you haven't altered much," he observed.

"I've grown an inch, and my dresses are quite long now. Besides, I have put up my hair. Didn't you notice?"

"I thought there was something. Turn your head round. About time you did, wasn't it? But why don't you make it stick out more? Other girls do, don't they?"

Katharine had not seen any other girls, and said so; whereupon Ted supposed it was all right, if she thought it was, and added conciliatingly, that at all events her new coat was "all there." They chattered in the same trivial manner all the rest of the way; it was like the old days, when they had never thought of making up a quarrel formally, but had just resumed matters where they had been broken off.

"Do you feel bad?" he asked, in his sympathetic way, when they stood at last on the well-worn doorstep of number ten, Queen's Crescent, Marylebone.

"Oh, I don't know! I've got to go through with it now, haven't I? It's just like you

The Making of a Prig

and me not to have touched on anything really important all the way; isn't it? And I've got such a heap of things to tell you," said Katharine, in a nervous tone; and she gave a little shiver as an east wind came rushing up the street and blew dirty pieces of paper against the dingy iron railings, whence they fluttered down into the area.

"Never mind; I'll look you up some evening soon. Let me know if you want bucking up or anything. Good-bye, old chum."

And she found herself inside a dimly lighted, distempered hall, face to face with a kindly looking maid, who was greeting her with the air of conventional welcome she had been told to assume towards strangers. It was supposed to support the advertisement that this was a home.

"Miss Jennings? No, miss; she won't be in, not before supper. And the lady what's in your cubicle ain't cleared out yet, miss, so I can't take your box up, neither. Will you come and have your tea, miss? This way, if you please."

Katharine followed her mechanically. The heroic notions that had sustained her for weeks were vanishing before this pleasant-faced maid and the dreary, distempered hall. For the

The Making of a Prig

first time in her life a feeling of shyness suddenly overwhelmed her, as the servant held open a door, and a hum of voices and clatter of plates came out into the passage. For the moment, she hardly knew where to look or what to do. The room into which she had been ushered was a bare-looking one, though clean enough, and better lighted than the hall outside. Long tables were placed across it, and around these, on wooden chairs, sat some twenty or thirty girls of various ages, some of whom were talking and others reading, as they occupied themselves with their tea. They all looked up when Katharine came into the room, but the spectacle did not present enough novelty to interest them long, and they soon looked away again and went on with their several occupations. "*She* won't be here long,— not the sort," Katharine overheard one of them saying to another, and the casual remark brought the colour to her cheeks, and made her assume desperately some show of courage.

"May I take this chair?" she asked, moving towards a vacant place as she spoke.

"It isn't anybody's; none of them are unless the plate is turned upside down," volunteered the girl in the next chair. She was

The Making of a Prig

reading "Pitman's Phonetic Journal," and eating bread and treacle.

"You have to get your own tea from the urn over there, and collect your food from all the other tables," she added in the same brusque manner, as Katharine sat down and looked helplessly about her. However, by following out the instructions thus thrown at her, she managed, with a little difficulty, to procure what she wanted from the food that was scattered incidentally about the room, and then returned to her seat by the girl who was eating bread and treacle.

"Isn't it rather late for tea?" she asked of her neighbour, who at least seemed friendly in a raw sort of way.

"It always goes on till seven; most of them don't get back from the office before this, you see."

"What office?" asked Katharine, who did not see.

"Any office," returned the girl, staring round at her. "Post office generally, or a place in the city, or something like that. Some of them are shorthand clerks, like me,—it's shorter hours and better paid as a rule; but it's getting overcrowded, like everything else."

"Do you like it?" asked Katharine. The

The Making of a Prig

girl stared again. The possibility of liking one's work had never occurred to her before.

"Of course not; but we have to grin and bear it, like the food here and everything else. I'm sorry for you if you mean to stop here long; you don't look as though you could stand it. I've seen your sort before, and they never stop long."

"Oh, I mean to stop," said Katharine decidedly. But her heroic mood had been completely dissipated by the leaden atmosphere of the place, and she could not repress a sigh.

"Butter bad?" asked her neighbour cheerfully. "Try the treacle; it's safer. You can't go far wrong with treacle. The jam's always suspicious; you find plum stones in the strawberries, and so on."

Katharine was obliged to laugh, and the shorthand clerk, who had not meant to make a joke, seemed hurt.

"I beg your pardon," said Katharine, "but your cynical view of the food is so awfully funny."

"Wait till you've been here three years, like I have," said the shorthand clerk, and she returned to her newspaper.

Katharine tried to stay the sinking at her

heart, and made a critical review of the room. What impressed her most was the twang of the girls' voices. Not that they were noisy,—for they seemed a quiet set on the whole; either daily routine or respectability had succeeded in subduing their spirits; but for all that they did not look unhappy, and Katharine supposed, as her neighbour had remarked, that it was possible to get used to it after a time.

"And the room is certainly clean," she reflected, as she made an effort to see the brighter side of things; "and the girls don't stare, or ask questions, or do anything unpleasant. I *couldn't* tell them anything about myself if they did. And I do wish, though I know it's awfully snobbish, that some of them were ladies."

Her neighbour broke in upon her thoughts, and Katharine came to herself with a start.

"Whose cuby are you going to have?" she was asking.

"I — I don't know. The servant said it was not empty yet. I should rather like to unpack."

"I don't suppose you will get a permanent one yet awhile," said the shorthand clerk, in the cheerful way with which she imparted all

The Making of a Prig

her unpleasant revelations; "they always move you about for a week or two first. I expect you are coming into our room for the present; Miss King is going up to Scotland by the night mail. Jenny will tell you when she comes in. Supper is at nine," she added, pushing back her chair and folding up her paper, "and there are two reception rooms upstairs, if you want to sit somewhere till your cubicle is empty."

Katharine thanked her, and felt more forlorn than ever when the shorthand clerk had gone. But the servant came to her rescue a few minutes later, and offered to take her to her room which was now empty.

"Is it Miss King's?" asked Katharine, and felt a little happier when she learned that it was. She would have one acquaintance in the same room at all events. But her heart sank again, when she found herself alone with her two boxes in a curtained corner of a dingy room, the corner that was the farthest from the window and the smallest of the four compartments. There was hardly room to move; and when she tried to unpack her boxes, she found that most of the drawers in the tiny chest were already occupied, and that there were no pegs for her dresses.

The Making of a Prig

"Could anything be more dreary?" she said aloud. "And the curtains are just horribly dirty, and I don't feel as though I *could* get into that bed. And what a tiny jug and basin!"

"Hullo, is that you?" said the voice of the shorthand clerk, who had come into her part of the room unobserved. "I guessed you'd feel pretty bad when you saw what it was like. They all do. But you might as well turn up the gas, and make it as cheerful as possible. That's better. Well, it's not much like the prospectus, is it?"

Katharine remembered the plausible statements of the prospectus, and broke into a laugh. There was a grim humour in her situation that appealed to her, though it seemed to be lost on her companion.

"Well, I'm glad you can laugh, though I never found it funny myself," she called out. "But don't stay moping here; come into the drawing-room until the bell rings for supper, won't you?"

Katharine followed her advice, and allowed herself to be taken into another bare looking room, over the dining-room. This was furnished with a horsehair sofa and three basket chairs, which were all occupied, several cane

The Making of a Prig

chairs, and two square tables, at which some girls sat writing. One of them looked up as the door opened, and asked the shorthand clerk to come and help her with her arithmetic.

"You know I'm no good, Polly. Where's Miss Browne?" asked the shorthand clerk, pushing a chair towards Katharine, and taking one herself.

"She's out; I think you might try," said the girl who had spoken to her, in a peevish tone. "I have got to finish this paper tonight; and I'm fagged now."

"Can I help?" asked Katharine. The other two looked at her, and seemed surprised.

"This is some one new," explained her first friend. "Let me introduce you: Miss Polly Newland, Miss— Why, I don't even know your name, do I?"

"Austen," said Katharine. "Won't you tell me yours?"

The girl said her name was Hyam,—Phyllis Hyam; and they returned to the subject of the arithmetic.

"Let's look at it, Polly," said Phyllis Hyam, and Miss Newland passed the paper across the table. The two girls bent over it, and Phyllis shook her head.

"I never understood stocks,—too badly

taught!" she said, and tilted her chair and began to whistle.

"Shall I try?" said Katharine, taking out a pencil. She worked out the sum to the satisfaction of Polly Newland, who then unbent a little, and explained that she was going up for the Civil Service examination in March.

"I say, you're clever, aren't you? Do you teach?" asked Phyllis Hyam, bringing the front legs of her chair down again with a bang.

"That is what I want to do; but I never have," replied Katharine. The other two looked at her pityingly.

"Any friends in London?" they asked.

"Only relations; and they won't help me."

"Of course not. Relations never do. Hope you'll get some work," said the shorthand clerk dubiously. Katharine changed the conversation, to hide her own growing apprehension.

"Where are the newspapers?" she asked, looking round.

"In the prospectus; never saw them anywhere else!" said Phyllis, with a short laugh.

"Did you expect to find any?" asked Polly Newland. "They all do," she added gravely.

The Making of a Prig

"It's like the baths, and the boots, and everything else."

"Surely, the bath-room is not a fallacy?" exclaimed Katharine in dismay.

"Oh, there is one down in the basement; but all the water has to be boiled for it, so only three people can have a bath every evening. You have to put your name down in a book; and your turn comes in about a fortnight."

"And the boots?" said Katharine, suppressing a sigh.

"You have to clean your own, that's all. They are supposed to provide the blacking and the brushes; but, my eye, what brushes! Of course you get used to it after a bit. When you get to your worst, you will probably wear them dirty."

"When does one get to one's worst?" asked Katharine.

"That depends," said Polly Newland, sucking the end of her pencil, and staring across in a curious manner at Katharine. "I should say you would get to it pretty soon, if you stop long enough."

"Of course I shall stop!" cried Katharine, a little impatiently. "Why do you both say that?"

The Making of a Prig

The two girls glanced at one another.

"You're not the sort," said Phyllis shortly; and Polly returned to her arithmetic.

Katharine relapsed into a dream. All her aspirations, all her hopes of making her father a rich man, had only landed her in number ten, Queen's Crescent, Marylebone! She looked round at the silent occupants of the room,—some of them too tired to do anything but lounge about, some of them reading novelettes, some of them mending stockings. She wondered if her existence would simply become like theirs,—a daily routine, with just enough money to support life, and not enough to buy its pleasures; enough energy to get through its toil, and not enough to enjoy its leisure. Ivingdon, with its recent troubles, its more distant happiness, seemed separated from this rude moment of disillusionment by a long stretch of years. A passionate instinct of rebellion against the circumstances that were answerable for her present situation made her unhappiness seem still more pitiable to her; and a tragic picture of herself, martyred and forgotten, ten years hence, brought sympathetic tears to her own eyes.

A piano began a cheerful accompaniment in the next room, and some one sang a ballad in

The Making of a Prig

a fresh, untrained soprano. The piano was out of tune, and the song was of the cheapest and most popular nature; but it made an interruption in the sound of the traffic outside on the cobble-stones, and Katharine glanced round the room characteristically, in search of an answering smile. But the other girls were as unaffected by the music as they had been by the dreariness that preceded it; and nobody looked up from what she was doing. Only one of them made a comment; it was Phyllis Hyam. "How that girl does thump!" she said.

But on Katharine the effect had been instantaneous. She was not cultured in music: with her it was an emotion, not an art; and the little jingling tune had already turned her thoughts into a happier channel. Her spirits rose insensibly, and the spell that the dingy surroundings had cast over her was broken. Why should she believe what these two girls told her? Surely, her conviction that she would make something of her life was not going to wear itself out in a miserable struggle to keep alive! She was worth something more than that: she was intellectual beyond her years; every one had told her so, until she had come to believe it was true; and her future was in her own hands. She would be a teacher of a new school; she would make a name for herself by her lectures; and then, some day, when she had acquired a fortune, and all the world was talking of her talent, and her goodness, and her beauty, — she was going to be very beautiful, too, in her dream, — these girls would remember that they had doubted her powers of endurance. She was even rehearsing what she would say to them in the hour of her triumph, when a touch on her shoulder brought her back abruptly to her present surroundings, and she looked up to see a little white-haired lady at her side, in a lace cap and a black silk apron.

"Miss Austen? Come down with me, and let us have a little chat together. I was sorry not to be back in time to receive you, my dear."

It was a sudden awakening; but she was able to smile as she followed her guide downstairs.

"She has the captivating manner of an impostor," she reflected. "She is just like Widow Priest! But it accounts for the prospectus."

CHAPTER VII

THE next day, she began a vigorous search for work. She did everything that is generally done by women who come up from the country and expect to find employment waiting for them; she answered advertisements, she visited agents, she walked over the length and breadth of London, she neglected no opportunity that seemed to offer possibilities. But she soon found that she had much to learn. She discovered that she was not the only girl in London, who thought there was a future before her because she was more intellectually minded than the rest of her family; and she found that every agent's office was full of women, with more experience than herself, who had also passed the Higher Local Examination with honours, and did not think very much of it. And she had to learn that an apologetic manner is not the best one to assume towards strangers, and that omnibus conductors do not mean to be patronising when they say "missy," and that a policeman is always open to the flattery

The Making of a Prig

of being addressed as "Constable." But what she did not learn was the extravagance of being economical; and it was some time yet before she discovered that walking until she was overtired, and fasting until she could not eat, were the two most expensive things she could have done.

But she found no work. Either there was none to be had, or she was too young; or, as they sometimes implied, too attractive. When this last objection was made to her by the elderly principal of a girl's school, Katharine stared in complete bewilderment for a moment or two, and then broke into an incredulous laugh.

"But, surely, my looking young and — and inexperienced would not affect my powers of teaching," she remonstrated.

"It would prevent my taking you," replied the principal coldly. "I must have some one about me whom I can trust, and leave safely with the children. Besides, what do I know of your capabilities? You say you have never even tried to teach?"

"But I know I can teach, — I am certain of it; I only want a chance. Why must I wait until I am old and unsympathetic, and can no longer feel in touch with the children, before

The Making of a Prig

any one will trust me with a class? It is not reasonable."

The elderly principal remained unmoved.

"The teaching market is overcrowded by such as you," she said. "I should advise your trying something else."

"I have not been trained to anything else," said Katharine. "That is where it is so hard. I might have got a secretaryship, if I had known shorthand. I never knew I should have to earn my own living, or I should be better qualified to do it. But I know I can teach, if I get the chance."

"Are you compelled to earn your living?" asked the principal, a little less indifferently. "Pardon me, but I have heard your tale so often before from girls who might, with a little forbearance, have remained at home."

"I am compelled," answered Katharine. "At least — "

A feeling of loyalty to her father, her lovable, faulty old father, who was so unconscious of her present difficulties, kept her silent and brought a troubled look into her face. The elderly principal was not unkindly, when circumstances did not force her to be academic; and Katharine, when she looked troubled, was very attractive indeed.

The Making of a Prig

"My dear," she said, with a severity that she assumed in order to justify her weakness in her own mind, "what are your friends thinking of? Go home; it is the right place for a child like you."

Katharine hurried away to conceal her desire to laugh. She did not go home, however; she went to a cheap milliner's in the Edgware Road, and ordered them to make her a severely simple bonnet. And when it came home the next evening, and she put it on, she hardly knew whether to laugh or to cry at the reflection of herself in the glass. "Whatever would daddy say?" she thought, and put it hastily back into the box; and if the other occupants of her room had happened to come in just then, they would certainly have modified their opinion of her pride and her coldness. But, after all, she was no better off than before; for the contrast of youth and age that her new bonnet made in her appearance was rather conspicuous than otherwise, and she found that her old countrified hat suited her purpose far better.

She saw very little of Ted at this time. He asked her to come out with him, once or twice, but she always refused. She was afraid that he would ask questions, and she shrank

The Making of a Prig

from telling any one, even Ted, of her failure to get on. On the few occasions that she went down to speak to him in the hall, she told him that she was getting along quite well, and would be sure to hear of some work very soon, and that she would prefer not to come out with him because it unsettled her. And Ted, in his humble-minded way, thought she had made new friends in the house and did not care to be bothered with him; and Katharine, who read him like a book, knew that he thought so, and made fresh efforts to get on so that she could spend all her leisure time with him. She wrote home in the same spirit, and said that she was sure of making her way soon, and that, meanwhile, she had everything she wanted, and nobody was to be anxious about her. And her father, with the quaint unworldliness of his nature, wrote back that he was glad to hear she was happy, and that he had no doubt the ten pounds he had given her would last until she earned some more, and that he had just picked up a perfect bargain in an old book shop for thirty shillings.

"Dear daddy," smiled Katharine, without a trace of bitterness. "Could any one be more economical for other people, and more extravagant for himself? I wonder if that is what makes me love him so? But, oh, what would I give for that thirty shillings!"

She counted her little store for the twentieth time, and sat thinking. Doubtless she had spent her money injudiciously at first; but the fact remained that, if she went on at her present rate of expenditure, she would have to return home in a fortnight. If she went without her midday meal, and economised in every possible way, she might manage to remain another month.

"That is what I must do," she said. "That will bring me to the middle of March, and I shall have been in London just nine weeks. And, after all, the food is so nasty that I sha'n't mind much. Besides, it is really very romantic to starve a little."

It grew less romantic as another fortnight went by. The food had never seemed less nasty than it did now; and she had to take long walks at dinner time to escape the appetising smell of the hot dishes. She had never realised before what a very healthy appetite she possessed; and she remembered with some regret how she had been too dainty, at first, to touch the food at all, and had lived for days almost entirely on bread and butter. But now she would have eaten any of it with a relish,—

The Making of a Prig

even a certain dish which was said to be stewed rabbit, but which she had derisively termed "a cat in a pie dish."

One day, she read an alluring advertisement of a new agency. She had lost her faith in agencies, and she had no more money for fees; but at least it was an object for a walk, and anything was better than waiting indoors for something to happen. To be idle in a place like Queen's Crescent was not an enviable position. And by this time she knew her London pretty well, and it fascinated her, and spoke to her of life, and work, and the future; and a walk through any part of it was always exhilarating. As she turned into the park at the Marble Arch, a carriage and pair rumbled out with two well-dressed women in it. Katharine stopped and looked after it, with an amused smile on her face.

"My aunt and cousin," she murmured aloud. "What would they say, if they knew? And once they came to stay with us, and they worried daddy no end, and said I wanted finishing, and ought to go to Paris! It seems to me that life is always a comedy, but sometimes it drops into a roaring farce!"

And pleased with the appositeness of her own remark, she continued her walk in better spirits

The Making of a Prig

than her worldly condition would seem to justify. The agency turned out to be on the top floor of some flats near Parliament Street; and the porter looked curiously at her as he took her up in the lift.

"Agency, miss? So they says, I'm told. Don't believe in agencies much myself, I don't; queerish kind of impostory places, I calls 'em. Don't you let yourself be took in, missy!"

Katharine remembered the condition of her purse, and felt that it was not likely. Her destination was marked by a large amount of information on the wall, headed by the inscription, "Parker's Universal Scholastic and Commercial Agency." She had not much time to study it, however, for an office boy hastened to answer her knock, as though he had been longing for the opportunity to do so for some time, and said that Mr. Parker was at liberty, if she would kindly step in. She fancied that he also stared critically at her, and she began to fear that something was wrong with her personal appearance. This naturally did not add to her self-possession; and when she found herself in a small inner room that smelt of stale tobacco and whiskey, she began to wish she had not come at all. A fair-haired man, with

The Making of a Prig

a moustache and an eyeglass, was sitting with his feet on the mantel-shelf when she entered the room; but he jumped up with a great deal of fuss, and offered her a chair, and asked her what he could do for her. Katharine faltered out her usual inquiry for teaching work; and the fact that Mr. Parker was adjusting his eyeglass and taking her in from head to foot all the time, completed her discomfiture.

"Teaching? To be sure," he said with a supercilious smile, and went at once to the door and told the boy to bring the books.

"There ain't no books, and you knows it," retorted the boy, who seemed disposed to be rebellious; and Mr. Parker vanished precipitately into the other room. When he returned, his smile was unaltered; and he sat down again, and twirled his drooping moustache.

"I have just looked through the books," he said, "and don't see anything good enough for you. Would you care to take anything else?"

"I don't quite know what else I could do," said Katharine doubtfully. She wanted to get away, and did not exactly know how to make a dignified exit.

"Book-keeping, for instance, or literary work? Have you ever tried being a secretary? Ah, I am sure you have! You are not the sort of young lady to lead the life of a humdrum governess, eh?"

"I was my father's secretary," said Katharine. Mr. Parker was leaning across the table and playing with the pens in the ink-stand, so that his hand almost touched her elbow.

"Of course you were. So I was right about you, wasn't I? Don't you think that was very clever of me, now?"

He leaned a little nearer to her, and Katharine drew back instinctively and took her elbow off the table. He found the straight look of her eyes a little disconcerting, and left off playing with the penholders.

"Speaking seriously," he said, donning an official air with alacrity, "would you care to take a post as secretary?"

He had dropped his eyeglass and his supercilious manner, and Katharine took courage.

"I should, immensely. But they are so hard to get."

"Of course they are not easy to pick up, but in an agency like ours we often hear of something good. Let me see, would you like to go out to South Africa? Hardly, I should think."

Katharine said she would not like to go out

The Making of a Prig

to South Africa; whereupon Mr. Parker offered New Zealand as an alternative.

"Your connection seems to lie principally in other quarters of the globe," Katharine felt obliged to remark; and in an unguarded moment she began to laugh at the absurdity of his suggestions. Mr. Parker at once ceased to look official, and laughed with her, and began playing with the pens in the inkstand again.

"Ah, now we understand each other better," he said, resuming his familiar tone. "What you want is a snug little berth with some literary boss, who won't give you too much to do, eh? A nice salary, and some one charming to play with; is n't that it?"

The sheer vulgarity of the man exposed the real nature of the situation to her. Her first impulse was to rush out of his sight, at any cost; but she restrained herself with an effort, and drew a sharp breath to gain time to collect her resources.

"I am afraid, Mr. Parker, that we don't understand each other at all," she said very slowly, trying to conceal the tremble in her voice; "and as I don't feel inclined to emigrate, I think I had better—"

"Now, now, what a hurry you are in, to be sure!" interrupted Mr. Parker, getting up and

The Making of a Prig

lounging round to her side of the table. "You have n't even heard what I was going to say. I've been looking out for a secretary myself, for some time, 'pon my oath I have; but never, until this blessed moment, have I set eyes upon a young lady who suited me so well as you. Now, what do you say to that, eh?"

Katharine had risen, too, and was turning imperceptibly towards the door. She glanced contemptuously round the room, that was so entirely devoid of the ordinary apparatus of business, and she walked swiftly to the door and opened it, before he had time to prevent her.

"You are most kind," she said sarcastically, emboldened by the presence of the office boy, "but I feel that the work would be very much too hard for me. A large business like yours must need so much looking after! Good morning."

Outside, while she was waiting for the lift, her composure completely deserted her, and she found she was trembling all over, and had to lean against the balusters for support.

"I knowed you was n't the sort to go a-mixing of yourself up with that kidney," observed the porter, who detected the tears in her eyes.

The Making of a Prig

"Why didn't you tell me he was such a horrid man?" asked Katharine. She was thoroughly unnerved, and even the porter's sympathy was better than none at all.

"It wasn't my business to hinterfere," said the porter, who was merely curious and not sympathetic at all; and Katharine dried her eyes hastily, and tried to laugh.

"Of course it is nobody's business," she said drearily, and gave him twopence for helping her to realise the fact. "And I shouldn't have cried at all, if I had had any lunch," she added vehemently to herself.

Some one was waiting to enter the lift as she stepped out of it. She looked up by chance and caught his eye, and they uttered each other's name in the same breath.

For a moment they stood silent, as they loosed hands again. Katharine had blushed, hopelessly and irretrievably; but he was standing a little away from her, with just the necessary amount of interest in his look, and the necessary amount of pleasure in his smile. Paul was a man who prided himself on never straining a situation; and directly he saw her agitation at meeting him, he assumed the conventional attitude, entirely for purposes of convenience.

The Making of a Prig

"This is very delightful. Are you staying in town?"

"Yes. At least—"

"Your father well, I hope? And Miss Esther? I am charmed to hear it. Supposing we move out of the draught; yes, cold, isn't it? Thanks, I won't go up now—" this to the porter, who was still waiting by the lift. "Which way are you going? Good! I have a call to pay in Gloucester Place, and we might go in the same cab."

It was pleasant to be ordered about, after taking care of herself for seven weeks, and Katharine yielded at once to the masterful tone, which had always compelled her compliance from the moment she had first heard it.

"Now, please, I want to hear all about it," he began briskly, as they drove westwards. His manner was no longer conventional, and his familiar voice carried her back over the weary months of last year to the spring when she had still been a child. Somehow she did not feel, as with Ted, that she could not tell him about her failures: it seemed as though this man must know all there was to know about her, whether it was pleasant for him to hear it or not; though, as she told him about her coming to town and her subsequent career there, she made her tale so entertaining that Paul was something more than idly amused, when she finally brought it to an end.

"Do you think I ought not to have done it?" she asked him, anxiously, as he did not speak. He looked at her before he answered.

"I cannot imagine how they let you do it!"

"Oh, don't! That is what that horrid old lady principal said. What could possibly happen to me, I should like to know?"

He looked at her again, with his provoking serenity.

"Oh, nothing, of course! At least, not to you."

"Why not to me, particularly?" she asked half petulantly. She did not know whether to be pleased or annoyed that he should credit her with the same infallible quality as every one else.

"Because things of that nature do not, I believe, happen to girls of your nature. But of course I may be wrong; I am quite ignorant in these matters."

She smiled at his show of humility; it was so characteristic of him to affect indifference about his own opinions. But she had learnt something already that day, and she remembered Mr. Parker, and thought that Paul very possibly was wrong on this occasion.

The Making of a Prig

"Every one tells me that. I can't see how I am different," she said thoughtfully.

"I shouldn't worry about it, if I were you. You could not be expected to see. But it is just that little difference that has probably carried you through."

Katharine remembered Mr. Parker again, and laughed outright.

"I don't think so," she said. "I think it is more likely to have been my sense of humour."

"You used to laugh like that when I first knew you," he said involuntarily. She knew that he had spoken without reflection, and she laughed again with pleasure. It was always a triumph to surprise him into spontaneity.

"How jolly it was in those days! Do you remember our tea in the orchard, how we watched Aunt Esther out of the front door, and then brought the things out through the back door?"

"Yes; and how you spilt the milk, and cook wouldn't let you have any more, and our second cups were spoilt?"

"Rather! And how you shocked Dorcas—"

"Ah," sighed Paul; "we can never do those delightful things again. We know one another too well, now."

They allowed themselves to become almost

The Making of a Prig

depressed, for the space of a moment, because they knew one another so well. "All the same," observed Katharine, "there is still one joy left to us. We can quarrel."

He became conventional again as he rang the bell for her at number ten, Queen's Crescent, Marylebone. He raised his hat, and gently pressed her hand, and supposed he should see her again soon. And Katharine, who was occupied in hoping that he did not notice the squalor of the area, and would not come inside the dull, distempered hall, only said that she supposed so too; and then blamed herself hotly, as he drove away, for not responding more warmly.

"He will think I don't want to see him again," she thought wearily, as she dragged herself up the uncarpeted stairs, and went into her dark and dingy cubicle. It had never seemed so dark or so dingy before; and she added miserably to herself, "I had better not see him again, perhaps. It makes it all so much worse afterwards."

She would have been surprised had she known what Paul really was thinking about her.

"She is more of a study than ever," he said to the cab horse. "Still so much of the

The Making of a Prig

innocent pose about her, with just that indication of added knowledge that is so fascinating to a man. She'll do, now she has got away from her depressing relations; and the touch of weirdness in her expression is an improvement. Wonder if Heaton would call her a schoolgirl now? It was quite finished, the careless way she said good-bye, as though it were of no consequence to her at all. Yes; she is a study."

About a week later, when Katharine came down to breakfast, Phyllis Hyam threw her a letter, in her unceremonious fashion.

"Look here!" she said. "I've kept you a chair next to mine, and I've managed to procure you a clean plate, too; so don't go away to the other table, as you did yesterday. Polly's gone; and I won't talk unless you want to. Come on!"

Katharine sat down absently on the hard wooden chair, and began to read her letter. She never wanted to talk at breakfast time, a fact which Phyllis good-naturedly recognised without respecting. To-day she was more silent than usual.

"No, I can't eat any of that stuff," she said to the proffered bacon. "Get me some tea, will you? I'll make myself some toast."

The Making of a Prig

Phyllis trotted off to the fire instead, and made it herself; and Katharine returned to her letter without noticing her further. Judging from the tense look on her face, it was of more than ordinary interest.

"Dear Miss Katharine," it ran,

A school in which I have a little influence is in want of a junior mistress. I have no idea as to the kind of work you want, but if it is of this nature, and you would like to consider it further, come up and see me about it in my chambers. I shall be in at tea-time, any afternoon this week. The best way for you to get here is to come to the Temple Station. Do not think any more about it, if you have already heard of something else.
Yours sincerely,
PAUL WILTON.

"Of course," said Katharine aloud, "I shall go this very afternoon." Then she paused, and looked smilingly into Phyllis Hyam's hot face. "No; I mean to-morrow."

"What?" said Phyllis, looking perplexed. "I thought you wanted it now, and I made it on purpose."

"You dear thing! of course I want it now. You are an angel of goodness, and I am a cross old bear," exclaimed Katharine, with a burst of unusual cordiality; and Phyllis was

The Making of a Prig

consumed with curiosity as to the writer of that letter.

It was not difficult to find Paul Wilton's chambers among the quaint old buildings of Essex Court; and Katharine, as she toiled up the massive oak staircase, stopping on every landing to read the names over the doors, felt that she had reached a delightful oasis of learning in the middle of commercial London.

"How splendid to be a man, and to have brains enough to live in a place like this," she thought enthusiastically; and then, with the cynicism that always dogged the steps of her enthusiasm, she added, "It probably only wants money enough, though."

Paul Wilton opened his own door to her. He looked really glad to see her, and Katharine flushed with pleasure when he kept hold of her hand and drew her into his room.

"This is most good of you," he said; and on the impulse of the moment Katharine let herself be surprised into an indiscretion.

"I was so glad to have your letter; I wanted to see you again dreadfully," she said, without reflection. She meant what she said, but she saw from his manner that she ought not to have said it. Any sentiment that was crudely expressed was always distasteful to him; and

The Making of a Prig

he at once dropped her hand, and pulled forward an arm-chair with a great show of courtesy.

"Is that comfortable, or do you prefer a high one? I thought you might come, one day; but I hardly expected you so soon. It is rather wet, too, is n't it?"

Something impelled her to meet his irritating self-assurance with ridicule.

"Very wet," she replied demurely. "In fact, now I come to think of it, there are a great many reasons why I should not have come. But the one that brought me here, in spite of them all, was a matter of business, if you remember."

If he minded being laughed at, he certainly did not show it, for his tone was much more natural when he answered her.

"Oh, yes, about the school! It is not far from you,—near Paddington, in fact. It is rather a swagger place, I believe; Mrs. Downing is the widow of an old friend of mine, who was killed out in Africa, and she started this concern after his death. She knows nothing about education, but a great deal about etiquette, and as this is also the position of the mothers of most of her pupils, she has no difficulty in convincing them of her capa-

The Making of a Prig

bilities. She is quite flourishing now, I believe. Can you teach arithmetic?"

They discussed the vacant appointment solemnly, with the result that Katharine agreed to accept it if Mrs. Downing approved of her. The salary was not large, but she had learnt by now not to be too particular, and it offered her an opening, at all events.

"I am sure she will like you all right. I told her about your people, and so on, and a clergyman is always a guarantee in such cases. And now for tea."

They talked about the historic associations of the Temple while the housekeeper was bringing in tea; and they talked very little about anything after she had left. Paul was in one of his unaccountable silent moods, and they were never conducive to conversation. He roused himself a little to show her some of his treasures,—an old bit of tapestry, some Japanese prints, a Bartolozzi; but the afternoon was not a success, and his depression soon communicated itself to Katharine.

"I must be going," she said at last, after an awkward pause that he showed no signs of breaking. They stood for a moment in the middle of the room.

"It was good of you to come like this,"

The Making of a Prig

he said, with the slightly worried look he always wore in his morose moods. "I was afraid, perhaps, that I ought not to have asked you."

Her questioning look invited him to continue.

"Not being sure what day you would come, I was unable to provide a chaperon, don't you see? But, of course, if you don't mind, that doesn't matter."

"Of course I don't mind," she said, with a reassuring smile. "Why should I? I know you so well, don't I?"

He continued his explanation, as though he had decided to make it beforehand, and did not mean to be deterred by her unwillingness to hear it.

"Under the circumstances," he said gravely, "you will see that it would be wiser for you not to come here again."

Katharine did not see, and she showed it in her face.

"If I were married," he continued, in a lighter tone, "it would be different; but there are many reasons which have made it impossible for me to marry, and there are still more now, which will prevent my ever doing so. And since I am a bachelor, it is obviously better for you to keep away."

The Making of a Prig

In spite of his assumed carelessness, Katharine felt instinctively that it was to hear this that he had asked her to come and see him to-day. And, like many another woman who has to face as embarrassing a disclosure from a man, her great desire at the moment was to conceal that she had ever entertained the idea of his marrying her at all.

"But does it matter, so long as I don't mind?" she asked, pulling on her gloves for the sake of the occupation. He bent down to button them for her, and their eyes met. "Let me come again," she said impulsively. "You know I think propriety is all rubbish. Besides, I want to come. We can go on being friends, can't we? *I* don't care what other people think!"

"I only care for your sake, not for my own. No, child, it is safer not; you are not the sort. Don't think any more about it. I am old enough to be your father, and have seen more of the world than you. I would not allow you, if you did wish it."

"It is all rubbish," repeated Katharine. "Why am I not the sort? I don't understand; I am tired of being told that. If that is all, I — I wish I were!"

Paul half wished it too, as she stood there

The Making of a Prig

in the firelight, with the glow all over her face and hair; but he laughed away the thought.

"You are an absurd child; you don't know what you are saying. It is lucky there is no one else to hear you. There, go away, and make it up with young Morton! Oh, no, I know nothing whatever about it, I swear I don't; but he won't do you any harm, and he isn't old, and worn out, and—"

"Don't, please don't!" said Katharine, imploringly. "Ted is only like my brother; I love him, but it is altogether different. Mayn't I really see you any more?"

She was threatening to become unpleasantly serious, and Paul switched on the electric light and fetched his coat hastily.

"Why, surely, lots of times, I expect. What a desperately solemn person you are! I believe you work too hard, don't you? Now, I am not going to let you walk to the station alone, so come along."

And Katharine realised, with a hot blush, that she had made a second blunder.

CHAPTER VIII

THE lady principal of the school near Paddington had too high an opinion of her distinguished and influential friend, Mr. Wilton, to refuse a teacher who was so warmly recommended by him, more especially as her junior mistress had left her most inconveniently in the middle of term; so Katharine found herself installed there, about three weeks before the Easter holidays, with a class of thirty children in her sole charge. The teaching was only elementary, but there was plenty to be done; and she soon found that, although she was ostensibly only wanted in the mornings, she had to spend most of her afternoons also in correcting exercises. But the work interested her, and she had no difficulty in managing the children,—a fact which surprised her as much as it did Mrs. Downing, who had expected very little from her youthful looking teacher, in spite of her recommendation by Mr. Wilton. Mrs. Downing was a well-

The Making of a Prig

dressed little woman, with charming manners and an unbounded belief in herself. By resolutely playing on the weaknesses of others, she concealed her own shallowness of mind; and she made up for her lack of brains by contriving to have clever people always about her. She had chatted herself into a fashionable and paying connection in that part of Bayswater which calls itself Hyde Park; and if she employed tact and dissimulation in order to entrap the mothers of the neighbourhood, she was, to do her justice, genuine in her love of their children. Katharine would have found it difficult to like such a woman, had not a two months' sojourn with working gentlewomen taught her to tolerate weaknesses which would formerly have excited her contempt; and she endured her smiles and her blandishments with a stoicism that arose from a knowledge of their harmlessness. But Mrs. Downing remained in ignorance of the fact that her youngest teacher, with the serious face and the childish manner, was able to see right through her; and the impenetrability which saved her from feeling a snub, also spared her the knowledge that Katharine was laughing at her.

One morning, about a week after she had begun her work as junior teacher, Katharine

The Making of a Prig

was interrupted in the middle of her first lesson by the precipitate entrance of the lady principal.

"My dear Miss Austen," she began effusively, and then paused suddenly; for there was something about Katharine, in spite of her youthful look, which warned intruders that she was not to be interrupted so lightly as the other teachers. On this occasion she finished explaining to the children that saying Mary Howard was "*in* the second piano" did not accurately express the fact that Mary Howard was practising in the second music-room; and then turned to see who had come in.

"My dear Miss Austen," began Mrs. Downing again, "so good of you to look after their English; they are apt to be so careless! I am always telling them of it myself, am I not, dear children? Ah, Carry, what an exquisite rose; such colouring; beautiful, beautiful! For me? Thanks, my sweet child; that is so dear of you! My dear Miss Austen, you are so obliging always, and my literature lecturer has suddenly disappointed me, and the first class will have nothing to do in the next hour. So tiresome of Mr. Fletcher! His wife is ill, and he is such a good husband,—quite a model! So I have set them an essay; I cannot *bear* to

The Making of a Prig

have the ordinary work interrupted; and would you be so good as to leave the door open between the two rooms, and give them a little, just a little supervision? That is so dear of you; it has taken a load off my mind. Dear children, listen with all your might to everything Miss Austen has to say, and you will soon be so clever and so wise — I beg your pardon, Miss Austen?"

"Isn't it rather a pity for them to miss their lecture altogether?" said Katharine, in the first breathing space. "I mean, I could give them one if you liked, on something else. My class is being drilled in the next hour, and I have nothing particular to do."

"But I should be charmed, delighted; nothing could be more opportune! My dear Miss Austen, I have found a treasure in you. Children, you must make the most of your teacher while she is with you, for I shall have to take her away from you, quite soon! Miss Austen, I shall come and listen to your lecture myself. I will go and prepare the girls —"

"I think, perhaps, something quite different would be best," said Katharine, detaining her with difficulty. "Would you like it to be on Gothic architecture?"

Mrs. Downing did not know the difference

The Making of a Prig

between a pinnacle and a buttress, but she hastened to say she would like Gothic architecture better than anything else in the world, and had, in fact, been on the point of suggesting it herself; after which, she went to interrupt the first class also, and Katharine devoted her energies to collecting the wandering attention of her own pupils.

At the end of her lecture the lady principal hastened up to her.

"How extremely interesting, to be sure! I had no idea those vaults, and pillars, and things, were so beautiful before. Where did you find out all that? I should like to learn it up myself in the holidays, and give a course of lessons on it to the first class next term."

Katharine tried not to smile.

"I have been learning it all my life, from my father. I don't think I know any textbooks; it would be difficult to read it up in a hurry, I should think." But the lady principal never allowed herself to be thwarted, when she had a fresh idea. Besides, Gothic architecture was quite new, and would be sure to take in the neighbourhood.

"Then you must give a course yourself to the whole school, my dear Miss Austen," she

The Making of a Prig

exclaimed. "I insist upon it; and we will begin the first Wednesday of next term."

Anything that promised an addition to her salary was sure to be agreeable to Katharine, and she was only too pleased to agree. But, meanwhile, her finances were in a deplorable condition. She found herself with nothing but the change out of half a sovereign, about ten days before the end of the term; and although she could easily have asked Miss Jennings to give her credit until she received her salary, she had all a woman's hyper-sensitiveness of conscience, and all her disregard of the importance of food as well; and she resolutely set to work to starve herself during those ten days. Fortunately, she was constitutionally strong, and she never reached the stage of privation when food becomes distasteful; but there was little consolation for her in the fact that she remained healthily hungry all the time, and had to run past the pastry-cooks' shops to escape their seductive display. Long walks at supper time did not compensate for a meal that was satisfying, if it was not very tempting; and the irony of it all was forced upon her with a somewhat grim significance by something that occurred, when she came up to bed one evening, tired out and dispirited. She noticed that the girls stopped talking directly she entered the room; but this would not have aroused her suspicions, if Phyllis Hyam had not made a point of conversing vigorously with her through the curtains, and being more brusque than usual when the others tried to interrupt her.

"Good old Phyllis," reflected Katharine. "They have evidently been abusing me. I wonder what I have done!"

Phyllis enlightened her somewhat unwillingly, the next morning, when the others had gone down to breakfast.

"Don't bother about them; *I* would n't. Mean cats! It's jealousy, of course. Fact is, Polly saw you in a hansom with a man, some time back; she came home full of it. Said you were no better than the rest of us, after all. I said you never pretended to be; it was our own look out, if we chose to think so. Besides, it was most likely your brother, I said. Polly said it was n't; you looked so happy, and he was smiling at you."

"Conclusive evidence," murmured Katharine, with her mouth full of hair-pins. "Did she describe the gentleman in question? It might be useful for future identification."

"Oh, yes, she did! Said he was rather like a corpse with a black beard; had a flavour of

The Making of a Prig

dead loves about him, I think she said; but I don't quite know what she was driving at. And I'm sure I don't care."

"I do. It is most entertaining. Was that all they said?"

Phyllis hesitated, said she was not going to tell any more, and finally told every detail.

"I said they were mean, despicable liars, especially Polly, considering how much you have done for her! And I said that if ever I had the chance—"

"But what did *they* say?" interrupted Katharine.

"Oh, bother! what does it matter? They are a pack of mean sneaks. They said you were never in to lunch now, or supper either; and Polly was sure she had seen you walking with some one, only yesterday evening, and that you went into a restaurant with him; and she declares you see him every day, and that you are going all wrong. I said I should like to kill her. And they all said you must have gone wrong, because you are never in to supper now. I said I should like to kill them all for telling such a false lie, whether it was true or not! It isn't their business whether you choose to come in to supper or not, is it? And then you came in, and— Why, whatever

The Making of a Prig

is the joke now? Mercy me; I thought you would be furious!"

For, of course, it was not to be supposed that she should know why Katharine was rolling on her bed in a paroxysm of laughter.

But the holidays came at last, and she congratulated herself proudly on not having given in once. She left school on the last day of the term with a light heart; everything had made her laugh that morning, from the children's jubilation at the coming holiday, to Mrs. Downing's characteristic farewell. "Don't overwork in the holidays, my dear Miss Austen," she had said, shaking Katharine warmly by both hands. "You look quite worn out; I am afraid you take things a little too seriously, do you not? When you have had *my* experience in school work, you will think nothing of a class like yours! Perhaps you do not eat enough? Take my advice, and try maltine; it is an excellent tonic for the appetite!" And Katharine walked out into the sunshine and the warm air, with a feeling of joy at the thought of the cheque she was to receive on the morrow. There was only one more day of privation for her; and she called herself greedy for thinking about it, and laughed at her own greediness, all in the same breath. She

The Making of a Prig

might easily have humbled her pride and gone home to lunch like a rational being, now that she saw her way to paying for it; but such a weakness as that never entered her head for a moment, and she walked gaily on instead, weaving a rosy dream of the feast she would have if her pocket were full of money. But it was nearly empty, and she only found twopence there when she put her hand in to feel; and she jingled the coppers together, and laughed again, and hurried on a little faster. At Hyde Park Corner a beggar pursued her with his studied tale of distress: he had no home, he whined, and he had eaten nothing for days. "Just my case," said Katharine cheerfully, and a spirit of recklessness impelled her to drop the two pennies into his grimy palm, and then hasten on as before.

"Well met," said a voice behind her. "But what a hurry you are in, to be sure! Where are you off to, now?"

She looked round and saw Paul Wilton, smiling unaffectedly at her in a way that recalled the old days at Ivingdon. Perhaps, the fine day had influenced him too; certainly, he had not been starving for a fortnight, nor would he have seen the humour of it, probably, if he had. But these reflections did not occur to Katharine; it was enough for her that he looked more pleased than usual, and that his manner had lost its constraint.

"I am not going anywhere. The spring has got into my head, that's all; and I felt obliged to walk. Besides, it is the first day of my first holidays!" and she laughed out joyously.

"Yes? You look very jolly over it, any way. Have you lunched yet?"

"Yes,—I mean, no. I don't want any lunch to-day," she said hastily. "Don't let us talk about lunch; it spoils it so."

"But, my dear child, I really must talk about it. I have had nothing to eat since supper last night, and I am going to have some lunch now. You've got to come along, too, so don't make any more objections. I'm not a healthy young woman like you, and I can't eat my three courses at breakfast, and then fast until it is time to spoil my digestion by afternoon tea. Where shall we go? Suppose you stop chuckling for a moment and make a suggestion."

"But I don't know any places, and I don't really want anything to eat," protested Katharine. She would not have been so independent, if she had been a little less hungry. "There's

The Making of a Prig

a confectioner's along here, that always looks rather nice," she added, remembering one she had often passed lately with a lingering look at its attractive contents.

"Nonsense! that's only a shop. Have you ever been in here?"

Katharine confessed that she had never lunched at a restaurant before; and the savoury smell that greeted them as they entered reminded her how very hungry she was, and drove away her last impulse to object.

"Never? Why, what has Ted been up to? Now, you have got to say what you like; this is your merrymaking, you know, because it is the first day of the holidays."

"Oh, but I can't; you must do all that, *please*. You don't know how beautiful it is to be taken care of again."

"Is it?" They smiled at each other across the little table, and the old understanding sprang up between them.

"You're looking very charming," he said, when he had given the waiter his preliminary instructions. "You may abuse the food at your place as much as you like, but it certainly seems to agree with you."

"I don't think," said Katharine carelessly, "that it has anything to do with the food."

The Making of a Prig

"Of course not; my mistake. No doubt it is natural charm triumphing over difficulties. Try some of this, to begin with; bootlaces or sardines?"

Katharine looked perplexed.

"What a delightful child you are," he laughed. "It's to give you an appetite for the rest. I advise the bootlaces. Nonsense! you must do as you are told, for a change. I am not one of your pupils. Besides, it is the first day of the holidays."

And Katharine, who had no desire for a larger appetite than she already possessed, ate the *hors d'œuvre* with a relish, and longed for more, and wondered if she should ever attain to the extreme culture of her companion, who was playing delicately with the sardine on his plate.

"Don't you ever feel hungry?" she asked him. "It seems to add to your isolation that you have none of the ordinary frailties of the flesh. I really believe it would quite destroy my illusion of you, if I ever caught you enjoying a penny bun!"

"You may preserve the illusion, if you like, and remember that I am not a woman. It is only women who— Well, what is it now, child?"

The Making of a Prig

"Do explain this," she begged him, with a comical expression of dismay. "Why is it red?"

"I should say because, fundamentally, it is red mullet. It would never occur to me to inquire more deeply into it; but the rest is probably accounted for by the carte, if you understand French. Don't you think you had better approach it, fasting and with faith?"

"Go on about your appetite, please; it is so awfully entertaining," resumed Katharine. "I believe, if you found yourself really hungry one day, force of habit would still make you eat your lunch as though you didn't want it a bit. Now, wouldn't it?"

"My dear Miss Katharine, you have yet to learn that hunger does not give you a desire for more food, but merely imparts an element of pleasure to it. Go on with your fish, or else the entrée will catch you up."

"I am glad," said Katharine, in the interval between the courses, "that I'm not a superior person like you. It must be so lonely, isn't it?"

"What wine will you drink? White or red?" asked Paul severely.

"Living with you," continued Katharine, leaning back and looking mischievously at

The Making of a Prig

what was visible of him over the wine list, "must be exactly like living with Providence."

"Number five," said Paul to the waiter, laying down the wine list. Then he looked at her, and shook his head reprovingly.

"You see you don't live with me, do you?" he said drily.

"No," retorted Katharine hastily. "I live with sixty-three working gentlewomen, and that is a very different matter."

"Very," he assented, looking so searchingly at her that she found herself beginning to blush. The arrival of the wine made a diversion.

"Oh," said Katharine, "I am quite sure I can't drink any champagne."

"If you had not been so occupied in firing off epigrams, you might have had some choice in the matter. As it is, you have got to do as you are told."

He filled her glass, and she felt that it was very pleasant to do as she was told by him; and her eyes glistened as they met his over the brimming glasses.

"I am so happy to-day," she felt obliged to tell him.

"That's right. Because it is the first day of the holidays?"

The Making of a Prig

"Because you are so nice to me, I think," she replied softly; and then was afraid lest she had said too much. But he nodded, and seemed to understand; and she dropped her eyes suddenly and began crumbling her bread.

"What makes you so nice to me, I wonder," she continued in the same tone. This time he became matter-of-fact.

"The natural order of the universe, I suppose. Man was created to look after woman, and woman to look after man; don't you think so?"

She understood him well enough, by now, to know when to take her tone from him.

"At all events, it saves Providence a lot of trouble," she said; and they laughed together.

Their lunch was a success; and Paul smiled at her woe-begone face when the black coffee had been brought, and she was beginning slowly to remember that there was still such a place as number ten, Queen's Crescent, and that it actually existed in the same metropolis as the one that contained this superb restaurant.

"It is nearly over, and it has been so beautiful," she sighed.

"Nonsense! it has only just begun. It is n't time to be dull yet; I'll tell you when it is,"

The Making of a Prig

said Paul briskly; and he called for a daily paper.

"What do you mean?" gasped Katharine, opening her eyes wide in anticipation of new joys to come.

"We're going to a matinee, of course. Let's see,— have you any choice?"

"A theatre? Oh!" cried Katharine. Then she reddened a little. "You won't laugh if I tell you something?"

"Tell away, you most childish of children!"

"I've never been to a theatre before, either."

They looked at the paper together, and laughed one another's suggestions to scorn, and then found they had only just time to get to the theatre before it began. And she sat through the three acts with her hand lying in his; and to her it was a perfect ending to the most perfect day in her life. He took her home afterwards, and left her at the corner of the street.

"I won't come to the door; better not, perhaps," he said, and his words sent a sudden feeling of chill through her. They seemed to have fallen back into the conventional attitude again, the most appropriate one, probably, for Edgware Road, but none the less depressing on that account.

"You are not going to be sad, now?" he

The Making of a Prig

added, half guessing her thoughts. She looked up in his face and made an effort to be bright.

"It has been beautiful all the time," she said. "I never knew anything could be so beautiful before."

"Ah," he said, smiling back; "it is the first day of your first holidays, you see. We will do it again some day." But she knew as he spoke that they never could do it again.

She saw him occasionally during the Easter holidays. He sent for her once about a pupil he had managed to procure her, and once about some drawing-room lectures he tried to arrange for her, and which fell through. But on both these occasions he was in his silent mood, and she came away infected by his dulness. Then she met him one day in the neighbourhood of Queen's Crescent, and they had a few minutes' conversation in the noise and bustle of the street, that left her far happier than she had been after a tête-à-tête in his chambers.

She went home for a few days, at the end of her holidays, but her visit was not altogether a success. It was a shock to her to find that home was no longer the same, now that she had once left it; and she did not quite realise that the change was in herself as much as in those she had left behind her. Her father had grown accustomed to living without her, and it hurt her pride to find that she was no longer indispensable to him. Her old occupations seemed gone, and there was no time to substitute new ones; she told herself bitterly that she had no place in her own home, and that she had burnt her ships when she went out to make herself a new place in the world. Ivingdon seemed narrower in its sympathies and duller than ever; she wondered how people could go on living with so few ideas in their minds, and so few topics of conversation; even the Rector irritated her by his want of interest in her experiences and by his utter absorption in his own concerns. Miss Esther added to her feeling of strangeness by treating her with elaborate consideration; she would have given anything to be scolded instead, for being profane, or for lying on the hearthrug. But they persisted in regarding her as a child no longer; and she felt graver and more responsible at home, than she had done all the time she was working for her living in London.

On the whole, she was glad when school began again; and she grew much happier when she found herself once more engrossed in the term's work, which had now increased very

The Making of a Prig

materially, owing to her own efforts as well as to those of Paul. Of him, she only had occasional glimpses during the next few weeks; but they were enough to keep their friendship warm, and she soon found herself scribbling little notes to him, when she had anything to tell,—generally about some small success of hers which she felt obliged to confide to some one, and liked best of all to confide to him. Sometimes he did not answer them; and she sighed, and took the hint to write no more for a time. And sometimes he wrote back one of his ceremonious replies, which she had learnt to welcome as the most characteristic thing he could have sent her; for, in his letters, Paul never lost his formality. It was a very satisfactory friendship on both sides, with enough familiarity to give it warmth, and not enough to make it disquieting. But it received an unexpected check towards the middle of June, through an incident that was slight enough in itself, though sufficient to set both of them thinking. And to stop and think in the course of a friendship, especially when it is between a man and a woman, is generally the forerunner of a misunderstanding.

It was the first hot weather that year. May had been disappointingly cold and wet, after

The Making of a Prig

the promise of the month before, but June came in with a burst of sunshine that lasted long enough to justify the papers in talking about the drought. On one of the first fine days, Paul was lazily smoking in his arm-chair after a late breakfast, when a knock at his outer door roused him unpleasantly from a reverie that had threatened to become a nap; and he rose slowly to his feet with something like a muttered imprecation. Then he remembered that he had left the door open for the sake of the draught, and he shouted a brief "Come in," and sank back again into his chair. A light step crossed the threshold, and paused close behind him.

"Who's there?" asked Paul, without moving.

"Well, you *are* cross. And on a morning like this, too!"

Paul got up again, with rather more than his usual show of energy, and turned and stared at his visitor.

"Really, Katharine," he said, with a slowly dawning smile of amusement.

"Oh, I know all that," exclaimed Katharine, with an impatient gesture. "But the sun was shining, and I had to come, and you'll have to put up with it."

The Making of a Prig

Paul looked as though he should have no difficulty in putting up with it; and he went outside, and sported his oak.

"Won't you sit down, and tell me why you have come?" he suggested, when he came back again. Katharine dropped into a chair, and laughed.

"How can you ask? Why, it is my half-term holiday; and the sun's shining. Look!"

"I believe it is, yes," he said, glancing towards the gently flapping blind. "Has that got anything to do with it?"

"Of course it has. I believe, I do believe you never would have known it was a fine day at all, if I had not come to see you!"

"I can hardly believe that you did come to see me for the purpose of telling me it was a fine day," said Paul.

Katharine leaned over the back of her chair, and nodded at him.

"Guess why I did come," she said. He shook his head lazily. She imparted the rest of her news in little instalments, to give it more emphasis. "It's my half-term holiday," she said again, and paused to watch the effect of her words.

"I think I heard you say that before," he observed.

The Making of a Prig

"And I'm going into the country for the whole day."

"Yes?" said Paul, who did not seem impressed.

"And I want you to come too. There! don't you think it was worth a visit?" Her laugh rang out, and filled the little room. Paul was stroking his beard reflectively, but he did not seem vexed.

"Really, Katharine," he said once more.

"Oh, now, don't be musty," she pleaded, resting her chin on her hands. "I just want to do something jolly to-day; and I've never asked you anything before, have I? Do, *please*, Mr. Wilton. I won't bother you again for ever so long; I promise you I won't."

"Are you aware," said Paul, frowning, "that it is not customary to come and visit a man in his chambers in this uninvited manner?"

"You know quite well," retorted Katharine, "that nothing ever matters, if I do it."

"Of course I know that you are beyond the taint of scandal, or the —"

She started up impatiently, and came over to the side of his arm-chair.

"Don't begin to be sarcastic. I never can

The Making of a Prig

think of the word I want, when you get sarcastic. I am not beyond anything, and I am certainly not above asking you a favour. Now, if you were to stop being superior for a few minutes—"

"And if you were to stop standing on one leg, and swinging the other about in that juvenile manner, a catastrophe might be—"

She seized a cushion and tried to smother him with it; but he was too quick for her, and the cushion went spinning to the other end of the room, and she found herself pulled on to his knee.

"You dreadful child! It is too hot, and I am too old for romping in this fashion," he observed lazily.

"Are you coming?" she asked abruptly. She was playing with his watch chain, and he did not quite know what to make of her face.

"Do you want me to?" he asked gently.

"Of course I do," she said, in a swift little whisper; and her fingers strayed up to his scarf pin, and touched his beard.

"I am being dreadfully improper," she said.

"You are being very nice," he replied, and weakly kissed her fingers. She did not move, and he gave her a little shake.

The Making of a Prig

"What a solemn child you are," he complained. "It is impossible to play with you, because you always take one so seriously."

"I know," said Katharine, rousing herself and looking penitent. "I am so sorry! I am made that way, I think. It used to annoy Ted. I think it is because I never had any fun at home, or any one to play with, except Ted. And then I began to earn my living, and so I never had time to be frivolous at all. I suppose I am too old to begin, now."

"Much too old," smiled Paul.

A knock came at the outer door. Paul put her away from him almost roughly, and glanced with a disturbed look round the room.

"You had better stay here," he said shortly, "and keep quiet till I come back."

"Who is it?" asked Katharine, in some bewilderment.

"I don't know. You don't understand," was all he said; and he went out and spoke for a few minutes to a man on the landing.

"It was about a brief," he said on his return. He still frowned a little, and she felt, regretfully, that his genial mood had fled.

"Was that all? Wouldn't he come in?" she asked.

Paul looked at her incredulously.

The Making of a Prig

"It wasn't likely that I should ask him," he said, turning his back to her, and rummaging among the papers on his desk. The colour came into her face, and she was conscious of having said something tactless, without exactly knowing what.

"Shall I go away again?" she asked slowly. The joy seemed suddenly to have been taken out of her half-term holiday.

"You see, it is not for myself that I mind," he tried to explain quietly; "but if you were to be seen in here alone, it would do for your reputation at once, don't you see?"

Katharine looked as though she did not see.

"But, surely, there is no harm in my coming here?" she protested.

"Of course not; no harm at all. It isn't that," said Paul hastily.

"Then," said Katharine, "if there is no harm in it, why should I not come? It is all rubbish, isn't it? I won't come any more if it bothers you; but that is another matter."

"My dear child, do be reasonable! It is not a question of my feelings at all. I like you to come, but I don't want other people to know that you do, because of what they might say. It is for your sake entirely that

The Making of a Prig

I wish you to be careful. That is why I don't come to see you at your place. Do you see now?"

Katharine shook her head.

"It is either wrong, or it isn't wrong," she said obstinately. "I never dreamed that there could be any harm in my coming to see you, or I should not have come. And it was so pleasant, and you have always been so nice to me. Why did you not tell me before? I don't see how it can be wrong, and yet it can't be right, if I have got to pretend to other people that I don't come. I hate hiding things; I don't like the feel of it. I wish I could understand what you mean."

"It is quite easy to understand," said Paul, beginning to realise that his case, as stated baldly by Katharine, was a very lame one. "It is not wrong, as far as you and I are concerned; but it is a hell of a world, and people will talk."

It was strong language for him to use; and she felt again that it was her stupidity that was annoying him. She sighed, and her voice trembled a little.

"I don't see what it has to do with other people at all. It is quite enough for me, if you like me to come; and as for my reputation, it seems to exist solely for the sake of

The Making of a Prig

the other people, so they may as well say what they like about it. *I* don't care. It is horrible of you to suggest such a lot of horrible ideas. According to you, I ought to be feeling ashamed of myself; but — I don't."

"Of course you don't," said Paul, smiling in spite of himself; and he put his hand out and drew her towards him. She was only a child, he told himself, and he was old enough to be her father.

"My dear little puritan," he added softly, "you were never made to live in the world as it is. If all women were like you, good heavens! there wouldn't be any sin left."

"And I believe you would be sorry for it, wouldn't you?" said Katharine suddenly. But when, instead of contradicting her, he tried to make her explain her meaning, she only shook her head resolutely.

"I don't think I could; I hardly know myself. It was only something that came into my head at the moment. It was something horrid; don't let us talk about it any more. Are you coming out with me, or not? Ah, I know you are not coming, now!"

She was swift to notice the least change in his expression, and it had grown very dark in the last ten minutes. He held her out at

The Making of a Prig

arms' length, by her two elbows, and smiled rather uncomfortably.

"I think I won't to-day, dear. Another time, eh? This brief must be looked to at once; and I have some other work, too. Go and enjoy your holiday, without me for a discordant element."

Katharine flushed up hotly, and loosed herself from his grasp. "I don't mind your not coming," she said, looking steadily on the ground, "but I don't think you need bother to invent excuses for *me*."

Paul shrugged his shoulders with an indifference that maddened her. "All right; I won't, then. Go and find some one else for a companion, and don't be a young silly. Can't Ted get off for to-day?"

"You have never said so many horrid things to me before," cried Katharine passionately.

"You have never been so difficult to please before," observed Paul coolly. "Besides, I was under the impression that I was making rather a good suggestion."

"You always drag up Ted when you are being particularly unkind! If I had wanted to go out with Ted, I shouldn't have come to you first."

The Making of a Prig

Paul began to fear a scene; and he had more than a man's horror of scenes. But he could not help seeing the tears in her eyes as she walked away to the door, and he caught her up just as she was opening it.

"Aren't you going to say good-bye? It may be some time before I see you again." He determined, as he spoke, that it should certainly be a very long time before he saw her again. But she disarmed him by turning round swiftly without a trace of her anger left.

"Oh, why must it be some time? You don't mean it, do you? Say you don't mean it, Mr. Wilton," she implored.

"No, no; I was only joking," he said reassuringly. "Quite soon, of course." And he dropped a kiss on the little pink ear that was nearest to him. But when he saw the look on her face, and the quick way in which her breath was coming and going, he blamed himself for his indiscretion, and pushed her playfully outside the door.

When Phyllis Hyam came home from the office, that evening, she found Katharine on the floor of her cubicle, mending stockings; while the rest of her wardrobe occupied all the available space to be seen. Katharine

The Making of a Prig

never did things by halves, and she very rarely had the impulse to mend her clothes.

"Hullo! do you mean to say you are back already?" cried Phyllis, tripping clumsily over the dresses on the floor.

"That hardly demands an answer, does it?" said Katharine, without looking up. She threaded her needle, and added more graciously, "I did n't go, after all."

"Oh," said Phyllis wonderingly. "I 'm sorry."

"You need n't bother, thanks. I did n't want to go. I stayed at home instead, and mended my clothes; they seemed to want it, rather. I shall be quite respectable, now."

"Oh!" said Phyllis again. "I should have left it for a wet day, I think."

"Perhaps your work allows you to select your holidays according to the weather. Mine does n't," said Katharine sarcastically.

Phyllis cleared the chair, and sat down upon it.

"You 've been crying," she said, with the bluntness that estranged all her friends in time. Katharine never minded it; it rather appealed to her love of truth than otherwise.

"Oh, yes! I was disappointed, that 's all. There was nothing really to cry about. I don't

The Making of a Prig

know why I did. Don't sit there and stare, Phyllis; I know I have made a sight of myself."

"No, you haven't. Poor old dear!" said Phyllis, with ill-timed affection. "I should like to tell him what I think of him, I know!" she added emphatically.

"What are you muttering about?" asked Katharine.

"Oh, nothing," said Phyllis. "Have you had any tea?"

"I don't want any tea, thank you. I wish you wouldn't bother. Go down and have your own."

"Guess I shall bring it up here instead, and then we can talk," said Phyllis. In about ten minutes she returned, very much out of breath, with a large tray.

Katharine looked up and frowned. "I said I didn't want any," she said crossly. However, she added that she believed there was some shortbread on the book-case, which Phyllis at once annexed; and her temper began slowly to improve.

"Phyllis," she asked abruptly, after a long pause, "what do you think of men?"

"That they are luxuries," returned Phyllis, without hesitation. "If you've nothing to do

The Making of a Prig

all day but to play about, you can afford to have a man or two around you; but if you're busy, you can't do with them, anyhow."

"Why not?" demanded Katharine. "Don't you think they help one along, rather?"

"Not a bit of it! First, they draw you on, because you seem to hold off; and then, when you begin to warm up, they come down with a quencher, and you feel you've been a sight too bold. And all that kind of thing is distracting; and it affects your work after a time."

"But surely," said Katharine, "a girl can have a man for a friend without going through all that!"

"Don't believe in it; never did; it doesn't work."

"I think it does, sometimes," observed Katharine. "Of course it depends on the girl."

"Entirely," said Phyllis cheerfully. "The man would always spoil it, if he could — without being found out."

Katharine leaned back on the pillow, with her arms behind her head, and her eyes fixed on the ceiling.

"That's just it," she said thoughtfully; "men are so much more conventional than women. I am glad I am not a man, after all.

The Making of a Prig

There is no need for a woman to be conventional, is there? She is n't afraid of being suspected, all the time. I 'm certain conventionality was made for man, and not man for conventionality, and that woman never had a hand in it at all."

"I don't know about that, though it sounds very fine," said Phyllis. "But of course men have to be more conventional than we are. It helps them to make some show of respectability, I guess."

"It is very horrible, if one analyses it," murmured Katharine. "According to that, the man who is openly bad is preferable to the man who is conventionally good. Of course Paul is not bad at all; but, oh! I do wish I did n't see through people, when they try to pretend things,—it always annoys them."

"Eh?" said Phyllis, looking up. "Your tea is getting cold."

"Never mind about the tea! Tell me, Phyllis, do you think any woman can attract any man, if she likes?"

"Of course she can, if she is not in love with him."

Katharine winced, and brought her eyes down to look at her unconscious friend, who was still munching shortbread with an

The Making of a Prig

expression of complete contentment on her face.

"I mean if she *is* in love with him, very much in love with him."

"Can't say; never was, myself. But I don't believe you can do anything, if you've got it badly; you have to let yourself go, and hope for the best."

"I don't believe you know any more about it than I do, Phyllis. I'll tell you what it is that is attractive to a man in a woman: it is her imperfections. He likes her to be jealous, and vain, and full of small deceptions. He hates her to be tolerant, and large-minded, and truthful; above all, he hates her to be truthful. I don't know why it is so, but it is."

"It is because she isn't too mighty big to worship him, then; nor cute enough to see through him," said Phyllis.

"If you can see through a man, you should never fall in love with him," added Katharine.

"Oh, I don't know!" said Phyllis. "You can always pretend not to see; they never know."

"A nice man does," said Katharine, smiling for the first time. The tea had made her feel more charitable; and she took up her pen, and wrote to her mother's connections, the Keeleys,

The Making of a Prig

who did not know she was in town, to ask them when she could call and see them.

She felt the need of knowing some one, now that she had made up her mind not to know Paul any more. For he had taught her the desire for companionship, and she shrank from being left entirely friendless.

CHAPTER IX

AT first she was surprised to find that it was so easy to get on without him. She persuaded herself that her indifference arose from her annoyance at his having imposed the conventional view of things upon her; but, in reality, it was due to her conviction that he would be the first to give in, and would soon write and ask her to go and see him. And she longed for an opportunity to write and refuse him. But when a fortnight passed by and no letter came from him, her righteous scorn deserted her and she became merely angry. The flatness of being completely ignored was unendurable; and she longed more than ever for a chance of showing him that her dignity was equal to his, although she was beginning to fear that he was not going to give her the necessary occasion. Then came days when she felt reckless, and determined to cease thinking about him at any cost; and she threw herself into any distraction that offered itself, and tried

The Making of a Prig

to think that she was quite getting over her desire to see him. It was in one of these moods that she went to call on the Keeleys, who had written to tell her that they were always at home on Thursdays. The fact of putting on her best clothes was in itself some satisfaction; it was a step towards restoring her self-respect, at all events, and she felt happier than she had been for some time past as she walked down Park Lane and found her way to their house in Curzon Street.

The Honourable Mrs. Keeley was the widow of a peer's son who had been a cabinet minister and had signalised his political career by supporting every bill for the emancipation of women, and his domestic one by impressing upon his wife that her true sphere was the home. The natural reaction followed after his death, when Mrs. Keeley broke loose from the restraint his presence had put upon her, and practised the precepts he had loved to expound in public. She became the most active of political women; she spoke upon platforms; she harried the ratepayers until they elected her favourite county councillor; she canvassed in the slums for the candidate who would vote for woman's suffrage. She had a passion for everything that was modern, irrespective of its value;

The Making of a Prig

and she spent the time that was not occupied by her public duties in trying to force her principles upon her only daughter. But Marion Keeley refused to be modern, except in her amusements; she accepted the bicycle and the cigarette with equanimity, but she had no desires to reform anything or anybody; she merely wanted to enjoy herself as much as possible, and she looked forward to making a wealthy marriage in the future. Her greatest ambition was to avoid being bored, and her greatest trial was the energy of her mother. She never pretended to be advanced; and she felt that she had been wasted on the wrong mother when she saw most of the girls of her acquaintance burning to do things in defiance of their old-fashioned parents. She chose her own friends from the idle world of Mayfair; and so it was that two distinct sets of people met in the Keeleys' drawing-room on Thursday afternoons and disapproved of each other.

Katharine received a warm reception from her hostess. The fact that she belonged to the class of working gentlewomen, about whom Mrs. Keeley had many theories but little knowledge, was a sufficient evidence of her right to be encouraged; and she found herself seated on an uncomfortable stool, and intro-

The Making of a Prig

duced to an East-end clergyman and a lady inspector of factories within five minutes of her entry into the room. She glanced rather longingly towards the back drawing-room, where her cousin Marion was looking very pretty and was flirting very charmingly with three smart-looking boys; but it was evident that her aunt had labelled her as one of her own set, and she resigned herself to her fate, and agreed with the East-end clergyman that the want of rain was becoming serious.

"My niece lectures, you know; strikingly clever, and *so* young," said Mrs. Keeley in a breathless aside to the lady inspector, as she came back from the opposite side of the room, where she had just coupled a socialist and a guardian of the poor.

"Indeed!" said the lady inspector; and Katharine began to lose her diffidence when she found that she smiled quite like an ordinary person. "Do you lecture on hygiene? Because Mr. Hodgson-Pemberton is getting up some popular lectures in his parish, and we are trying to find a lecturer for hygiene?"

Mr. Hodgson-Pemberton became animated for a moment; but when Katharine said, apologetically, that her subjects were merely literary, he took no further interest in her and

The Making of a Prig

resumed his conversation with the lady inspector of factories. Katharine was left alone again, and relapsed into one of her dreams, until Marion recognised her and came and fetched her into the back drawing-room.

"Isn't it refreshing?" she said to the boys, who had now increased in number: "Kitty doesn't know anything about politics, and she doesn't want to be with the fogies at all, do you, Kitty? And, for all that, she is dreadfully clever, and gives lectures on all sorts of things to all sorts of people. Oh, dear, I do wish I were clever!"

"Oh, please don't be clever, Miss Keeley! you won't know me any longer if you are," said her favourite boy, imploringly.

"You are far too charming to be clever," added another boy, who had been her favourite last week, and was trying to regain his position by elaborate compliments.

"That's rubbish," said Marion crushingly; "and not very polite to my cousin, either."

The dethroned favourite did his best to repair his blunder by assuring Katharine that he would never have supposed her to be clever, if he had not been told so. And when she laughed uncontrollably at his remark, he chose to be offended, and withdrew altogether.

The Making of a Prig

"You shouldn't laugh at him. He can't help it," said Marion, and she introduced a third admirer to Katharine to get rid of him. He had very little to say, and when she had confessed that she did not bicycle, and never went in the park because she was too busy, he stared a little without speaking at all, and then contrived to join again in the conversation that was buzzing around Marion. Most of the other people had left now, and Katharine was trying to summon up courage to do the same, when her aunt came up to her again, and presented her to a weary-looking girl in a big hat.

"You ought to know each other," she said, effusively, "because you are both workers. Miss Martin does gesso work, and has a studio of her own; and my niece gives lectures, you know."

They looked at one another rather hopelessly, and Katharine resisted another impulse to laugh.

"The knowledge of our mutual occupations doesn't seem to help the conversation much, does it?" she said; and the weary-looking girl tried to smile.

"That's right," said Mrs. Keeley, resting for a moment in a chair near them. "I knew

The Making of a Prig

you two would have plenty to say to each other. That's the best of you working-women; there is such a bond of sympathy between you."

"Is there?" said Katharine, remembering the sixty-three working-women at Queen's Crescent, and her feelings towards them. But Mrs. Keeley had ideas about women who worked, and meant to air them.

"It is so splendid to think that women can really do men's work, in spite of everything that is said to the contrary," she continued.

The weary-looking girl made no attempt to contradict her, but Katharine was less docile.

"I don't think they can," she objected. "They might, perhaps, if they had a fair chance; but they haven't."

"But they are getting it every day," cried Mrs. Keeley, waxing enthusiastic. "Think of the progress that has been made, even in my time; and in another ten years there will be nothing that women will not be able to do in common with men! Isn't it a glorious reflection?"

"I don't think it will be so," persisted Katharine. "It has nothing to do with education, or any of those things. A woman is

The Making of a Prig

handicapped, just because she is a woman, and has to go on living like a woman. There is always home work to be done, or some one to be nursed, or clothes to be mended. A man has nothing to do but his work; but a woman is expected to do a woman's work as well as a man's. It is too much for any one to do well. I am a working-woman myself, and I don't find it so pleasant as it is painted."

"I'm *so* glad you think so," murmured Marion, who had come up unobserved, with her favourite in close attendance. "I was afraid you would be on mamma's side, and I believe you are on mine, after all."

At this point the weary-looking girl got up to leave, as though she could not bear it another minute, and Katharine tried to do the same; but she was not to be let off so easily.

"Tell me," said her aunt earnestly, "do you not think that women are happier if they have work to do for their living?"

"I suppose it is possible, but I haven't met any who are," answered Katharine. "I think it is because they feel they have sacrificed all the pleasures of life. Men don't like women who work, do they?"

The eyes of Marion met those of her fa-

The Making of a Prig

vourite admirer; and Marion blushed. But Mrs. Keeley returned to the charge.

"Indeed, there are many in my own acquaintance who have the greatest admiration for working-women."

"Oh, yes," laughed Katharine, "they have lots of admiration for us; but they don't fall in love with us, that's all. I think it is because it is the elusive quality in woman that fascinates men; and directly they begin to understand her, they cease to be fascinated by her. And woman is growing less mysterious every day, now; she is chiefly occupied in explaining herself, and that is why men don't find her such good fun. At least, I think so."

"You know us remarkably well, Miss Austen, you do, really," drawled the favourite boy.

"Oh, no," said Katharine, really getting up this time, "I don't pretend to. But I do know the working gentlewoman very well indeed, and I don't think she is a bit like the popular idea of her."

She was much pleased with herself as she walked home; and even the bustle of Edgware Road and the squalor of Queen's Crescent failed to remove the pleasant impression that her excursion into the fashionable world had left with her. It comforted her wounded

The Making of a Prig

feelings to discover that she could hold her own in a room full of people, although the only man whose opinion she valued held her of no more account than a child.

"Hullo! you seem pleased with yourself," said Polly Newland, as she entered the house. The cockney twang of her voice struck unmusically on Katharine's ear, and she murmured some sort of ungracious reply and turned to rummage in the box for letters. There was one for her, and the sight of the precise, upright handwriting drove every thought of Polly, and the Keeleys, and her pleasant afternoon out of her head. Even then something kept her from reading it at once, and she took it upstairs into her cubicle, and laid it on the table while she changed her clothes and elaborately folded up her best ones and put them away. Then she sat down on the bed and tore it open with trembling fingers, and tried to cheat herself into the belief that she was perfectly indifferent as to its contents.

"Dear child," it ran:—

What has become of you? Come round and have tea with me to-morrow afternoon. I have some new books to show you.

Yours ever,
Paul Wilton.

The Making of a Prig

Here at last was the opportunity she had wanted. He should know now that she was not a child, to be laughed at because she was cross, to be ignored when she was hurt, and to be coaxed back into good humour again by a bribe. She would be able to show him now that she was not the sort of woman he seemed to consider her, and she told herself several times that she was overjoyed at being given the chance of telling him so. But when it came to the point, she found that the cold, dignified letter she had been composing for weeks was not so easy to write; and she spent the rest of the evening in thinking of new ones. First of all, it was to be very short, and very stiff; but that was not obvious enough to gratify her injured feelings, and she set to work on another one that was mainly sarcastic. But sarcasm seemed a sorry weapon to use when she had reached such a crisis in her life as this; and she thought of another one in bed, after the light was out, in which she determined that he should know she was unhappy as well. And this one was so pathetic that it even roused her own pity, and she felt that it would be positively inhuman to send such a letter as that to any one, however badly he had behaved.

The Making of a Prig

In the end, she did not write to him at all. It was more effective, she thought, to remain silent. So she went to school the next morning as usual, and gave her lessons as usual; though she looked in the glass at intervals to see if she were pale and had a sad expression, which certainly ought to have been the case. But even her head did not ache, which it did sometimes; and Nature obstinately refused to come to her assistance. She reached home again about four o'clock, and the aspect of the doorsteps and the area completed her discomfiture. If they had only been a little less squalid, a little more free from the domination of cats, she might have retained her dignified attitude to the end. But there was something about them to-day that recalled the cosy little room in the Temple by vivid contrast; and she flung her pile of exercise books recklessly upon the hall table, and hastened out of the house again, without allowing herself time to think.

"I was afraid you were not coming," he said, and he greeted her with both hands. She never remembered seeing him so unreserved in his welcome before; and she marvelled at herself for having attempted to keep away from him any longer.

The Making of a Prig

"It was because of the cats," she said, laughing to hide her emotion. But she could not hide anything from him; he knew something of what she was thinking, and he bent down and deliberately kissed her.

"Why did you do that?" she asked, trying to free her hands to cover her burning face.

"Because you didn't stop me, I suppose," he replied, lightly.

"But I didn't know you were going to."

"Because I knew you wouldn't mind, then."

She did not speak, and her eyes were lowered.

"Did you mind, Katharine?"

"No," she whispered.

"Now, tell me why I am indebted to the cats," he said, as he rang the bell for tea; and for the rest of the afternoon they talked, as Katharine laughingly said, "without any conversation."

There was no explanation on either side, no attempt at facing the situation; and she felt when she left him that she had thrown away her last chance of controlling their friendship. There had been a tacit struggle between their two wills, and his had triumphed. She could never put him out of her life now, unless he

The Making of a Prig

broke with her of his own accord; and she realised bitterly, even while she was glad, that he did not care enough for her to do that.

She saw him constantly all through the hot months of July and August. She gave up her original intention of going home for the summer holidays, on the pretext of reading for her next term's lectures at the British Museum; but she did very little work in reality, and she spent whole days in the reading-room, regardless of the people around her, sometimes even of the book before her, and dreamed long hours away, making visions in which only two people played any prominent part,—and those two people were Paul and herself. Her whole life seemed to be a kind of dream just then, with a vivid incident here and there when she met him or went to see him, and the rest a vague nebula, in which something outside herself made her do what was expected of her. Sometimes she felt impelled to work furiously hard for a day or two, or to take long walks by herself, as though nothing else would tire her restless energy; and then she would relapse into her lethargic mood again, and do nothing but watch vigilantly for the post, or haunt the streets where she had sometimes met him. And all the while she thought she was happy,

The Making of a Prig

with a kind of weird, passionate happiness she had never known before; and it seemed to compensate for the hours of suspense and anxiety she went through when he took no notice of her. For his conduct was as inexplicable as ever; and for one day that he was demonstrative and even affectionate, she had to endure many of indifference that almost amounted to cruelty.

"We are horribly alike; it hurts me sometimes when I suddenly find myself in you," she said to him one day, when he was in an expansive mood.

"I am much honoured by the discovery, but I fail to see where the likeness lies," was his reply.

"It is not very definite," she said, thoughtfully. "I think it must be because I feel your changes of mood so quickly. We laugh together at something, and everything seems so fearfully nice; and then, suddenly, I feel that something has sprung up between us, and I look up and I see that you feel it too, and all at once there is nothing to talk about. Haven't you ever noticed it?"

"I think you are an absurdly sensitive little girl," he said, smiling.

"Of course," she continued, without heeding

The Making of a Prig

his remark, "on the surface, no two people could be more unlike than we are. You are so awfully afraid of showing what you feel, for instance; but I always tell you everything, don't I?"

"My dear child, what nonsense! I am of the most artless and confiding nature; while you, on the contrary, never give yourself away at all. Why, you never tell me anything I really want to know! Whatever put such an idea into that curious head of yours?"

"Oh, don't!" she cried. "You make me feel quite hysterical! You have no right to upset all my views on my own character, as well as on yours. I *know* I am stupidly demonstrative. I have often blushed all over because I have told you things I never meant to tell any one. How can you say I am reserved? I only wish I were!"

"The few confidences of a reserved person are always rash ones," observed Paul. "The same might be said of the reflections of an impulsive person, or the impulses of a reflective one. It all comes from want of habit. You can't alter your temperament, that's all."

"But I can't believe that I am reserved," she persisted; "it seems incredible. And it makes us more alike than ever."

The Making of a Prig

"Really, Katharine, I beg you to rid your mind of that exceedingly fallacious notion," said Paul, laughing. "I assure you I am to be read like a book."

"A book in a strange language, then. I don't think I shall ever be able to read it," said Katharine, shaking her head. And she drew down a rebuke upon herself for being solemn.

They had a tacit unwillingness to become serious, about this time; their conversation was made up of trivialities, and he never kissed her except on the tips of her fingers. They avoided any demonstration of feeling that might have revealed to them the anomaly of their position, and they mutually shrank from defining their relations towards one another.

They were standing together at the window, one day, looking down into Fountain Court, which was as hot and as dusty as ever in spite of the water that was playing into the basin in the middle.

"What are you thinking about?" he asked her, so suddenly that she was surprised into an answer.

"I was thinking how queer it is that you and I should be friends like this," she replied, truthfully.

"What's the matter with our friendship,

The Making of a Prig

then?" he asked, in the prosaic manner he always assumed when she showed any sentiment. She laughed.

"There's nothing the matter with it, of course. You are the most unromantic person I ever knew. You seem to delight in divesting every little trivial incident of its sentiment. What makes you such a Vandal?"

"But, surely, you are not supposing that there *is* any romance in our knowing each other, are you?"

"I never dreamed of such a thing," retorted Katharine. "I think there is more romance in your cigarette holder than in the whole of you!"

Sometimes she wondered if he were capable of deep feeling at all, or if his indifference were really assumed.

"I envy you your utter disregard of circumstance," she once exclaimed to him. "How did you learn it? Do you really never feel things, or is it only an easy way of getting through life?"

"I'm afraid I don't see what you are driving at. I dare say you are being very brilliant, but I fail to discern what I am expected to say."

"You are not expected to say anything," she said, playfully. "That is the best of being a gigantic fraud like yourself; nobody ever does expect you to fulfil the ordinary requirements of every-day life. You might be a heathen god, who grins heartlessly while people try to propitiate him with the best they have to offer, and who eats up their gifts greedily when they are not looking."

"Has all this any reference to me, might I ask?"

"I don't believe you've got any ordinary human feeling," pursued Katharine. "I don't believe you care for anybody or anything, so long as you are left alone. Why don't you say something, instead of staring at me as though I were a curiosity?"

"If you reflect, you will see that there has not been a single pause since you began to speak. Besides, why shouldn't you be catechised as well as myself? Where do you keep all your deep feeling, please? I haven't seen much of it, but perhaps I have no right to expect such a thing. No doubt you keep it all for some luckier person than myself."

His tone was one of raillery, as hers had been when she began to talk. But she startled him, as she did sometimes, by a sudden change of mood; and she flashed round upon him indignantly.

The Making of a Prig

"It is horrible of you to laugh at me. You know you don't mean what you say; you know I have any amount of deep feeling. I hide it on purpose, because you don't like me to show it, you know you don't! I — I think you are very unkind to me."

He reached out his hand and stroked her hair gently; she was sitting a little away from him, and he could see the sensitive curve of her lower lip.

"Don't, child! One never knows how to take you. Another time you would have seen that I was only joking."

"You have no right to joke about such a serious matter. You know it was a serious matter, now; wasn't it?"

"The most serious in the universe," he assured her; and he brought his hand gently down her cheek, and laid it against her throat.

"You are only laughing; you always laugh at me," she complained; but she bent her head, and kissed his hand softly. "I feel like a wolf, sometimes," she added, impetuously.

"Didn't you have enough tea?" he said. But she knew by his tone that he was not laughing at her now, and she went on recklessly.

"I am certain I could not love any one very

much, without hating him too. It is a horrible dual feeling that tears one to pieces. Is it the badness in me, I wonder? Other people don't seem to feel like that when they are in love. Why is it?"

"Because it is the same emotion, or set of emotions, that inspires both love and hatred," said Paul. "Circumstance does the rest, or temperament."

"It is inexplicable," said Katharine solemnly. "I can understand killing a man, because he could not understand my love for him; or casting off my own child, because it was bored by my affection. I am quite sure," she added, quaintly, "that I should bore any one in a week, if I really loved him."

"Oh, no," said Paul politely; and they again laughed away a crisis.

CHAPTER X

At the beginning of October Paul went abroad. She had thought that life without him would be unendurable, and she could not analyse her own feelings when she found that she could laugh with as much enjoyment as ever, and that her fits of depression were less frequent than before. In fact, she had often been far more unsettled if a letter from him had failed to arrive when it was due; and a new sensation of freedom went far to cure her of the restlessness that had possessed her all the summer. She began to probe into her truth-loving soul, to try and discover whether her feeling for him was not an illusion after all; but she found no satisfactory explanation of the problem that was puzzling her, and she put it voluntarily away from her, and turned to her work as a healthy antidote. And she had a good deal of work just then. Thanks to the influence of the Honourable Mrs. Keeley, her private pupils were increasing in number, and these, with her lectures at the school, were producing

The Making of a Prig

a salary that relieved her of all financial worry for the present. She was making new friends too, and it added to her contentment to find that people asked her to go and see them because they liked her. For the first time since her arrival in town, she felt sure of being on the way to success; and the sensation was a very thrilling one. Phyllis asked her, one day, why she was looking so happy. Katharine laughed, and pondered for a moment; then answered frankly that she did not know why. "I only know that I have never been so gloriously happy in my whole life," she added; and she wondered, as she spoke, whether the mad, feverish happiness of the summer months had really been happiness at all. But Phyllis, who felt that she had no share in this strange new life of hers, looked back regretfully on the earlier days when Katharine had been lonely and in need of her sympathy. Even Ted told her she was looking "very fit," and this was the highest term of praise in his vocabulary. For, since the beginning of October, she had seen a good deal of Ted. It was very restful to come back to him, after the state of high pressure in which she had been living lately; and when she grew accustomed to his being a West-end young man, instead of an easy-going

The Making of a Prig

schoolboy, she found him the same delightful companion as of old. He did not allude to her many weeks of silence, nor ask her how she had spent them; he came at her bidding, and when he found that she liked him to come he came again. He was as humble as ever, except in matters of worldly knowledge, and there he showed a youthful superiority over her which amused her immensely. His laziness, which had always been more or less an assumption with him, had developed into the fashionable pose of indifference; and she tried in vain to spur him on to doing something definite with his life, instead of letting it drift away in a city office.

"Girls don't understand these things," he would say with good-natured obstinacy. "Of course I loathe the beastly hole; any decent chap would. But I may as well stop there. It's not my fault that I was ever born, is it? I get enough to live on, with what my cousin allows me; and I'm not going to grind all I know, to get a rise of five bob a week. It isn't good enough. I'm sure I'm very easily contented, and my wants are few enough. Oh, rats! I must have a frock coat; every decent chap has. And you couldn't possibly call that extravagant, because I sha'n't think of squaring it for a year at least. Of course I don't expect you to understand these things, Kitty; it's impossible for a man to do the cheap, like a woman."

And Katharine, who always wanted to reconstitute society, with a very limited knowledge of its first principles, would strike in with a vigorous denunciation of his comfortable philosophy; and he would listen and laugh at her, and make no effort to support his own opinion which he continued to hold, nevertheless. He was the best companion she could have had just then; he never varied, whatever her mood was, and he kept her from thinking too much about herself, which was a habit she had acquired since she last saw him. Besides, he was a link with her childhood, that period of vague existence which had held no problems to be solved, and had never inspired her with a wish to reform human nature. So they spent many evenings and half-holidays together, and they went frequently to the theatre and sat in the gallery, which often entertained them as much as the play itself; and he loved to pay for her, with a manly air, at the box office, and always made the same kind of weak resistance afterwards, when Katharine insisted on refunding her share, under the lamp at the corner of

The Making of a Prig

Queen's Crescent, Marylebone. Sometimes, when they were unusually well off, they would dine at an Italian restaurant first, where they could have many wonderful dishes for two shillings, and a bottle of tenpenny claret. On one occasion — it was Ted's birthday, and his cousin had sent him a five-pound note — they had more than an ordinary jubilation.

"Buck up, and get ready!" he had rushed into the little distempered hall to say. "We'll go to a new place, where the waiters aren't dirty, and the wine isn't like sulphuric acid. And, Kitty, put on that hat with the pink roses, won't you?"

They did their best, on that memorable evening, to reduce the five pound-note, and to behave as though they were millionaires. They drove in a hansom to the restaurant in question, which was a very brilliant little one close to the theatres, where they had a waiter to themselves instead of the fifth part of a very distracted and breathless one. The state of Ted's pockets could always be estimated by the amount of attention he exacted from the waiter; and this evening there was absolutely nothing he would do for himself, from the disposal of his walking stick to the choice of the wine.

The Making of a Prig

"It's a very good tip to start by taking the waiter into your confidence," he assured Kitty, when it had just been settled for them that they were to have *bisque* soup.

"It's convenient, sometimes, when everything is written in French," observed Katharine. Ted changed the conversation. On his twenty-second birthday he felt inclined, for once in a way, to assert himself.

"I'm rather gone on this place; pretty, isn't it?" he continued. "All the candle-shades are red, white, and blue; mean to say you didn't twig that? You're getting less alive every day, Kit! Awfully up-to-date place, this! I don't suppose there is a single decent woman in the room, bar yourself."

He said this with such pride in the knowledge, that she would not have robbed him of his satisfaction for the world.

"They look much the same as other women to me," she observed, after a quick survey of the little tables.

"That's because you don't know. How should you? Women never do, bless them! Do you like fizz?"

"Oh, Ted, don't! Isn't it a pity to spend such a lot just for nothing?" she remonstrated. She had visions of all the unpaid bills he had

The Making of a Prig

disclosed to her in one of his recent pessimistic moods.

"My dear Kitty, you really must learn to enjoy life. Don't be so beastly serious over everything. Bills? What bills? There are n't any to-night. The art of living is knowing when to be extravagant."

And she had to acknowledge, for the rest of the evening, that he had certainly mastered the art of living. They went to a music hall, and sat in the stalls; and Katharine enjoyed it because Ted was there, and because he was so funny all through,—first, in his fear of being asked by the conjurer for his hat which was a new one, or his watch which was only represented by his watch chain; and secondly, because he tried so hard to distract her attention from the songs that were inclined to be risky. And Ted enjoyed it because it was the thing to do, and because there would be hardly any of that fiver left by the time he got home.

"Then you 'll look me up at the office at five to-morrow; you won't forget?" he asked rather wistfully, when they parted on the doorstep.

"Of course I won't forget," she answered, hastily. "Dear old Ted, I have enjoyed it so much!"

The Making of a Prig

"Good-night, dear," he said, as he turned away. And his tone haunted her rather, as she groped her way up to bed in the dark. She began to feel half afraid, with some annoyance at the thought, that this pleasant state of things could not go on for ever, and that Ted was going to spoil it all again as he had done once before, by taking their relationship seriously. So she prepared to meet him, the next afternoon, with a reserve of manner that was meant to indicate her displeasure; but he disconcerted her very much by asking her bluntly why the dickens she was playing so poorly; and she felt unreasonably annoyed to find that her fears were groundless. So for some time longer they went on as before, in the same happy-go-lucky kind of way that had always characterised them. She learned to know several of his friends, most of them genuine boyish fellows, who appealed to her more by their affection for Ted than by any qualities they possessed themselves. They seemed very much alike, though she was bound to acknowledge that this impression may have been conveyed by the cut of their clothes and the shape of their hats, which did not differ by so much as a hair's breadth. But Ted always shone by

The Making of a Prig

comparison with the best of them. He was the only one of his set who did not take himself seriously; he had a sense of humour, too, and this compensated for the exhausted manner which he felt obliged to assume as a mark of fellowship with them.

He asked her, one night, with some diffidence, if she would mind coming to tea in his chambers on the following Sunday.

"I should n't think of asking you to come alone," he hastened to add; "but Monty is going to bring his sister along, so that's all square as long as you don't mind."

"Mind! Why, of course not," said Katharine, in frank astonishment. "What is there to mind? I want to see your chambers very much. I have often wondered why you never asked me before."

Ted stared at her for a moment, and then began tracing what remained of the pattern in the linoleum with his walking stick. They were standing, as usual, in the hall of number ten, Queen's Crescent.

"What a babe you are, Kitty!" he said, without looking up; and Katharine reddened as she suddenly realised his meaning. Of course Ted was no longer a boy, and she was no longer a child; and she was on precisely the

The Making of a Prig

same footing with him in the eyes of the world as she was with Paul Wilton. Unconsciously, she compared the attitude of the two men under similar circumstances; Paul, who was unscrupulous in letting her visit him as long as no one knew of it; and Ted, who had no views on the matter at all but merely wished to spare her any annoyance.

"I see," she said. "Who is Monty?" She always felt nervous when he offered to introduce her to any of his friends; because she knew very well that he warned them all beforehand that she had "ideas," and this put her at a distinct disadvantage to begin with.

"Oh, Monty's awfully smart! He knows no end. You'll like Monty, I expect. He wants to meet you, awfully; says he likes the look of your photograph. I told him how bally clever you were, and all that. Monty's clever, too; he reads Ibsen."

Katharine received this proof of Monty's intellectual ability with some cynicism which, however, she was careful to conceal.

"I shall be delighted to meet him," she said. "What time shall I come?"

"Oh, any time; four will do. And, I say, Kit, I suppose I must have cream, must n't I? You can't give Monty milk that's been sitting

The Making of a Prig

for hours, and spoof him that it's cream. I've done that sometimes, but you can't spoof Monty."

"Oh, I'll bring the cream. I know a shop where they'll let me have it on Sunday," said Katharine confidently; and Ted left comforted.

After all, Monty's sister could not come; but Ted's sense of the fitness of things was satisfied by his having asked her, and, as Monty himself came and did not seem afraid of Katharine as all his other friends were, he felt that his tea-party was a success. The only thing that marred his enjoyment was the fact that Katharine, for some unaccountable caprice, refused to be intellectual in spite of the efforts of Monty, whose real name proved to be Montague, to draw her out. Monty was a young man with a gentlemanly view of life, tempered by a great desire to be thought advanced; and he began the conversation with a will.

"Awfully clever new thing at the Royalty! Suppose you've seen it, Miss Austen?" he began. "Awfully plucky of the Independent Theatre to put it on, it is really."

"Is it?" smiled Katharine. "I haven't seen it yet. Ted and I hate those advanced plays,—they're so slow as a rule. Comic operas, we like best."

The Making of a Prig

Monty seemed surprised; and Ted was a little disconcerted by this frank avowal of his own ordinary tastes.

"You see, Kit only goes to those things to please me," he said, apologetically. "She's just as keen on all those humpy plays as you are, don't you know?"

Monty was not sure that he knew, but he turned to another branch of art.

"Talking about posters," he said,—which was only his favourite method of opening a conversation, for nobody was talking about posters at all,—"have you seen that awfully clever one of the new paper, 'The Future'? It's by quite a new man, in the French style, so bold and yet so subtle. But of course you must have seen it."

"Oh, yes," laughed Katharine, "I should think I had! You mean the red one, don't you, with a black sun and a cactus thing, and a lot of spots all over it? Ted and I were laughing at it, only yesterday. Do you really think it is good?"

Monty said he really did think so; and Ted, who was torn in two by his admiration for both of them, came to his rescue.

"You had better be careful, Kitty," he said, anxiously. "Monty does know."

The Making of a Prig

"Of course," said Katharine politely, "it is only a matter of taste, is n't it, Mr. Montague?"

"Quite so," replied Monty, concealing his feelings of superiority as well as he could. "By the way, talking of taste, what do you think of the new Danish poet? Rather strong, don't you think?"

Katharine sighed, and glanced nervously at Ted.

"Oh, I suppose he's all right," she said, with the exaggerated solemnity that would have betrayed to any one who knew her well how close she was to laughter; "but he is n't a bit new, is he? I mean, he only says the same things over again that the old poets said ever so much better. Don't you think so?"

"They all give you the hump, any way," put in Ted. But Monty ignored his remark, and said that he never read any of the old poets; he preferred the new ones because they went so much deeper.

"Hang it all, Kitty; what a rum girl you are!" said Ted, in a disappointed tone. "A chap never knows where to have you. I did think you were advanced, if you could n't be anything else."

At this point, Katharine yielded to an irresistible desire to laugh; and Ted looked

The Making of a Prig

anxiously at the friend to whom he had given such a false impression of her "ideas." But, to his surprise, the great Monty himself joined in her laughter, and seemed inexpressibly relieved to find that she was not nearly so intellectual as she had been painted, and it was therefore no longer incumbent on him to sustain the conversation at such a high pitch.

"Now that we have settled I am not advanced," said Katharine, turning up her veil, "supposing we have some tea." And for the rest of the afternoon they behaved like rational beings, and discussed the low comedians and the comic papers.

"All the same," Ted complained, when Monty had gone, "he's awfully clever, really. You may rot as much as you like, but Monty does know about things. You don't know what a fool he makes *me* feel."

"He needn't do that," said Katharine. "It would be the kindest thing in the world not to let him read another magazine or newspaper for six months. I think he is very nice, though, when he lets himself go."

Ted looked at her a little sadly.

"You seemed to be getting on beastly well, I thought," he said.

"He is certainly very amusing, and it was

The Making of a Prig

nice of you to ask me to meet him," continued Katharine, innocently. Ted walked to the fireplace, and studied himself silently in the looking-glass.

"I wish I wasn't such a damned fool," he burst out savagely. Katharine stood still with amazement.

"Ted!" she cried. "Ted! What do you mean?"

Ted planted his elbows on the mantel-shelf, and buried his face in his hands.

"Ted!" she said again, with distress in her voice. "What do you mean, Ted? As if I — oh, Ted! And a man like *that*! You know piles more than he does, old boy, ever so much more. You don't put on any side, that's all; and he does. You mustn't say that any more, Ted; oh, you mustn't! It hurts."

"You know you are spoofing me," he said, in muffled tones. "You know you only say that just to please me. You think I am a fool all the time, only you are a good old brick and pretend not to see it. As if I didn't twig! I ought never to have been born."

Katharine walked swiftly over to him, and laid her hand on his arm. She did not reason with herself; she only knew that she wanted to comfort him at any price.

The Making of a Prig

"Ted," she said, earnestly, "*I* am glad you were born."

He turned round suddenly, and looked at her; and she started nervously at the eagerness of his expression. He had not looked like that when he made love to her in the summer-house.

"Do you mean that, dear?"

"Oh, don't be so serious, Ted! Of course I mean it; of course I am glad you were born. Think how forlorn I should have been without you; it would have been awful if I had been alone." He looked only half satisfied; and she went on desperately, caring for nothing but to charm away the miserable look from his face. "Dear Ted, you know what you are to me; you know I don't care a little bit for Monty, or anybody else, either."

"Do you mean that, Kitty?" he asked again, in a voice that he could not steady. "Not anybody else, dear?"

Something indefinable, something that made her long for another man's voice to be trembling for love of her, as his was trembling now, seemed to come between them and to strike her dumb. He looked at her searchingly for a moment, then shook off her hand and pushed her away from him. She shivered as the suspi-

The Making of a Prig

cion crossed her mind that he had guessed her thoughts, though she knew quite well that the renewal of her friendship with Paul was unknown to him. She went up to him again, and let him seize her two hands and crush them until she could have cried out with the pain.

"You are the best fellow in the world, Ted," she said. "But you must n't look like that; oh, don't! I am not worth it, Ted; I am not nearly good enough for you, dear,—you know I am not. I am never going to marry any one; I am not the sort to marry; I am hard, and cold, and bitter. Sometimes, I think I shall just work and fight my way to the end. I know I shall never be happy in the way most women are happy. But I will be your chum, and stick to you always, Ted. May I?"

"Oh, shut up!" said Ted, almost in a whisper; and the tears sprang to her eyes. She stood on tiptoe, and impetuously kissed the only place on his cheek she could reach. At the moment, it seemed the only right and proper thing to be done.

"I could n't help it. I had to; and I don't care," she said, defiantly. And Ted wrung her hands again, and let them go.

"I suppose none of it is your fault, Kit, but—"

The Making of a Prig

There was a pause, and Katharine avoided his eyes, for the first time in her life.

"It's time to go," she said. "Will you see me home?"

She fetched him his hat and coat, and Ted gave himself a shake.

"He didn't take cream, after all," he said, with a poor attempt at a laugh.

CHAPTER XI

A LETTER came from Paul, just before Christmas, to say that he was going to remain at Monte Carlo for another month. Knowing his passion for warmth and sunshine, she was not surprised; she was hardly even disappointed. She began to wonder what her feelings would have been if he had decided to remain another year instead of another month; and again she was obliged to own that the solution of her own state of mind was beyond her. The Keeleys went abroad about the same time, which took away her chief centre of amusement; and her former mood of satisfaction was succeeded by one of serene indifference, in which she continued until she went home for the holidays. At Ivingdon the dulness of four weeks, passed almost entirely in the company of her father and Miss Esther, caused the old unsatisfied feeling to return to her; and she longed for a vent for the restless energy that wore her out as long as there was no work to be done. She grew impatient once more for a

The Making of a Prig

glimpse of Paul Wilton, for the touch of his thin, nervous hand, and the sound of his quiet, unemotional voice; and she acted over and over again, in her mind, how they would meet once more in the little room overlooking Fountain Court, what he would be sure to say to her, and what she knew she would say to him. No letter came from Paul all through those weary days, and she only wrote to him once. The pathetic note was very prominent in that one letter, and she consoled herself with her own unhappiness while she awaited the answer to it; but when no answer came her pride revolted, and she wished passionately that she had never sent it.

"Can't you stay another week, child?" said Miss Esther, as the end of the holidays drew near. "You don't look much better than when you came, though it's not to be expected you should, working away as you do. I never heard such nonsense, and all to no purpose! When I was a girl— But there, what's the use?"

And Katharine, who had heard it all before, explained over again with increasing impatience that her work was a definite thing and required her presence on a certain day. She

The Making of a Prig

had never felt less pleased with herself than on the day of her departure, when she left the home that had once been the whole world to her, and took leave of the people who no longer believed in her. But as she neared London a sensation of coming events dispelled the atmosphere of disapproval which had been stifling her for a whole month, and she once more felt the mistress of her own situation and her own future. Here was life and activity, work and success, and some of it was going to be hers. And Paul Wilton would soon be coming home again. They told her at Queen's Crescent how well she was looking, when she appeared in the dining-room at tea-time; and she laughed back in reply as she contrasted their greeting with her aunt's farewell words.

"Just a year since I first came," she said to Phyllis. "What a lot has happened since then! I don't believe it was myself at all; it must have been somebody else. Oh, I am glad I am different now!"

"I remember," said Phyllis, who never rhapsodised. "Your face was smutty after your journey, and you looked as though you would kill any one who spoke to you."

"And you were eating bread and treacle,"

retorted Katharine. "Let's have some now, shall we?"

"By the way," said Phyllis presently, "there's a letter for you upstairs. It came about a week ago, and I clean forgot to forward it. I'm awfully sorry, but I don't suppose it matters much because it's got a foreign postmark."

The laughter died out of Katharine's face, as she put down her teacup and stared speechlessly at her friend.

"Shall I go and fetch it?" continued the unconscious Phyllis, as she deluged her last morsel of bread with more treacle than any force of cohesion would allow it to hold. "Perhaps you're ready to come up yourself, though? I've prepared a glorification for you — Hullo! what are you in such a desperate hurry about?"

When she arrived breathless at the top of the house, Katharine was already in her cubicle, turning everything over in a wild and fruitless search.

"Go away!" she said shortly, when Phyllis came in. "It was the only thing I asked you to do, and I thought I could trust you. I shall know better another time. What are all these things doing here?"

The Making of a Prig

She knocked her head, as she spoke, against a string of Chinese lanterns. There were flowers on the mantel-shelf, and a look of festivity in the dingy little room; but it was all lost on Katharine, who continued to open and shut the drawers with trembling hands, and to search in every likely place for her letter, until Phyllis put an end to her aimless task by bringing it to her in eloquent silence. Then she stole away again; and Katharine sat down in the midst of the confusion she had created, and became absorbed in its contents. It was very short, and there was hardly any news in it that could not have been extracted from a guide-book; but she spent quite half an hour in reading it and pondering over it, until she knew every one of its stilted phrases by heart. He was very well and it was very hot, and he was sitting by the open window looking down on the orange groves, and the sea was a splendid colour, and there were some very decent people in the hotel, and amongst them her relations the Keeleys. It was hard to look up at last, with dazed eyes, and to discover that she was in Queen's Crescent, Marylebone, instead of being where her thoughts were, in the sunny South of France.

"Hullo," said Phyllis, who was standing at the end of the bed.

The Making of a Prig

"Yes?" said Katharine, smiling. "Do you want anything?"

"Oh, no," said Phyllis, and crept away again. Katharine sat and pondered a little while longer. Presently, she shivered and made the discovery that she was cold, and she jumped up and stretched herself.

"I suppose I must unpack," she said, still smiling contentedly. "Where has Phyllis gone, I wonder?"

She went to the door and made the passage ring with her voice, until Phyllis hurried out of a neighbouring room and apologised for not being there when she was wanted.

"I believe you were there when I didn't want you," said Katharine candidly. "Wasn't I cross to you or something?" Her foot touched one of the discarded Chinese lanterns. "Hullo! I thought there were some lanterns somewhere. Where are they gone?"

"Oh, no!" said Phyllis, going down on her knees before the box. "You must have been dreaming."

"I wasn't dreaming, and you're a foolish old dear, and I am a selfish pig," cried Katharine penitently.

"Oh, no!" said Phyllis again. "I was the pig, you see, because I forgot your letter.

The Making of a Prig

You'll rumple my hair, if you do that again."

Katharine did hug her again, nevertheless, and accused herself of all the offences she could remember, whether they related to the present occasion or not; and Phyllis silenced her in a gruff voice, and the unpacking proceeded by degrees.

"Don't you think," said Katharine irrelevantly, "that women are much more selfish than men, in some ways?"

"What ways?"

"I mean when they are absorbed in anything. Now, a man wouldn't behave like a cad to his best friend, just because he happened to be in love with a girl, would he? But a woman would. She would betray her nearest and dearest for the sake of a man. I am certain I should. Women are so wolfish, directly they feel things; and they seem to lose their sense of honour when they fall in love. Don't they?"

"Where do the stockings go?" was all Phyllis said.

"Perhaps," continued Katharine, "it is because a woman really has stronger feelings than a man."

"I shouldn't wonder," said Phyllis. "Who

The Making of a Prig

packed the sponge bag next to your best hat?"

"I don't think it matters," said Katharine mildly. "I was saying— What are you laughing at?"

"Nothing. Only, it is so delightful to have you back again, moralising away while I do all the work," laughed Phyllis.

Katharine owned humbly that Phyllis always did all the work, and Phyllis bluntly repudiated the charge, and insisted that Katharine was the most unselfish person in the world, and Katharine ended in allowing herself to be persuaded that she was; and the rest of the evening passed in an amicable exchange of news. Even the "cat in the pie dish" seemed appetising that evening.

Her feeling of satisfaction was increased when she arrived at school the next morning and found that Mrs. Downing was anxious to speak to her. An interview with the lady principal at the beginning of term generally foreboded some good.

"I want you to give up the junior teaching this term, my dear Miss Austen," she began, after greeting her warmly. "You are really too good for it, far too good. Mr. Wilton was quite right when he told me how cultured

The Making of a Prig

you were, quite right. At the time, I must confess to feeling very doubtful; you seemed so inexperienced, — so very young, in fact. But I have come to think that in your case it is no drawback to be young; indeed, the dear children seem to prefer it. Their attachment for you is extraordinary; pardon me, I should have said phenomenal. And the way you manage them is perfect, quite perfect, — just the touch of firmness to show that your kindness is not weakness. Admirable! I am most grateful to Mr. Wilton for introducing you to me, most grateful. Such a charming man, is he not? So distinguished!"

She paused for breath, and Katharine murmured an acknowledgment of Mr. Wilton's distinction.

"To come to the point, my dear Miss Austen, I should be charmed, quite charmed, if you would take the senior work this term, — English in all its branches, French translation, Latin, and drawing. I think you know the curriculum, do you not? Thank you very much; that is so good of you! Did you have a pleasant holiday? There is no need to ask how you are, — the very picture of health, I am sure! And the architecture lectures, too; I should be more than grateful if you would continue them as before. Thank you so much — Ah, I beg your pardon?"

Katharine here made a desperate inroad into the torrent of words, and mentioned that she knew no Latin and had never taught any drawing.

"Indeed? But you are too modest, my dear Miss Austen; it is your one failing, if I may say so. Of course, if you wish — then let it be so. But I am convinced you would do both as well as Miss Smithson, quite convinced. However, that can easily be arranged. The salary I think you know, and the lectures will be as before. Indeed, we are most fortunate to have so delightful a lecturer, most fortunate. Ah, there is one more thing," continued Mrs. Downing, leading her towards the door. The rest of her speech was said on the landing which happened, fortunately, to be empty. "This is between ourselves, my dear Miss Austen, — quite between ourselves. I should be more than grateful if you would act as chaperon to the music master this term. It may appear strange that I should ask you to do this, — indeed, I may say peculiar; but I do so in the conviction that I can trust you better than any one else. Of course you will not mention what I have said! I am sure

The Making of a Prig

you understand what I mean. That is so charming of you! Thank you so much!"

And the lady principal returned to say very much the same thing over again to the next teacher whom she summoned. But Katharine, who had long since learnt to regard her insincerity as inevitable, merely congratulated herself on the practical results of her interview, and thoroughly enjoyed the contest that ensued when her new pupils found they were going to be taught by a junior mistress. She felt very elated when she came out of it victorious; and for the next week or two everything seemed to go well with her. She had made a position for herself, although every one had told her it would be impossible; there were people who believed in her thoroughly, and there were others, like Ted and Phyllis Hyam, who did not understand her but worshipped her blindly. It was all very gratifying to her, after the dull month she had spent at home; and for the first time she threw off the reserve she usually showed, though unconsciously, towards the working gentlewomen of Queen's Crescent, and talked about herself in a way that astonished them not a little. Work to them was a sordid necessity, and they were a little jealous of this brilliant girl, with the youth

The Making of a Prig

and the talent, who found no difficulty in winning success where they had barely earned a living, and who seemed to enjoy her life into the bargain.

"Who is that girl with the jolly laugh and the untidy hair?" she overheard a stranger asking Polly Newland one day.

"That one?" was the reply, given in a contemptuous tone. "Oh, she's a caution, I can tell you! Nice? Oh, I dare say! She's a prig, though. Phyllis Hyam — that's the other girl in our room — thinks all the world of her; but I can't stand prigs, myself."

It was a little shock to her self-esteem to hear herself described so baldly, though she consoled herself by the reflection that Polly had never liked her, and there was consequently very little value to be attached to her opinion. But she was careful to remain silent about her own affairs for the next day or two; and she startled Ted, one evening, by asking him suddenly, between the acts of a melodrama, what was meant by a "prig."

"A prig? Oh, I don't know! It's the same thing as a smug, isn't it?"

"But what is a smug?"

"Well, of course, a smug is — well, he's a

The Making of a Prig

smug, I suppose. He has n't got to be anything else, has he? He's a played-out sort of bounder, who wants to have a good time and has n't the pluck, don't you know?"

"Are all prigs bounders?" asked Katharine, in a voice of dismay.

"Oh, I expect so! It does n't matter, does it? At least, there's a chap in our office who is a bit of a prig, and he is n't a bounder exactly. He's a very decent sort of chap, really; I don't half mind him, myself. But they always call him a prig because he goes in for being so mighty saintly; at least, that's what they say. I don't think he is so bad as all that, myself."

"Is it priggish to be good, then? I thought one ought to try."

"My dear Kit, of course you are a girl; don't worry yourself about it. It's altogether different for a girl, don't you see?"

"Then girls are never prigs?" said Katharine eagerly.

"Bless their hearts," said Ted vaguely; and she did not get any further definition from him that evening.

And so the days grew into weeks, and her life became filled with new interests, and she told herself she was learning to live at last.

The Making of a Prig

But she had her bad days, as well; and on these she felt that something was still wanting in her life. And the end of February came, and Paul Wilton had not yet returned to his chambers in Essex Court.

CHAPTER XII

THE courts had just risen, and the barristers in their wigs and gowns were hastening through the Temple on the way to their various chambers. It was not a day on which to linger, for a pitiless east wind swept across Fountain Court, making little eddies in the basin of water where the goldfish swam, and swirling the dust into little sandstorms to blind the shivering people who were using the thoroughfare down to the Embankment. The city clocks were chiming the quarter after four, as Paul Wilton came along with the precise and measured step that never varied whatever the weather might be, and mounted the wooden staircase that led to his rooms. A man rose from his easiest chair as he walked into his sitting-room, and they greeted one another in the cordial though restrained manner of men who had not met for some time.

"Sorry you've been waiting, Heaton. Been here long?" said Paul, throwing off his gown with more rapidity than he usually showed.

The Making of a Prig

"Oh, no matter; my fault for getting here too early," returned Heaton cheerily, as he sat down again and pulled his chair closer to the fire. He never entered anybody's house without making elaborate preparations to stay a long while.

"Fact is," he continued, "it's so long since I saw you that, directly I heard you were back, I felt I must come round and look you up. It was young Linton who told me,—you remember Linton? Ran across him in the club, last night; he knows some friends of yours,— Kerry, or Keeley, or some such name as that; just been calling on them, apparently, and they told him you had travelled back with them. Suppose you know the people I mean?"

Paul admitted that he knew the people he had been travelling with, and Heaton rattled on afresh.

"We were talking about you at the club, only the other afternoon; coincidence, wasn't it? Two or three of us,— Marston, and Hallett, and old Pryor. You remember old Pryor, don't you? Stock Exchange, and swears a lot — ah, you know; he wanted to know what had become of you and your damned career; it was a damned pity for the most brilliant man at the bar, and the only one with a con-

The Making of a Prig

science, to be wasted on a lot of damned foreigners, and so on. You know old Pryor. Of course I agreed with him, but it was n't my business to say so."

He paused a little wistfully, as though he expected Paul to say something to explain his long absence; but the latter only smiled slightly, and walked across to his cupboard in the corner.

"I'm going to have some tea," he observed, "but I don't expect you to join me in that, Heaton. There's some vermuth here, Italian vermuth; or, of course, you can have whiskey if you prefer it."

"Thanks, my boy," laughed the other. "I'm glad to see that five months in the infernal regions have n't spoilt your memory. Claret for boys, brandy for heroes, eh?"

He helped himself to whiskey, and then leaned back in his chair to survey Paul, who was making a cigarette while the water boiled. There was one of the long silences that were inevitable with Paul, unless his companion took the initiative; and for the next five minutes the only sounds to be heard were the singing of the kettle, the rise and fall of footsteps in the court below, and the occasional rattle of the window sash as the wind wrestled with it.

The Making of a Prig

Paul made the tea, and brought his cup to the table, and flung himself at full length on the sofa beside it.

"Well," he said at last, "haven't you any news to tell me? Who is the last charming lady you have been trotting round to all the picture galleries, — the one who is more beautiful, and more intellectual, and more sympathetic than any woman you have ever met?"

Heaton laughed consciously.

"Now, it's odd you should happen to say that," he said in his simple manner. "Of course I know it's only your chaff, confound you, but there *is* just a smattering of truth in it. By Jove, Wilton, you must come and meet her; you never saw such a figure, and she's the wittiest creature I ever ran across! I'm nowhere, when it comes to talk; but she's so kind to me, Wilton, — you can't think; I never met such a sympathetic woman. Really, she has the most extraordinary effect upon me; I haven't been so influenced by any woman since poor little May died, 'pon my word I haven't. I can't think how it's all going to end, I tell you I can't. It's giving me a lot of worry, I know."

"Ah," said Paul gravely. "Widow?"

"Her husband was a brute," said Heaton

The Making of a Prig

energetically. "Colonel in the army, drank, used her villainously I expect, though she does n't say much; she's awfully staunch to the chap. Women are, you know; I can't think why, when we treat them so badly. That's where they get their hold over us, I suppose. But her influence over me is wonderful. I would n't do anything to lose her respect, for the world."

He blinked his eyes, and drank some more whiskey. Perhaps it occurred to him that his companion was even less responsive than usual, for there was more vigour and less sentiment in his tone when he resumed the conversation.

"You never tell me anything about yourself," he complained, rather pathetically. "You draw me out, and I 'm ass enough to be drawn; and then you sit and smile cynically, while I make a fool of myself. How about *your* experiences, eh? 'Pon my word, I don't remember a single instance of your giving me your confidence! You 're such a rum, reserved sort of chap. Well, I dare say you 're right to keep it all to yourself. It does me good to tell things; but then, I 'm different."

"My dear fellow, I 've nothing to tell," replied Paul, smiling. "You forget that my

The Making of a Prig

life is not full of the charming experiences that seem to fall so continually to your lot. And your conversation is so much more interesting than mine would be, that I prefer to listen; that's all. I'm not secretive; I have merely nothing to secrete."

"That's all very well, said Heaton, shaking his head; "but I'm older than you, so that won't wash. You should have heard what those fellows at the club were saying about you."

"Yes? It doesn't interest me in the least," said Paul coldly. But tact was not the strong point of his friend's character, and he went on, notwithstanding.

"Of course I didn't say much,—it isn't my way; besides, you know I think you're always right in the main. But it's enough to make fellows talk, when a man like you, who always sets his career before his pleasure, goes away out of the vacation, and stays away all these months. You must own it's reasonable to speculate a little; it's only in man's nature."

"Some men's," said Paul, as coldly as before. "I should never dream of speculating about anybody's course of action, myself."

"No, no, of course not; I quite agree with you, quite," said Heaton. "By the way," he added, with bland innocence in his expression,

The Making of a Prig

"what sort of people are these Kerrys you have been travelling with? An old married couple of sorts, I suppose!"

Paul raised himself on his elbow and drank his tea straight off, as though he had not heard the question. He was always divided, in his conversations with Heaton, between a desire to snub him and a fear of wounding his sensitiveness.

"You haven't told me the charming widow's name," he said, dropping back into his former position. The other man's face brightened, and the conversation again became a monologue until even Heaton's prosiness was exhausted, and silence fell upon them both. And then, very characteristically, as soon as he was quite sure he was not expected to say anything, Paul suddenly became communicative.

"The Keeleys are rather nice people," he observed, taking his cigarette out of his mouth and staring fixedly at the lighted end of it. "Mother and daughter, you know, just abroad for the winter. Nice little place in Herefordshire, I believe, but they come to town for the season,—Curzon Street."

Heaton was wise enough to remain silent; and Paul went on, after a pause.

The Making of a Prig

"Sat next to them at table d'hôte, and that sort of thing. One is always glad of a compatriot abroad, don't you know! And the mother was really rather nice," he added, as an afterthought.

"And what was the daughter like?" asked Heaton.

"Oh, just an ordinary amusing sort of girl! She's pretty, too, in a sort of way, but I don't admire that kind of thing much, myself. And I think she found me very dull." He paused, and looked thoughtful. "I must take you there when they come up to town, Heaton. You'd get on with them, and the girl is just your style, I fancy. She is really very pretty," he added, becoming thoughtful again.

"Nothing I should like better! Delightful of you to think of it!" exclaimed Heaton, with a warmth that was a little overdone. His want of a sense of proportion was always an annoyance to Paul. "You take me there, that's all," he said, chuckling; "and let me have my head—"

"Which is precisely what you wouldn't have," said Paul drily. "And I'm sure I don't know why you want to know them; they are quite ordinary people, and don't possess every grace and virtue and talent,

The Making of a Prig

like all your other lady friends. However, I shall be very pleased if you really care about it. But you'll be disappointed."

Heaton agreed to be disappointed, and as another pause seemed imminent, he began to think about taking his departure. But Paul did not notice his intention, and seized the occasion to start a new subject.

"Look here, Heaton," he began, so suddenly that the elder man sat down again with precision; "you say I never tell you anything about my experiences. Does that mean that you really think I have anything to tell?"

Heaton looked at him dubiously.

"I'm hanged if I know," he said.

Paul smiled, a little regretfully.

"After years of renunciation," he murmured, "to be merely accounted a riddle! Then you think," he continued, with an interested expression, "that I am not the sort of man women would care about, eh? Well, I dare say you're right. But then, why do they ever care for any of us? I never expect them to, personally."

Heaton was looking at him in a perplexed manner.

"Perhaps I didn't express myself quite clearly," he hastened to say, with his usual wish to compromise. "I only meant that I sometimes think you never can have cared for any one seriously. But I've no doubt I'm wrong. And I never said that nobody had ever cared for *you;* I think that's extremely unlikely. In fact— Do you really want me to say what I think?"

"It would be most interesting," said Paul, still smiling.

"Well," said Heaton decidedly, "I think you're the sort of man who would break a woman's heart and spare her reputation, and perhaps not discover that she liked you at all. I know what women are, and they just love to pine away for a man like you who would never dream of giving them any encouragement. And you have such a fascinating way with you that you just lead them on, without meaning to in the least. You can curse, if you like, Wilton; it's great impertinence on my part, eh?"

"My dear fellow," was all Paul said. As a matter of fact, he had never liked him better than he did at that moment, and his words had set him thinking. But Heaton's next remark undid the good impression he had unwittingly made.

"The fact is," he said, "a woman's reputation is worth only half as much to her as her happiness."

And his worldly wisdom jarred on Paul's nerves, and sounded unnecessarily coarse to him in his present mood; and he did not try to detain him again, when Heaton rose for the second time to take his leave. When he had gone, Paul strolled to the window-seat and smoked another cigarette, looking down into the wind-swept court. And his thoughts deliberately turned to Katharine Austen. He had not seen her for five months, he had not written to her for two, and her last letter to him was dated six weeks back. It had not occurred to him, until he drew it from his pocket now and looked at it, that it was really so long as that since she had written to him; and he became suddenly possessed of a wish to know what those six weeks had held for her. Out there in the orange groves of the South, walking by the side of the beautiful Marion Keeley, with the rustle of her skirts so close to him and the shallow levity of her conversation in his ears, it had been easy to forget the desperately earnest child who was toiling away to earn her living in the dullest quarter of a dull city. But here, where she had so often sat and talked to him, where they had loved to quarrel

The Making of a Prig

and to make it up again, where she had given him rare glimpses of her quaint self and then hastily hidden it from him again, where she had been whimsical and serious by turns, where he had sometimes kissed her and felt her cheek warm at his touch,— here, all sorts of memories rushed back into his mind, and made him wonder why he had yielded so easily to the persuasions of the Keeleys, and remained so long away from England. It was impossible to name Marion Keeley in the same breath with this curiously lovable child who had held him in her sway all last summer, who had never used an art to draw him to her, and yet had succeeded, by force of qualities that she did not know she possessed, in gaining his sincere affection. Yet he had hardly thought of her for two months, and she had not written to him for six weeks. What had she been doing in those six weeks? It had not seemed to matter, when he walked by the side of Marion Keeley, how Katharine was passing her time in London; but now that Marion was no longer near him, now that he was free from her fascination and the necessity of replying to her banalities, it suddenly became of the first importance to him to know what had happened to Katharine in those six weeks. He had

The Making of a Prig

gone away, he told himself, because he had taken fright at the situation, because he could not analyse his own feelings for her, because everything, in the eyes of the world, was hurrying them on to marriage,—and of marriage he had the profoundest dread. And he had allowed himself to be captivated almost immediately, by the ordinary beauty of an ordinary girl, some one who knew how to play upon a certain set of his emotions which Katharine had never learnt to touch. An expression of distaste crossed his face as he threw away his cigarette only half smoked, and looked down at the fountain as he had so often stood and looked with her in the hot days of last July. Heaton's words returned to his mind with a new significance: "Their reputation is worth only half as much to them as their happiness." He remembered how he had parted from Katharine in this very room, before he went abroad; and how he had congratulated himself afterwards on having refrained from kissing her. But he had a sudden recollection now of the look on her face as she turned away from him; and, for the first time, he thought he understood its meaning.

He had never acted on an impulse in his life, before, nor yielded to a wish he could not ana-

The Making of a Prig

lyse; but this afternoon he did both. It was about an hour later that Phyllis Hyam strolled into Katharine's cubicle with the announcement that a gentleman was in the hall, waiting to speak to her.

"Bother!" grumbled Katharine, who was correcting exercises on the bed. "He never said he was coming to-night."

"It is n't Mr. Morton," volunteered Phyllis, from behind her own curtain. "I've never seen him before. He's tall, and thin, and serious looking, with a leathery sort of face, and a dear little fizzly beard."

She made a few more gratuitous remarks on the gentleman in the hall, until she began to wonder why she received no reply to them, and then made the discovery that the occupant of the neighbouring cubicle was no longer there.

Paul was already regretting his impulse. He had never been inside the little distempered hall before, and it struck a feeling of chill into him. A good many girls came in at the door while he was waiting, and they all stared at him inquiringly, and most of them were dull looking. He remembered the sumptuous house in Mayfair that would soon contain Marion Keeley, and he shuddered a little.

The Making of a Prig

"I don't think I should like to live with working-women much," he said, when Katharine came running down the wooden stairs.

It was the only remark that came easily to him, when he felt the warm clasp of her hand and saw the glad look in her eyes.

CHAPTER XIII

She was looking rather tired, he thought, when he examined her more critically; her eyes seemed larger, and her expression had grown restless, and she had lost some of the roundness of her face. But she had gained a good deal in repose of manner; and her voice, when she answered him, was more under control at the moment than his own.

"I shouldn't think you would," she laughed. "I shocked them all at breakfast, this morning, by saying I should like to try idle men for a change!"

It struck him that she would not have made such a remark when he left her last autumn; and again he would have liked to possess a chronicle of the last six weeks. But her laugh was the same as ever, and her hand was still grasping his with a reassuring fervour.

"Come back with me," he said, spontaneously. "We can't talk here, can we? I

The Making of a Prig

dare say I can knock up some sort of a supper for you, if you don't mind a very primitive arrangement."

"It will be beautiful," she said; and the throb of pleasure in her voice allayed his last feeling of suspicion.

They found that, after all, they had very little to say to one another; and they were both glad of the occupation of preparing supper, when they arrived at the Temple and found that the housekeeper had gone out for the evening. They made as much fun as they could over the difficulties of procuring a meal, and avoided personal topics with a scrupulous care, and did not once run the risk of looking each other in the face. And afterwards, when they had made themselves comfortable in two chairs near the lamp and conversation became inevitable, an awkward embarrassment seized them both.

"It's very odd," said Katharine, frowning a little; "but I have been bottling up things to tell you for weeks, and now they seem to have got congested in my brain and I can't get one of them out. Why is it, I wonder? I can't have grown suddenly shy of you; but we seem to have lost touch, somehow. Oh, it's queer; I don't like it!"

The Making of a Prig

She gave herself a little shake. Paul laughed slightly.

"What an absurd child you are! It is only because we have not been together lately, and so we've lost the trick of it. You are always turning yourself inside out, and then sitting down a little way off to look at it."

"I believe I do," owned Katharine. "I always want to know why certain things affect me in certain ways."

"Did you want to know why you were glad to see me, this evening?"

She looked up quickly at him for the first time.

"No," she said, frankly. "At least, I don't think I thought about it."

"Good child!" he said. "Don't think about it." And she wondered why he looked so pleased.

"Why not?" she asked him. "Please tell me."

"Oh, because it isn't good for you to be always turning yourself inside out; certainly not on my account. Besides, it spoils things. Don't you think so?"

"What things?"

"Oh, please! I'm not here to answer such a lot of puzzling questions. Who has

The Making of a Prig

been getting you into such bad habits, while I have been away?"

"Nobody who could answer any of my puzzling questions," she replied, softly; and Paul asked hastily if she would make the coffee. He had fetched her here as an experiment, a kind of test of his own feelings and of hers; and he had a sudden fear lest it should succeed too effectually. She went obediently and did as she was told, and brought him his coffee when it was ready; and he submitted to having sugar in it, since it compelled her to brush his hair with her sleeve as she bent over him with the sugar basin.

"Well?" he asked, in the next pause. She was balancing her spoon on the edge of her cup, with a curious smile on her face.

"Oh, nothing!"

"Nothing must be very interesting, then. But I don't suppose I have any right to know. Have I?"

The spoon dropped on the floor with a clatter.

"Of course you have! I wish you would n't say those things! They hurt so. I was only thinking,— it was n't anything important, but — I'm so awfully happy to-night."

The Making of a Prig

"But that is surely of the very first importance. Might one know why? Or is that some one else's secret, too?"

She disturbed his composure by suddenly pushing her coffee away from her; and there was an angry light in her eyes, as she sprang to her feet and stood looking down at him.

"Sometimes I think I hate you," she said; and the words struck him as being strangely inadequate to the occasion. They might have been spoken by a petulant child, and the moment before he had felt that she was a woman. He put his cup down too, and went towards her.

"Does sometimes mean now?" he asked jestingly. He was trying, impotently, to prevent her from going any farther. But she took a step backward, and did not heed his intention.

"Yes, it does," she said, angrily. "I am tired of being treated like a child; I am tired of letting you do what you like with me. One day you spoil me; and another, you hurt me cruelly. And you don't care a little bit. I am a kind of amusement to you, an interesting puzzle, a toy that does n't seem to break easily; that's all. And I just let you do it,—it is my own fault; when you hurt me

The Making of a Prig

I hide what I feel, and when you are nice to me I forget everything else. Oh, yes, of course I am a fool; do you think I don't know it? You have only to touch my face, or to look at me, or to smile, and you know I am in your hands. I despise myself for it; I would give all I know to be strong enough to put you out of my life. But I can't do it, I can't! And you know I can't; you know I am bound up in you. Everything I feel seems to be yours; all my thoughts seem to belong to you, directly they come into my head; I can't take the smallest step without wondering what you will think of it. Oh, I hate myself for it; you don't know how I hate myself! But I can't help it."

"Stop," said Paul, putting out his hand. But she waved him away, and went on talking rapidly.

"I must say it all now; it has been driving me mad lately. At first, it seemed so easy to get on without you; but it grew much harder as it went on, and when you stopped writing to me, I — I thought I should go mad. It was so awful, too, when I had got used to telling you things; there was no one else I could tell things to, and the loneliness of it was so terrible! I wanted to kill

The Making of a Prig

myself, those days; but I was too big a coward. So I got along somehow; and some days it was easier than others, but it was always hard. Only, nobody ever guessed. Oh, if you knew how I have learnt to deceive people! And there was always my work to get through, as well; it has been horrible. And I could no more help it than I could help breathing. I wanted to kill myself!"

"Don't," half whispered Paul, and he came a little nearer to her. But she turned and leaned against the mantel-shelf for support, and clasped the cold marble with her fingers.

"I must say it, Paul. If you like, I will go away afterwards and never see you again. But I cannot let it spoil my life any longer; I feel as though you had got to hear it *now*. When I wrote you that last letter, I said that if you did not answer it I would not write to you again, or think about you, or come and see you any more. And you did n't answer it. I got to loathe the postman's knock, because it made my face hot, and I was afraid people would find out. But they never did! I came down to breakfast every day, in the hope of finding a letter from you; and when there was n't one, and everything seemed a blank,— oh, don't I know the awful look of that dining-room when there isn't a letter from you!—I just had to pretend that I hadn't expected to find one at all." She paused expectantly, but this time Paul made no attempt to speak. "I was never any good at pretending, before," she went on in a gentler tone, "but I believe I could deceive any one now. Only, I never succeeded in cheating myself! I used to find out new ways to school, because the old ones reminded me of you; and I had to do all my crying in omnibuses, at the far end up by the horses, because I dare not do it at Queen's Crescent, where I might have been seen. For I did cry sometimes." Her voice trembled, and she ended with a little sob. She buried her face in her hands.

"So that is what you have been doing for these six weeks?" said Paul, involuntarily.

"Do you find it so amusing, then?" asked Katharine in a stifled tone. He stepped up behind her, and twisted her round gently by the shoulders, so that she was obliged to look at him. The hardness went from her face, and she held out her hands to him instinctively. "Paul," she said, piteously, "I couldn't help it. Aren't you a little bit sorry for me? What have I done that I should like the wrong person? Other girls don't do these

The Making of a Prig

things. Am I awfully wicked, or awfully unlucky? Paul, say something to me! Are you very angry with me? But I couldn't help it, I couldn't indeed! I have tried so hard to make myself different, and I can't!"

He bit his lip and tried to say something, but failed.

"And after all," she added in a low tone, "when I had been schooling myself to hate you for six weeks, I nearly went mad with joy when Phyllis came and told me you were in the hall. Oh, Paul, I know I am dreadfully foolish! Will you ever respect me again, I wonder?"

There was a quaint mixture of humour and pathos in her tone; and he gathered her into his arms and kissed her tenderly, without finding any words with which to answer her. She clung to him, and kissed him for the first time in return, and forgot that she had once thought it wrong to be caressed by him; just now, it seemed the most natural thing in the world that he should be comforting her for the suffering of which he himself was the cause. And her passionate wish to rouse him from his apathy had ended in a weak desire to regain his tolerance at any cost.

"You are not angry with me? I haven't

The Making of a Prig

made you angry?" she asked him in an anxious whisper.

"No, no, you foolish child!" was all he said as he drew her closer.

"But it was dreadful of me to say all those things to you, wasn't it?"

"I like you to say dreadful things to me, dear."

She swayed back from him at that, with her two hands on his shoulders.

"Do you mean that, really? But — you *must* think it dreadfully wicked of me to let you kiss me, and to come and see you like this? It is dreadfully wicked, isn't it? Oh, I know it is; everybody would say so."

"I can't imagine what you mean. You are a dear little Puritan to me. You don't know what you are saying. Come, there are all those things you have got to tell me. I want to hear everything, please; whom you have been flirting with, and all sorts of things. Now, it is no use your pretending that you are going to hide anything from me, because you know you can't!"

He had resumed his former manner with a rather conscious effort, and drew her down beside him on the sofa. She tried to obey him, but she could think of very little to say;

The Making of a Prig

and towards ten o'clock, Paul looked at his watch.

"My child, you must go," he said. Katharine rose to her feet with a sigh.

"I don't want to go," she said, reluctantly.

"Has it been nice, then?" he asked, smiling at her dejected face.

"It has been the happiest evening I have ever spent," she said, looking away from him.

"Surely not!" laughed Paul. "Think of all the other evenings at the theatre, with Ted and Monty and all the rest of them!"

"You know quite well," she said indignantly, "that I like being with you better than with any one else in the world. You know I do, don't you?" she repeated, anxiously.

"It is enough for me that you say so," replied Paul; and they stood silent for a moment or two. "Come, you really must go, child," he said again. Katharine still remained motionless, while he put on his coat.

"Must I?" she said, dreamily. He came back to her and gave her a gentle shake.

"What is it, you strange little person? I believe you would have been much happier if I had not come back to bother you, eh?"

She denied it vehemently, and exerted herself to talk to him all the way home in the

The Making of a Prig

cab. She was solemn again, however, when the time came to say good-bye.

"May I see you again soon?" she asked him wistfully.

"Why, surely! We are going to have lots of larks together, aren't we? Well, what is it now?"

"Oh, I was only thinking!"

"What about?"

She unlocked the door with her latch-key before she replied.

"It seems so odd," she said, "that I care more about your opinion than about anybody else's in the whole world; and yet I have given you the most reason to think badly of me. Isn't it awfully queer?"

She shut the door before he had time to answer her. And Paul walked home, reflecting on the futility of experiments.

CHAPTER XIV

THE Sunday afternoon on which the Honourable Mrs. Keeley gave her first reception, that season, was a singularly dull and sultry one. The room was filled with celebrities and their satellites; and Katharine's head was aching badly, as she struggled with difficulty through the crowd and managed to squeeze herself into a corner by the open window. She was always affected by the weather; and to-day, she felt unusually depressed by the absence of sunshine. A voice from the balcony uttered her name, and she turned round with a sigh, to be met by the complacent features of Laurence Heaton. For a moment she did not recognise him; and then, the sound of his voice carried her back to Ivingdon, and she smiled back at him for the sake of the associations he brought to her mind.

"Is it really two years?" he was saying. "Seems impossible when I look at your face, Miss Austen. Two years! And what have you been doing with yourself all this time, eh?

The Making of a Prig

And how do you contrive to look so fresh on a day like this? I am quite charmed to have this opportunity of renewing so pleasant an acquaintance."

He forgot that, when he had known her before, she had annoyed him by not being in his style. And Katharine answered him vaguely, while her eyes wandered over the crowd of faces; for Paul had told her he was going to be there, and she felt restless.

"Small place the world is, to be sure," continued Heaton, with the air of a man who says something that has not been said before. "Who would have expected you to turn up at my old friends', the Keeleys'? Most curious coincidence, I must say!" Katharine, who knew of his very recent introduction to the house, explained her own relationship demurely. But her companion was quite unabashed, and changed the conversation skilfully.

"Wilton often comes here, he tells me. You remember Wilton, don't you? Ah, of course you do, since it is to him that I owe your charming acquaintance," he said, gallantly. "He met them at Nice, or somewhere. Astonishing how many people one meets at Nice! Wilton always meets every

The Making of a Prig

one, though, and every one likes him; he's so brilliant, don't you think? Yes, brilliant exactly describes him. Ever seen him since he stayed in your delightful rural home?"

"Oh, I see him here sometimes. And my aunt is expecting him to-day, I believe."

"I have no doubt of it, no doubt of it whatever!" smiled Heaton, nodding his head wisely. "If I'm not very much mistaken, Wilton is often the guest of Mrs. Keeley, is he not?"

The meaning in his remarks was wasted on Katharine, for most of her attention was still concentrated on the doorway. But Heaton, to whom she was more of an excuse than a reason for conversation, rambled on contentedly.

"Nice fellow, Wilton, to bring me here, pretending he wanted me to know her! Not much chance of that, I fancy! I haven't had two words with her since I first called here with him, three weeks ago. Ah, well, I mustn't be surprised at that,—an old fellow like me; though I would have you know, Miss Austen, that I am still young enough to admire the charms of a beautiful woman! But it is amusing, all the same, to watch how a serious fellow like Wilton suddenly forgets all

The Making of a Prig

his prejudices against marriage, and behaves like every one else. If it had been me, now — but then, I'm a marrying man, and I've had two of the sweetest wives God ever gave to erring man — Ah, I beg your pardon?"

"I — I don't quite understand," said Katharine.

"Nobody does, my dear young lady; nobody does. It is impossible to understand a clever, quiet sort of chap like Wilton. To begin with, he doesn't mean you to. But I'm heartily glad he has made such a fortunate choice; he is an old friend of mine, and my friends' happiness is always my happiness. He is lucky, for all that; beauty and money and influence, all combined in one charming person, are not to be despised, are they? She is so sweet, too; and sweetness in a woman is worth all the virtues put together, don't you agree with me? Now, tell me, — woman's opinion is always worth having, — do you consider her so very pretty?"

"I don't know whom you mean," said Katharine. She was wishing he would take his idle chatter away to some one else. But Heaton was accustomed to inattention on the part of his hearers, and he was not disconcerted by hers.

The Making of a Prig

"Why, the beautiful Miss Keeley, to be sure," he replied. "For all that," he added, hastily, "I think she is rather overrated, don't you?" This was meant to be very cunning, for he prided himself on being an accomplished lady's man. But Katharine's reply baffled him.

"Do you mean Marion? I think she is beautiful," she said, warmly. "I am not surprised that every one should admire her."

"Just so, just so; quite my view of the case!" exclaimed Heaton, at once. "I call her unique, don't you? 'Pon my word, I never felt more pleased at anything in my life! What a future for Wilton, with the Honourable Mrs. Keeley for a mother-in-law, and her beautiful daughter for a wife; why, we shall see him in Parliament before long! The Attorney-General of the future,—there's no doubt about it. Ah, I see you are smiling at my enthusiasm, Miss Austen. That is because you do not know me well enough to realise how much my friends are to me. All the real happiness in my life comes from my friends, it does indeed. But I am boring you with this dull conversation about myself. Come along with me, and I'll see where

The Making of a Prig

the ices are to be found. Young people always like ices, eh?"

And she yielded to his kindly good-nature, even while she felt indignant with him for spreading such an absurd piece of gossip. And what had Paul been doing, to allow such an idea to take root in his foolish old head? He had known nothing of the rumour on Wednesday, for she had been to a concert with him then, and he had never once alluded to her cousin. Of course, it was ridiculous to give it another thought, and she roused herself to chatter gaily to her companion as they slowly made their way downstairs.

But, as she stood in the crowded dining-room, wedged between the table and Heaton who was occupied for the moment in seeking for champagne cup, she became again the unwilling hearer of that same absurd piece of gossip. It sounded less blatant, perhaps, from the lips of the two magnificent dowagers who were lightly discussing it, but it was hardly less vulgar in its essence; and Katharine ceased to be gay, and shrank instinctively away from them.

"Who is he? I seem to know the name, but I never remember meeting him anywhere. Surely her mother would not throw her away on a nobody? She expects such great things

The Making of a Prig

from Marion, one is always led to believe; though she is just the sort of girl to end in being a disappointment, don't you think so?"

"My dear, it is a *fait accompli*, and he is not a nobody at all. He would not visit here if he were; at least, not seriously. His name is Wilton,—something Wilton, Peter or Paul or one of the apostles, I forget which. He belongs to a very good Yorkshire family, I am told. His father was a bishop, or it may have been a canon; at all events, he was not an ordinary person. Mr. Wilton, this one, is one of our rising men, I believe,—a lawyer, or a barrister, or something of that sort. He defended the plaintiff in the Christopher case, don't you remember? And with Mrs. Keeley to back him up, he will soon be in the front rank,—there is no doubt about that. They always ice the coffee too much here, don't they? Have you seen Marion to-day?"

"Yes. She's over there in the same green silk. Wonderful hair, isn't it? A little too red for my taste, but any one can see it is wonderful. He's over there too, but you can't see him from here. He is much older than Marion, and delicate looking. I shouldn't like a child of mine to marry him, but that's another matter. And, of course, all *my* girls were so particular about looks. How insufferably hot it is! Shall we go upstairs?"

Laurence Heaton had a second glass of champagne cup, and when he had drunk it he found that Katharine was gone. He dismissed her from his mind without any difficulty, however, and fought his way upstairs to find some one who was more to his taste. He certainly did not connect her disappearance with his gossip, nor yet with his old friend, Paul Wilton.

And Katharine could not have told him herself why she had slipped away so abruptly. Of course, the rumour was not true; she did not believe a word of it; and it was disloyal to Paul even to be annoyed by it. But it was disquieting, all the same, to hear his name so persistently coupled with her cousin's; and she wondered if her aunt knew any of his views against marriage, to which she had been so often a humble listener. And it was equally certain that he was one of the most rising men of the day; she did not want to be told that by a number of society gossips, who had never even heard of him until he paid his attentions to one of their set,—just the ordinary attentions of a courteous man to a beautiful woman. Had he not repeatedly told her that she knew more about his real life and his real self, more

The Making of a Prig

about his ambition and his work, than any one else in the world? He had chosen her out of all his friends for a confidant; and yet, she might not even acknowledge her friendship for him. He only trifled with Marion, teased her about the number of her admirers, talked to her about the colour of her hair, and the daintiness of her appearance; he had told her that, too. Marion knew nothing of his aspirations; she would not understand them, if she did. And yet it was common talk that he admired Marion, while *she* was to make a secret of her intimacy with him. Something of the old feeling of rebellion against him, which had been dead ever since the evening they had supped together in his chambers, was in her mind as she left the house where he was sitting with Marion, and walked aimlessly towards the park. The sun had completely vanished in a dull red mist; and the intense heat and lurid atmosphere did not tend to raise her spirits. A nameless feeling of impending trouble crept over her, and she felt powerless to shake it off. She wandered along the edge of the crowds as they listened to the labour agitators, past groups of children playing on the grass, past endless pairs of lovers in their Sunday garments, until the noisy tramp of footsteps began

The Making of a Prig

to grate upon her nerves; and she turned and fled from the park, as she had fled from Curzon Street. Something at last took her towards the Temple, and an hour later she was knocking furtively at the door of Paul's chambers. She had never been there on a Sunday before, and the deserted look of the courts, and the silk dress of the housekeeper whom she met on the stairs, depressed her still further. Would she come in and wait, the housekeeper suggested, as Mr. Wilton was out, and had not said when he would be back? But Katharine shook her head wearily, and turned her face homewards. Even the solitude of Queen's Crescent could not be worse than the unfriendliness of the deserted London streets. She went out of her way to walk down Curzon Street, without knowing why she did so, and took the trouble to cross over to the side opposite her aunt's house, also without a definite purpose in her mind. It was not much after eight, but the storm was still gathering, and there was only just enough daylight left to show the figure of a girl on the balcony. It was Marion, beyond any doubt Marion, who was leaning forward and looking down into the street as though she expected to see some one come out of the house. The front door opened, and a man

The Making of a Prig

came down the steps; he looked up and raised his hat, and lingered; and Marion glanced hastily around, kissed her fingers to him, and vanished indoors. The man walked away down the street with a leisurely step, and Katharine stepped back into the shadow of the portico. But her caution was quite unnecessary, for neither of them had noticed her.

For the second time that evening Katharine knocked gently at the door of Paul's chambers in the Temple. This time, he opened to her himself.

"Good heavens!" he was startled into exclaiming. "What in the name of wonder has brought you here at this time of night? It is to be hoped you didn't meet any one on the stairs, did you?"

He motioned her in as he spoke, and shut the door. Katharine walked past him in a half-dazed kind of way. There had been only two feelings expressed in his face, and one was surprise, and the other annoyance.

"What is it, Katharine? Has anything gone wrong?" he demanded in his low, masterful tone. Katharine turned cold; she had never realised before how pitilessly masterful his tone was.

The Making of a Prig

"I couldn't help coming,—I was so miserable! They were all saying things about you, things that were not true. And I wanted to hear you say they were not true. I couldn't rest; so I came. Are you angry with me for coming, Paul?"

She faltered out the words, without looking at him. Paul shrugged his shoulders, but she did not see the movement.

"It was hardly worth while, was it, to risk your reputation merely to confirm what you had already settled in your own mind?"

She opened her eyes, and stared at him hopelessly. Paul walked away to look for some cigarette papers in the pocket of a coat.

"Was it?" he repeated, with his back turned to her. Katharine struggled to answer him.

"You have never spoken to me like that, before," she stammered at last.

"You have never given me any cause, have you?" said Paul, rather awkwardly.

"But what have I done?" she asked, taking a step towards him. "I didn't know you would mind. I always come to you when I am unhappy; you told me I might. And I was unhappy this evening; so I came. Why

The Making of a Prig

should it be different this evening? I don't understand what you mean. Why are you angry with me? You have never been angry before. What have I done?"

"My dear child, there is no occasion for heroics," said Paul, speaking very gently. "I am not angry with you at all. But you must own that it is at least unusual to call upon a man, uninvited, at this unearthly hour. And hadn't you better sit down, now you have come?"

Katharine did not move.

"What does it matter if it is unusual?" she asked. "You know I have been here sometimes, as late as this, before. There is no harm in it, is there? Paul! tell me what I have done to annoy you?"

Paul gave up rummaging in his coat pocket, and came and sat on the edge of the table, and made a cigarette.

"I seem to remember having this same argument with you before," he observed. "Don't you think it is rather futile to go all through it again? You know quite well that it is entirely for your sake that I wish to be careful. Hadn't we better change the subject? If you are going to stop, you might be more comfortable in a chair."

The Making of a Prig

Katharine clenched her hands in the effort to keep back her tears.

"I am not going to stay," she cried, miserably. "I can't understand why you are so cruel to me; I think it must amuse you to hurt me. Why do you ask me to come and see you sometimes, quite as late as this, and then object to my coming to-night? I don't know what you mean."

Paul lighted his cigarette before he answered her.

"You have quite a talent, Katharine, for asking uncomfortable questions. If you cannot see the difference between coming when you are asked, and coming uninvited, I am afraid I cannot help you. Would you like any coffee or anything?"

All at once her brain began to clear. For two hours she had been wandering aimlessly through the streets, in a strange bewilderment of mind, not knowing why she was there nor where she was going. Then she had found herself in Fleet Street; and habit, rather than intention, had brought her to the Temple. And now his maddening indifference had touched her pride, and her deadened faculties began slowly to revive under the shock. She put her fingers over her eyes, and tried to

The Making of a Prig

think. The blood rushed to her face, and she thrilled all over with a passionate instinct of resistance. He did not know what to make of her, when she stepped suddenly in front of him and faced him unflinchingly.

"You must not expect me to see the difference," she said, proudly. "I shall never understand why I have to make a secret of what is not wrong, nor why you allow me to do it at all if it is wrong. I think you have been playing with my friendship all the time; I can see now that you have not valued it, because I gave it you so freely. But I didn't know that; I wasn't clever enough; and I had never liked anybody but you. I didn't know that I ought to hide it, and pretend that I didn't like you. Perhaps, if I had done that you would have gone on liking me."

He was going to interrupt her, but she did not give him time.

"Would you ask Marion Keeley to come and see you, as you have asked me?"

Paul's face grew dark, and she trembled suddenly at her own boldness.

"I fail to see how such a question can interest either of us," he said, coldly.

"But would you ask her?" she repeated.

"I am perfectly assured," he replied, quietly,

"that if I were to forget myself so far as to do so, Miss Keeley would certainly not come."

"Then you mean to say that it has always been dreadfully wrong of *me* to come?"

"Really, Katharine, you are very quarrelsome this evening," said Paul, with a forced laugh. "I have repeatedly pointed out to you that a man chooses some of his friends for pleasure, and others for business. I really fail to see why I should be subjected to this minute catechism at your hands."

"Then you chose Marion — for business? It is true, then, what they said! I wish — oh, I wish you had never chosen me — for pleasure!"

The anger had died out of her voice; he could hardly hear what she said; but he made a last attempt to treat the matter lightly.

"I really think, my child, that any comparison between you and your cousin is unnecessary," he began in a conciliating manner.

"I thought so too, until to-day," she replied, piteously.

"But what has happened to-day to put you in this uncomfortable frame of mind?"

"It is what every one is saying about you and Marion, — all those horrid people, and Mr. Heaton, and everybody. I want to know if it is true. Everything is going wrong, every-

The Making of a Prig

where. I wish I were dead! I came to ask you if it is true; I thought I might do that; I thought I knew you well enough. I didn't know you would mind. If you like, I will go away now, and never come and see you any more, or bother you, or let you know that I care for you so awfully. Only, tell me first, Paul, whether it is true or not?"

Her voice had risen, as she went on, and it ended full of passionate entreaty. The stern look on his face deepened, but he did not speak.

"I wish I knew the meaning of it all," she continued, relentlessly as it seemed to him. "I wish it were easier to like the right people, and to hate all the others. Why was I made the wrong way? If I had never wanted to like you, it would have been so simple. It would not have mattered, then, that you did not really care for me. But I wish I understood you better. Why did you tell me that you wanted me for your friend, always; and that you didn't believe in marriage, and those things? I believed you so, Paul; and I was content to be your friend; you know I was, don't you? And now you have met Marion, and she is beautiful, and she can help you to get on, to become one of the first men in the

The Making of a Prig

country, they said. And you have forgotten all about your views against marriage; and you allow people to talk as though you were making a kind of bargain. Oh, it is horrible! But it is n't true, Paul, is it?"

"Who has been telling you all these things?" he asked.

"Then it is true? You are going to marry her, because of the position, and all that? I wish it was n't so difficult to understand. Is it a crime, I wonder, to like any one so desperately as I like you? But I can't help it, can I? Oh, Paul, do tell me what to do?"

He winced as she turned to him so naturally for protection, even though it was against himself that she asked it.

"Don't talk like that, child," he said, harshly. And the hand she had held out to him appealingly fell down limply at her side.

"I can't expect you to think anything of me, after what I have just said to you," she went on in the same hopeless voice. "Girls are never supposed to tell those things, are they? It does n't seem to me to matter much, now that it has all got to stop, for always. I only wish — I wish it had stopped before. I — I am going now, Paul."

Although she turned away from him, she

The Making of a Prig

still half expected him to come and comfort her. For a couple of seconds she stood quite still, possessed with a terrible longing to be comforted by him. But he sat motionless and silent on the table; even his foot had ceased swinging. She walked unsteadily to the door.

"Stop," said Paul. "You cannot go out in this storm."

A peal of thunder broke over the house as he spoke. She had not noticed the rain until then.

"I must go," she said dully, and fumbled at the fastening of the door. Paul came and took her by the arm, and led her back gently.

"I want to explain, first," he said.

"There is nothing to explain," said Katharine. "I understand."

"Not quite, I think," said Paul. They were standing together by the table, and he was nervously caressing the hand he held between his own. "You have only been talking from your own point of view; you have forgotten mine altogether. You do not seem to think that I, too, may have had something to suffer."

"You? But you do not care—as I do."

He did not heed the interruption.

"It is the system that is at fault," he said. "A man has to get on at the sacrifice of his

The Making of a Prig

happiness; or he has to be happy at the sacrifice of his position. It is difficult for a woman to realise this. She never has to choose between love and ambition."

"And you have chosen — ambition," said Katharine bitterly.

"My child, when you are older you will understand that the very qualities you affect to despise in man now, are the qualities that endear him to you in reality. You are far too fine a woman, Katharine, to love a man who has no ambition. Is it not so?"

She quivered, and lowered her eyes.

"I don't know," she said. "It seems so hard."

"It is terribly hard for both of us," continued Paul, looking down too. "But believe me, there would be nothing but unhappiness before us if it were otherwise. I am thinking of you, child, as much as of myself. Marriage for love alone is a ghastly mistake. There, I have said more to you than I have ever said to any woman; I felt you would understand, Katharine."

He mistook her silence for indifference, and put his arms round her. But she clung to him closely, and lifted her face to his and broke out into a desperate appeal.

The Making of a Prig

"Paul, don't say those horrid, bitter things! They are not true; I will never believe they are true. Why must you marry for anything so sordid as ambition? Why must you marry at all? Can't we go on being friends? I want to go on being your friend. Paul, don't send me away for ever. I can't go, Paul; I can't! I will work for you, I will be your slave, I will do anything; only don't let it all stop like this. I can't bear it; I can't! Won't you go on being nice to me, Paul?"

He threw back his head and compressed his lips. He had grown quite white in the last few moments. She sobbed out her entreaties with her face hidden on his shoulder, and wondered why he did not speak to her.

"Why did you never look like that before?" he asked in a hoarse whisper. She raised her head and stared at him with large, frightened eyes.

"Like what, Paul? What do you mean?"

He flung her away from him almost roughly.

"You must go," he said, "at once."

She laid her hand on his arm, and looked into his face.

"Why are you so angry?" she asked, wonderingly. "Is it because I have told you all these things?"

The Making of a Prig

"My God, no! You must go," he repeated, vehemently, and pushed her towards the door. She stumbled as she went, and he thought he heard her sob. He sprang to her side instantly, and took her in his arms again.

"Why did n't you go quickly?" he gasped, as he crushed her against him.

His sudden change of manner terrified her. None of the tenderness or the indifference, or any of the expressions she was accustomed to see on his face were there now, and his violence repelled her. She struggled to free herself from his grasp.

"Let me go, Paul!" she pleaded. "I don't want to stop any more. What is the good of it all? You know I have got to go; don't make it so difficult. Paul, I — I *want* to go."

He looked searchingly into her eyes, as though he would have read her inmost thoughts; but he did not see the understanding he had almost hoped to find there, and he laughed shortly and relinquished his hold of her.

"There, go!" he said in an uncertain tone. "Why did I expect you to know? Your day has n't come yet. Meanwhile — Ah! what am I saying?"

"I have annoyed you again," said Katharine sorrowfully. "What ought I to have known?"

"Oh, nothing," said Paul, flinging open the door. "You can't help it. Now and again Nature makes woman a prig, and it is only the right man who can regenerate her. Unfortunately, circumstances prevent me from being the right man. Are you ready to come, now?"

He spoke rapidly, hardly knowing what he said. But Katharine walked past him without speaking, with a set look on her face. He talked mechanically about the storm and anything else that occurred to him, as they went downstairs, but she did not utter a word, and he did not seem to notice her silence. She held out her hand to him as they stood in the doorway.

"You will let me see you to a cab?" he said. "Oh, very well, as you like; but, at least, take an umbrella with you."

She shook her head mutely, and plunged out into the rain and the storm. It was on just such a night as this, more than two years ago, that she had first gone out to meet him. Paul called after her to come back and take shelter; and some one, who was walking swiftly by, turned round at the sound of his voice. The dim lamp above shed its uncer-

The Making of a Prig

tain light for a moment on the faces of the three, whom circumstances had thus strangely brought together in the fury of that June thunder-storm. It was only for a moment. Paul drew back again into the doorway, and Katharine stumbled blindly against the man outside.

"Ted!" she cried, with a sob of relief. "Take me home, Ted, will you? Something terrible has happened to me; I can't tell you now. Oh, I am so glad it is you!"

She clung to his arm convulsively. Some clock in the neighbourhood was striking the hour, and it struck twelve times before Ted spoke.

"Kitty!" he said.

She waited, but not another word came. Exhaustion prevented her from resisting, as he led her to a hansom, and paid the driver, and left her. Then she remembered dimly that he had not spoken to her, except for that one startled exclamation.

It seemed to Katharine as though nothing could be wanting to complete her wretchedness.

CHAPTER XV

But, humiliated as she was, the predominant feeling in her mind was astonishment. Could it be true that she was a prig? Was that the final definition of the pride and the strength in which she had gloried until now? Was that all that people meant when they told her she was not like other girls? It was an odious revelation, and for the moment her self-respect was stunned by it. She had boasted of her success; and to be successful was merely to be priggish. She had been proud of her virtue; and virtue, again, was only an equivalent for priggishness. She wondered vaguely whether there was a single aspiration left that did not lead to the paths of priggishness. A prig! He had called her a prig! She had thought it such a fine thing to be content with his friendship, and this was the end of it all. All the wretchedness of her solitary drive home was centred in those last cruel words of his; all the bitterness of that long, miserable Sunday was concentrated in that covert insult.

The Making of a Prig

She could have borne his indifference, or even his displeasure; but she could have killed him for his contempt.

And Ted? She did not give a thought to Ted. Even the reason for his curious behaviour had not fully dawned upon her yet. It had only seemed in keeping with the rest of her misfortunes, just like the rain, which she allowed to beat in upon her, with a kind of reckless satisfaction. In the fulness of her more absorbing personal trouble, Ted would have to wait. It had been her experience that Ted always could wait. It was not until she stood once more within the familiar hall of number ten, Queen's Crescent, that the recollection of Ted's astonished look returned to her mind; and then she put it hastily away from her, as something that would have to be faced presently.

As she walked into her room, too weary to think any more, and longing for the temporary oblivion of a night's rest, the first thing that met her eye was the unmade condition of her bed. The desolate look of the tiny compartment was the crowning point of her day of woe; and the tears, which she had kept back until now, rushed to her eyes. It seemed a little hard that, on this day of all others,

The Making of a Prig

Phyllis should have neglected to make her bed. She gave it an impatient push, and it scraped loudly over the bare boards.

"Stop that row!" said Polly's sharp voice from the other end of the room. "You might be quiet, now you *have* come in."

"Is Phyllis asleep?" asked Katharine shortly.

"Can't you be quiet?" growled Polly. "Haven't you heard she is worse? Don't see how you should, though,—coming in at this hour of the night!"

"Worse?" With an effort, Katharine's thoughts travelled back over the absorbing events of the day, to the early morning; and she remembered that Phyllis had stayed in bed with a headache. "What is the matter with her?" she asked, faintly. Everything seemed to be conspiring against her happiness to-day.

"Influenza. A lot you care! Nothing but my cousin's funeral would have taken me out to-day, I know. I had to show up for that. Of course, I thought you would look after her; I asked you to."

Katharine had pushed aside the curtain, and was looking at the flushed, unconscious face of her friend. She dimly remembered saying she would stop with her; and then a letter

The Making of a Prig

had come from Paul, asking her to meet him in the park, and she had thought no more of Phyllis. She had not even succeeded in meeting him; and again her eyes filled with tears at her own misfortunes.

"I couldn't help it," she said, miserably. "How was I to know she was so bad? Have you taken her temperature?"

"Hundred and three, when I last took it. It's no use standing there and pulling a long face. She doesn't know you; so it's rather late in the day to be cut up. You'd better go to bed, I should say; you look as though you'd been out all day, and half the night, too!"

She ended with a contemptuous sniff. Katharine rubbed the tears out of her eyes. The weariness had temporarily left her.

"Let me sit up with her," she said.

"You? What could you do? Why, you'd fall asleep, or think of something else in the middle, and she might die for all you cared," returned Polly contemptuously. "Can you make a poultice?"

Katharine shook her head dumbly, and crept away. Her self-abasement seemed complete. She lay down on her untidy bed, and drew the clothes over her, and gave way to her grief. There did not seem a bright spot in her existence, now that Phyllis was not able to comfort her. She hoped, with a desperate fervour, that she would catch influenza too, and die, so that remorse should consume the hearts of all those who had so cruelly misunderstood her.

A hand shook her by the shoulder, not unkindly.

"Look here! you must stop that row, or else you will disturb her. What's the good of it? Besides, she isn't as bad as all that either; you can't have seen much illness, I'm thinking."

"It isn't that," gasped Katharine truthfully. "At least, not entirely. I was dreadfully unhappy about something else, and I wanted to die; and then, when I found Phyllis was ill, it all seemed so hopeless. I didn't mean to disturb any one; it was dreadfully foolish of me; I haven't cried for years."

Polly gave a kind of grunt, and sat down on the bed. It was more or less interesting to have reduced the brilliant Miss Austen to this state of submission.

"Got yourself into trouble?" she asked, and refrained from adding that she had expected it all along.

Katharine began to cry again. There was

The Making of a Prig

so little sympathy, and so much curiosity, in the curt question. But she had reached the point when to confide in some one was an absolute necessity; and there was no one else.

"I haven't done anything wrong," she sobbed. "Why should one suffer so awfully, just because one didn't *know!* We were only friends, and it was so pleasant, and I was so happy! It might have gone on for ever, only there was another girl."

"Of course," said Polly. "There always is. How did she get hold of him?"

Katharine shrank back into herself.

"You don't understand," she complained. "He isn't like that at all. He is clever, and refined, and very reserved. He doesn't flirt a bit, or anything of that sort."

"Oh, I see," said Polly, with her expressive sniff. "I suppose the other girl thought herself a toff, eh?"

"She is the most beautiful girl I have ever seen," said Katharine simply. "But I never knew he cared about that. He had views against marriage, he always said; and he wasn't always talking about women, like some men. I did not think he would end in marrying, just like every one else."

"More innocent you, then! I always said

you ought to have stopped at home; girls like you generally do come the worst cropper. You surely did n't suppose he would go on for ever, and be content merely with your friendship, did you?"

"Yes, I did," said Katharine wearily. "Why not? I was content with his."

Polly gave vent to a stifled laugh.

"My dear, you're not a man," she said in a superior tone. It added considerably to the piquancy of the conversation that the subject was one on which she was a greater authority than her clever companion.

"But he really cared for me, I am certain he did," Katharine went on plaintively; and her eyes filled with tears again.

"Then why is he marrying the other girl instead of you? If she is so beautiful, you're surely very good-looking too, eh? That won't wash anyhow, will it?"

Katharine was silent. She felt she could not reveal the full extent of his infamy just then; there was something so particularly sordid in having been weighed against the advantages of a worldly marriage and found wanting; and she felt a sudden disinclination to expose the whole of the truth to the sharp criticism of Polly Newland.

The Making of a Prig

"I haven't done anything wrong," she said again. "I don't understand why things are so unfairly arranged. Why should I suffer for it like this?"

"Don't know about that," retorted the uncompromising Polly. "I expect you've been foolish, and that's a worse game than being bad. Going about town with a man after dark, when you're not engaged to him, isn't considered respectable by most, even if it's always the same man. I'm not so particular as some, but you must draw the line somewhere."

"I didn't go about with him much," said Katharine, making a feeble attempt to justify herself. "He didn't care about it; he was always so particular not to give people anything to talk about. He didn't care for himself, he said; it was only for me. So I used to go to his chambers instead. I couldn't be more careful than that, could I? And I should have gone in the daytime, if I had had more time; but there was all my work to get through,—so what else could I do? There wasn't any harm in it."

She could not see her companion's face, and was so full of her own reflections that she failed to notice her silence. Polly did not even sniff.

The Making of a Prig

"Then there's Ted," Katharine continued presently. "Even Ted was strange to-night; and Ted has never been like that to me before. I can't think what has come over everybody. What have I done to deserve it all?"

"Mercy me!" cried Polly suddenly. "Is there another of them? Who on earth is Ted?"

"Ted? Why, you must have seen him in the hall sometimes; he often comes to take me out. I have known him all my life; he is only a little older than I am, and I am devoted to him. I would not quarrel with Ted for anything in the whole world; it would be like quarrelling with myself. And to-night I ran into him, just as I came out of — of the other one's chambers; and I was so glad to see him, because Ted is always so sweet to me when I am in trouble; and — and Ted was quite funny, and he wouldn't speak to me at all, and he just put me into a hansom and left me to come home alone. I can't think why he behaved so oddly. I know he used not to get on with — with the other one, and that is why I never told him I had met him again up here in London; and I suppose he caught sight of him to-night in the doorway, — there was a lamp just above, — but still, he need not have been hurt

The Making of a Prig

until he had heard my explanation, need he? Why has every one turned against me at once?"

Polly remained silent no longer. She turned and stared at the prostrate figure on the bed, with all the power of her small, watery blue eyes.

"I really think you beat everything I ever knew," she exclaimed.

"What?" said Katharine, who had turned her face to the wall, and was occupied in meditating miserably on the problem of her existence. "What do you mean?"

Polly lost all control over herself.

"Do you mean to tell me that you never saw any harm in all this?" she cried emphatically. "Do you really mean to say that you have been carrying on anyhow with two men at once, going to their chambers late at night, and letting yourself be seen in public with them, without knowing that it was unusual? Didn't you ever see the danger in it? You are either the biggest fool in creation or the biggest humbug! One man at a time would be bad enough; but two! My eye!"

"But—there wasn't any harm," pleaded Katharine. "Why does no one understand? It seemed quite natural to me. They were so

The Making of a Prig

different, and I liked them in such opposite ways, don't you see? I have known Ted all my life; he is a dear boy, and that is all. But Paul is clever and strong; he is a man, and he knows about things. And I never knew it was wrong; I did n't *feel* wicked, somehow. I wonder if that was what Paul was thinking, when he said I was a prig? Oh, dear! oh, dear! I have never been so wretched in my whole life!"

"Did he say that about you? Well, I don't wonder."

Katharine looked hopelessly at her unsympathetic profile, with the snub nose and the small chin, and the hair twisted up into tight plaits and the ends tied with white tape; and her eyes wandered down the red flannel dressing-gown to the large slippered feet that emerged from beneath it.

"You called me a prig, too," she said, humbly. "I overheard you."

"I thought so then," said Polly gruffly.

"Do you think so now? Is it true? Am I a prig?" She awaited the answer anxiously. Polly gave her another pitiless stare.

"I'm bothered if I know," she said. "But if you're not, you ought to be in the nursery. Only don't go telling people the things you've

The Making of a Prig

been telling me to-night, or you might get yourself into worse trouble. You'd better go to sleep now, and leave it till to-morrow. My conscience! you'd make some people sit up, you would!"

Katharine felt she had endured as much contempt as she could bear that evening; but she made a last attempt to recover some of her self-respect.

"I wish you would tell me why it is wrong to do things that are not really wrong in themselves, just because people say they are wrong?" she asked, rather sleepily.

"Because people can make it so jolly unpleasant for you if you don't agree with them," said Polly bluntly. "And if you fancy you're going to alter all that, you must make up your mind to be called a prig. You can't have a good time and defy convention as you've been doing, and then expect to get off scot free without being called a prig; it isn't likely. Most people are content to take things as they are; it's a jolly sight more comfortable, and it's good enough for them. Good-night."

"I sha'n't sleep," Katharine called after her. And Polly sniffed.

And the next thing that Katharine remembered was being awakened by her in the early

The Making of a Prig

morning, and told in a gruff voice that she might sit with Phyllis if she liked, until some one came to relieve her.

"All right," she replied, drowsily. "How tired you look; didn't you sleep well?"

"Sleep? There wasn't much chance of that, when she was talking gibberish all the time. She's quieter now, and you can fetch Jenny if you want anything. I must be off; I shall be late as it is. Just like my luck to get my early week when she is ill!"

And there by the bedside of Phyllis Hyam, before any one else in the house was astir, Katharine sat and pondered again over the events of the day before. They seemed just as tragic as ever, separated as they were from her by a few hours of forgetfulness; and she wondered miserably how she was going to take up her life as usual, and go about her work as though nothing had happened. "That is why it is so hard to be a woman," she murmured, full of pity for her own troubles. And yet, when Miss Jennings came and took her post in the sick-room, and she was free to go to school, she found that it was a relief to be compelled to do something, and her work seemed easier to her than she had ever found it before. She had never given a better lecture

The Making of a Prig

than she gave that morning; and something that was outside herself seemed to come to her assistance all day, and remained with her until her work was done. But when she returned home in the evening, the full significance of her unfortunate situation stared her again in the face; and the news that Phyllis was worse and was not allowed to see any one was so in keeping with her feelings, that she felt unable even to make a comment upon it.

"I always said that Miss Austen hadn't a spark of feeling in her," observed the girl who had given her the information; and Katharine overheard her, and began to wonder mechanically if it were true. Every faculty she possessed seemed deadened at that moment; she had no longer the inclination even to rebel against her fate. She sat on the stairs, outside the bedroom she was not allowed to enter, and took a strange delicious pleasure in dwelling upon the whole of her intercourse with Paul. There was not a conversation or a chance meeting with him, that she did not go through in her mind with a scrupulous accuracy; the pain of it became almost unendurable at moments, and yet it was an exquisite torture that brought her some measure of relief. She even forced herself to recall her last meeting with

The Making of a Prig

him, and was surprised in an apathetic sort of way when she found that she did not want to cry any more.

And from thinking of Paul, she naturally fell to thinking of Ted too. And it slowly dawned upon her, as she considered it in the light of her present mood, that what Polly had said in her vulgar, uncompromising manner, was the truth. For a whole year she had been living in a false atmosphere of contentment; she had deluded herself into the belief that she was superior to convention and human nature combined, and she had ended in proving herself a complete failure. Paul had seen through her self-righteousness, he had nothing but contempt for her, and he had found it a relief to turn from her to the human and faulty Marion Keeley. In the depths of her self-abasement, she had even ceased to feel angry with Marion.

And Ted had found her out. That was the worst of all. On the impulse of the moment, she fetched some paper and wrote to him at once, sitting there on the uncarpeted stairs, while the people passed up and down unheeded by her. It was a very humble letter, full of pleading confession and self-accusation,— such a letter as she had never sent him before, and written from a standpoint she had never

The Making of a Prig

yet been obliged to assume towards him. It was a relief at the moment to be doing something; but she regretted her action the whole of the following day, and hardly knew how to open his reply when she found it awaiting her, on her return home in the evening. It was very short.

"Dear Kitty," it ran:—

Don't mind about me. It's a rotten world, and I'm the rottenest fool in it. I was only hit up the other night because I was so surprised. Of course you're all right, and I ought never to have been born. I knew all the time that you were spoofing me when you pretended to care for me; but I did n't know you cared for any one else, least of all Wilton. He always seemed so played to me, but then I'm not clever. Only, I advise you not to go hanging round his chambers at night; people are so poor, and they might talk. Let me know if you want me or anything. I won't bother you otherwise.

TED.

He still believed in her, then; only it was more from habit than conviction. But she had destroyed his love for her. She realised these two facts in the same breath, and she rebelled passionately at the loss of the affection that had been hers for so long, though she had valued it so lightly.

The Making of a Prig

"I do want you, now," she scribbled to him in pencil. "Will you come here to-morrow evening? Miss Jennings has promised me the use of her sitting-room. I shall expect you about seven."

It seemed quite in harmony with the general wretchedness of those few days that Phyllis should be seriously ill all the time. The sixty-three working gentlewomen, who had never pretended to care for the brusque shorthand clerk when she was in good health and trampled without a scruple on their tenderest susceptibilities, now went about on tiptoe, and conversed in whispers on all the landings, and got in the way of the doctor when he came downstairs. And they one and all condemned Katharine for her indifference, because she refused to enlarge on the subject at every meal.

"The conversation is never very exhilarating, at the best of times; but when all those women take to gloating over a tragedy, it simply isn't bearable," she was heard to exclaim; and the unlucky remark cost her the last shred of her popularity at Queen's Crescent.

She was waiting at her usual post on the stairs, when they came to tell her that Ted was downstairs. He had come at her bidding;

The Making of a Prig

that was consoling, at all events. But when she walked into Miss Jennings' private room and saw his face as he stood on the hearthrug, her heart sank again, and she knew that she was not to find consolation yet. He held out his hand to her silently, and pulled forward a slender, white-wood chair tied up with yellow ribbons, and imperilled a bamboo screen crowded with cheap crockery, and finally sat down himself on the edge of the chintz-covered sofa. Neither of them spoke for a moment or two, and Ted cleared his throat uncomfortably, and stared at the ferrule of his walking-stick.

"I got your letter," he said at last, "and I've come."

"Yes," said Katharine, "you've come."

Having delivered themselves of these two very obvious remarks, they again relapsed into silence; and Katharine glanced at the cuckoo clock, and marvelled that so much concentrated wretchedness could be crowded into something under five minutes.

"Ted," she forced herself to say, in a voice that did not seem to be hers, "Ted, will you never come and see me any more?"

He lifted his head and looked at her; then looked away again.

The Making of a Prig

"Not unless you want me to do anything for you," he said. "I don't want to bother, you see."

She longed to cry out and tell him that he never bothered her; that she wanted to see him more than she wanted anything in the whole world. But something new and strange in his face, that told her he was no longer a boy and no longer her willing slave, seemed to paralyse her. To be proved inferior to the man she had always considered inferior to her, was the hardest blow she had yet had to endure.

"I don't know what you mean," she said, lamely.

Ted hastened to be apologetic.

"I'm beastly sorry," he said, and cleared his throat again.

"I — I wish you would explain," she went on.

"Oh, that's all right, isn't it?" said Ted vaguely.

"It isn't all right; you know it isn't," she cried. "What makes you so strange to me? You've never looked like that before. Is it I who have changed you so, Ted?"

"Oh, it's nothing," he said. "You've hit me up rather, that's all. Don't bother

The Making of a Prig

about me. Did you want me for anything particular?"

She looked in vain for any signs of relenting in his manner; but he sat on the edge of the sofa, and played with his walking-stick, and cleared his throat at intervals. In spite of the changed conditions of their attitude towards one another, she felt that she was expected, as usual, to take the initiative.

"I wanted to tell you all about it, to explain," she faltered. "I thought you would help me."

"If it's all the same to you, I would rather not hear," said Ted, with unexpected promptitude. "I know as much about it as I care to know, thanks. *He* wrote to me this morning, too."

"He wrote to you? Paul?"

"Wilton, yes," he replied, shortly, and glanced at her again. His under lip was twitching, as it always did when he was hurt or embarrassed.

"What for?" she asked, wonderingly.

"Oh, to explain, and all that! Hang the explanation! I didn't want him to tell me he hadn't been a blackguard; I knew you,— so that was all square. But I don't understand it now, and I don't want to. I can't

The Making of a Prig

see any great shakes, myself, in playing about with a girl when you're engaged to some one else. But I suppose that's because I'm such a rotten ass. It's none of my business, any way; only, I think you'd better be careful. But you know best, so that's all right."

Again she longed to tell him that she was not so bad as he thought her, and yet, much worse than he thought her; but the words would not come, and she sat self-condemned.

"You don't understand," she stammered presently. "I didn't know he was engaged till yesterday. I saw no harm in it all; I only liked him very much, as a friend. I liked you in quite a different way, I—"

"You didn't know he was engaged?" said Ted, rousing himself suddenly. "Do you mean to say he has been playing fast and loose with you, the blackguard? If I had thought that—"

"No, no!" she cried, in alarm at the fierceness of his expression. "He never treated me badly; he made everything quite clear from the beginning. It was my fault if I misunderstood him. But I never did; I always knew we were just friends, and it was pleasant, and I let it go on. Haven't you and I been

The Making of a Prig

friends, too, Ted? There was no harm in that, was there?"

"Oh, no," he said, bitterly. "There was no fear of any harm in it!"

She realised his meaning, and blushed painfully as she felt that he had spoken the truth.

"Ted, do you hate me, I wonder?" she murmured.

"What? Oh, that's all right. Don't bother about me. I was a rotten ass ever to expect anything else."

"But, I mean, because — because of the other?" she went on anxiously.

Ted bit his lip, but did not speak.

"Do you think it was wrong of me?" she pleaded. "Ted, tell me! I didn't know; I didn't really. It seemed quite right to me; I couldn't see that it mattered, just because of what people said. Would you think it wrong of a girl to come and see you, if she liked coming, and didn't care what people said?"

Ted rose from his seat hurriedly, and picked up his hat.

"I never said you were wrong, did I?" he said, gently. "You see, you're clever, and I'm not, and it's altogether different. I was only sorry, that was all; I didn't think you went in for that sort of thing, and I was hit up, rather. But it was my fault entirely; and of course you're right,—you always are. I sha'n't bother you any more, now I know."

"Ted, don't go," she said, imploringly, as he touched her hand again and turned towards the door. "Don't you understand, Ted, that —that *he* only appealed to half of me, and— I do care, Ted, and I want you to come and see me again; I do really, Ted, I—"

But he only smiled as incredulously as before, and spoke again in the same gentle tone.

"Thanks, awfully. But don't bother to spoof yourself about me; I shall be all right, really. It was always my fault; I won't bother you any more. Good-bye."

And, haunted by his changed manner and his joyless smile, she went back to her seat on the stairs, and sat with her hands clasped over her knees and her eyes staring vacantly into space, as she tried in vain to discover what her real feelings were. "Perhaps I haven't got any," she thought to herself. "Perhaps I am incapable of loving any one, or of feeling anything. And I have sent away the best fellow in the whole world, and it doesn't seem to matter a bit. I wonder if

The Making of a Prig

anything could make me cry now?" And she took a gloomy pleasure in conjuring up all the incidents of the last unhappy week, and laughed cynically when she found that none of them had any effect upon her.

"Why don't they light the gas?" complained the working gentlewomen, when they came downstairs to supper. And when Katharine explained that she had promised to light it herself and had forgotten to do so, they passed on their way, marvelling that any one with so little feeling should have her moments of abstraction like every one else. After they had all gone down, she had a restless fit, and paced up and down the landing until Polly Newland came out of the sick room, and stopped her.

"You might choose another landing, if you want to do that," she said, crossly. "You've woke her up now; but you can come in if you like. She has just asked for you."

Katharine followed her in, rather awkwardly, and sat down on the chair that was pointed out to her, and tried to think of something appropriate to say. It was difficult to know how to begin, when she looked round the room, and noted all the objects that seemed to have belonged to some distant period in her

The Making of a Prig

life, before the world had become so hard and cheerless. But Phyllis was looking the same as ever, except that she was rather white, and her hair was strangely tidy. She was the first to speak.

"Hullo," she said. "I've been wanting to see you. What's the matter with you, child?"

The incongruity of being asked by the invalid for the cause of her own malady did not immediately occur to Katharine. But the familiar tone of sympathy went straight to her heart, and she broke down completely. She had a dim notion that Polly remonstrated angrily, and that Polly was sent out of the room; and after that she was conscious of nothing except of the comfort of being able to cry undisturbed, until Phyllis said something about red eyes, and they joined in a spasmodic laugh.

"Poor old girl, what have they been doing to you?" she asked.

"Everything has been horrid," gasped Katharine. "And you were ill, and nobody understood, and oh, Phyllis!— I am a *prig!*"

CHAPTER XVI

Marion Keeley lay in an indolent attitude on the sofa by the window. Her mother was addressing circulars at the writing-table, with the anxious haste of the fashionable woman of business. Both of them looked as though the London season, which a royal wedding had prolonged this year, had been too much for them.

"He is coming again to-night," said Marion, throwing down a letter she had been reading. Her tone was one of dissatisfaction.

"I know," replied her mother. "I asked him to come."

Marion made a gesture of impatience.

"Don't you think," she said, "that you might occasionally, for the sake of variety, wait until his own inclination prompted him to come?"

"I don't understand you," said Mrs. Keeley, absently. "I asked him because I wanted to make final arrangements with him about Lady Suffolk's drawing-room meeting, at which he has promised to speak to-morrow."

The Making of a Prig

"It seems to me," observed Marion sarcastically, "that it would save a lot of trouble if you were to marry him yourself."

"It is very surprising," complained her mother, "how you persist in dragging the frivolous element into everything. If you were only like your cousin, now,— so earnest and so sympathetic! How is it that you are really my daughter?"

"I'm sure I don't know; in fact, I think it is the only subject on which you have allowed me to remain ignorant," returned Marion, calmly. "But you need n't bother about me; I am going out to dinner in any case to-night, so you will be able to make your arrangements with Paul without the distraction of the frivolous element. Meanwhile, can't we have some tea?"

The Honourable Mrs. Keeley returned to her circulars with a sigh.

"One might almost think, to hear you talk, that you did not want to marry him at all," she exclaimed.

"One almost might," assented Marion; and she tore her letter into little pieces, and threw them deftly into the waste-paper basket. Her mother looked at her a little apprehensively.

"How you can, even in fun, pretend to ig-

The Making of a Prig

nore the merits of a character like Paul Wilton's is beyond my comprehension," she grumbled. "What more can you want in a man, I should like to know?"

"More? I don't want any more; I want a good deal less. I'm not ignoring his merits; I only wish I could. I would give anything to find a few honest human imperfections in him. It is his eternal excellence that is driving me to distraction. What a fool I was ever to let him take me seriously! Of course I never should have done, if he had not provoked me by being so difficult to fascinate. He is one of those awful people who are going to make heaven unbearable!"

"Judging by your aggravating behaviour in this world, you won't be there to help him," said her mother, who was losing her patience rapidly after having wrongly addressed two wrappers.

"I hope I sha'n't. If all the people go to heaven who are popularly supposed to be *en route*, I should think even the saints would be too bored to stop there. As for Paul, I grant you that he is eminently fitted for a son-in-law, but I don't see why I should be the victim of his heaven-sent vocation."

"You are not married to him yet; and if

The Making of a Prig

you continue in this strain much longer, I doubt if you ever will be."

"Oh," said Marion, with sudden animation, "do you really think there *is* a chance of his breaking it off?"

The opportune arrival of Katharine at this moment restored some of Mrs. Keeley's good-humour. She approved very decidedly of Katharine, not only because she was a working-woman, but also on account of her patience as a listener. Katharine, she felt, would have made an ideal daughter; Katharine understood the serious aspect of the political situation, and she showed no signs of being bored when people gave her their opinion of things. So she received her with genuine cordiality.

"I am so glad you have come," said Marion, offering her a perfunctory embrace. "You have interrupted mamma, and made tea inevitable. It is quite providential."

"I am glad to be the unwitting cause of so many blessings," said Katharine drily. "I really came to say good-bye. I am going home to-morrow."

"Holidays already?" exclaimed Mrs. Keeley, as though she grudged even the working gentlewoman her moments of relaxation.

The Making of a Prig

"They have not come too soon for me," observed Katharine, to whom the last six weeks had seemed an endless period of waiting. "But I am leaving town for good; so I suppose I shall not see you again for some time. I mean to say, I have given up my teaching, and—"

"How charming of you!" exclaimed Marion, who felt that the last barrier to a warm friendship with her cousin was now removed. "Are you really going to be like everybody else, now?"

But the Honourable Mrs. Keeley was bitterly disappointed.

"It is incredible," she said. "Do you mean to say that you are going to throw up your life's work, just as you are on the point of being a brilliant success?"

"I think, on the contrary, I have merely been a failure," said Katharine, with a patient smile. "You see, there are hundreds of people who can do just what I am doing. But I am wanted at home, and I am going back to my father; I ought never to have left him."

"Oh, these girls!" sighed Mrs. Keeley. "What is the use of trying to make them independent? And I thought you were so different; I held you up as an example to my own daughter—"

The Making of a Prig

"I am so sorry," murmured Katharine, in parenthesis. Marion only laughed.

"I was proud to own you as my niece," pursued Mrs. Keeley, increasing in fervour as she went on. "You were doing what so few women succeed in doing, and I had the keenest admiration for your courage and your talent. And to give it all up like this! Surely, you have some excellent reason for such an extraordinary course of action?"

"It seems to me quite sufficient reason that I am more wanted at home than here," replied Katharine, with the same air of gentle endurance. She had gone through a similar explanation more than once lately, and it was beginning to blunt the edge of her newly made resolutions. It also took away most of the picturesqueness of being good.

"But, indeed, you are very much mistaken," her aunt continued to urge. "Who has been putting this effete notion of *duty* into your head? I thought we working-women had buried it for ever! Consider what you are doing in throwing up the position you have carved out for yourself; consider the bad effect it will have upon others, the example,— everything! Your place is the

The Making of a Prig

world, Kitty, the great world! There cannot be any work for you to do in a home like yours."

"There is always plenty to do in the village, and nobody to do it," said Katharine. "I have considered the matter thoroughly, Aunt Alicia, and my mind is quite made up. Anybody can do my work up here in London; you know that is so."

"Indeed, you are mistaken," said her aunt, vehemently. It seemed particularly hard that her favourite protégée should have deserted her principles, just as she had been driven to the last limit of endurance by her own daughter. "Every woman must do her own work, and no one else can do it for her."

"Then why do you always say the labour market is so overcrowded?" asked Marion, making a mischievous application of the knowledge she had so unwillingly absorbed. But she was not heeded.

"It is the mass we have to consider, not the individual," continued the Honourable Mrs. Keeley, as though she were addressing the room from a platform. "It is for lesser women than ourselves to look after the home and the parish; there is a far wider sphere reserved for such as you and I. It would be a

The Making of a Prig

perfect scandal if you were to throw yourself away on the narrowness of the domestic circle."

Katharine felt a hysterical desire to laugh, which she controlled with difficulty. She spoke very humbly, instead.

"It must be my own fault, if I have allowed you to think all these things about me," she said. "There is nothing great reserved for me; I am just a complete failure, and that is the end of all my ambition and all my conceit. I wish some one had told me I was conceited, before I got so bad."

The Honourable Mrs. Keeley was silenced at last. None of her experience of working gentlewomen helped her to meet the present situation. A woman with a great future before her had obviously no right to be humble. But Marion realised gleefully that she had gained a new and unexpected ally.

"I always said you were much too jolly to belong to mamma's set," she observed; at which the angered feelings of her mother compelled her to seek comfort in solitude, and she made some excuse for retiring to her boudoir, and left the two rebels together. They looked at one another and broke into mutual merriment. But Marion laughed the loudest,—a fact that she herself was the first to appreciate.

The Making of a Prig

"Kitty," she said suddenly, growing grave, "I am so sorry, dear! What's up, and who has been treating you badly?"

She strolled away immediately to pour out tea, and Katharine had time to recover from surprise at her unusual penetration.

"How did you know?" she asked, slowly.

"I guessed, because — oh, you looked like it, or something! Don't ask me to give a reason for anything I say, *please*. It isn't my business, of course, and I don't want to know a thing about it if you would rather not tell; only, I'm sorry if you're cut up, that's all. Did you chuck him, or did it never get so far as that? There, I really don't want you to tell me about it. Of course, he was much older than you, and much wickeder, and he flirted atrociously with you and you were taken in by him, you poor little innocent dear! I know all about it, and the way they get hold of girls like you who are not up to their wiles. He was married, too, of course? They always are, the worst ones."

It was too much trouble to correct her assumptions, and Katharine allowed her to go on. After all, her sympathy was genuine, if it was a little crudely expressed.

"I shouldn't think any more about him,

The Making of a Prig

if I were you," continued Marion. "They're not worth it, any of them; go and get another, and snap your fingers at the first. You're not tied to one, as I am."

"No," said Katharine, scalding herself with mouthfuls of boiling tea. "I'm not."

"I know I would give anything to get rid of mine," said Marion sorrowfully. "May you never know the awful monotony of being engaged!"

"I don't fancy I ever shall," observed Katharine.

"Always the same writing on the breakfast table," sighed Marion; "always the same face on the back seat of the carriage; always the same photograph all over the house,—oh, it's maddening! You wouldn't be able to stand it for a day, Kitty!"

"Perhaps not," said Katharine. "Then your engagement is publicly announced now?"

"I should rather think so! I am tired of being congratulated by a lot of idiots, who don't even take the trouble to find out whether I want to be married or not. And then, the boys! Bobby is going to shoot himself, he says; but of course Bobby always says that. And Jack has gone to South Africa; I don't exactly know why, except that every

The Making of a Prig

one goes to South Africa when there isn't any particular reason for staying in town. And Tommy — you remember Tommy, don't you? He was my best boy for ever so long; I rather liked Tommy. Well, he has gone and married that stupid Ethel Humphreys, and he always said she *pinched*. I know why he did it, too. He was being objectionably serious, one day, and said he would do anything on earth for me; so I asked him to go and marry mamma, because then I should get eight hundred a year. And he didn't like it a bit; Tommy always was ridiculously hot-tempered. Oh, dear, I'm sick of it all! I believe you're the only person I know, who hasn't congratulated me."

"Apparently, you do not consider yourself a subject for congratulation," said Katharine, smiling faintly.

"Oh, you're not like all the others, and I should like to be congratulated by you. You would mean what you said, anyhow."

"I certainly should," exclaimed Katharine.

"How earnestly you said that! It's frightfully nice of you to care so much, though. I was telling Paul what a good sort you were, the other day, and he quite agreed."

The Making of a Prig

"Was n't it rather dull for him?"

"Oh, no, I 'm sure it was n't; he takes a tremendous interest in you; he says you are the cleverest woman he knows, and the pluckiest. He does, really!"

"I have no doubt of it. He has always thought me clever and plucky," said Katharine.

"Well, it's more than he thinks about me, anyhow," said Marion ruefully. "He does n't think I am good for anything, except to play with."

"And to fall in love with," added Katharine softly.

"Why did n't you come and meet him the other evening?" continued Marion. "He seemed so disappointed. So was I; I wanted you to come, for lots of reasons. I get so bored when I am left alone with him! I like him ever so much better if there is some one else there; and you are the only girl I know who would be safe not to flirt with him. Bobby said, only the other day, that you were much too nice to flirt with. And girls are so mean, sometimes, — are n't they? I was really sorry when you refused."

"If you had told me the real reason for your invitation, instead of the conventional one, I

The Making of a Prig

might have made more effort to come," said Katharine.

"You old dear, don't be sarcastic; I never can endure sarcasm. But you will come next time, won't you? Oh, dear, I am forgetting all about your own trouble; what a selfish wretch I am! Are you sure there is nothing I can do for you?"

"Nothing, thanks; at least, nothing I would let you do."

"Sure? Well, let me know if there is. Are you really very gone on him, Kitty?"

"Please don't," said Katharine.

"All right, I won't. But I wish you would try a course of boys for a time; it would make you feel so much happier. They're so fresh and harmless."

"Even when they shoot themselves?" said Katharine.

"Oh, that's only Bobby. Must you really go? You old dear, you have done me such a lot of good. What is it, Williams?"

Mr. Wilton was in the library, the man announced, and would be glad to see either Mrs. Keeley or her daughter for a moment, and he would rather not come upstairs, as he was in a hurry. Marion gave a petulant little stamp.

The Making of a Prig

"Oh, send mamma to him! How like Paul, not to care which of us he sees! Just fancy, if it were Tommy, now! Stop, though, show him up here, Williams. You will be able to congratulate him, Kitty; it will put him in a good humour. Oh, nonsense! you can wait just for that, and I haven't anything to say to him that he hasn't heard hundreds of times before."

So Katharine found herself shaking hands with him once more, and congratulating him on being engaged to her cousin, Marion Keeley. She had not seen him since the night of the thunderstorm, when he had stood in the old doorway in Essex Court, with the lamplight on his face.

"You are very good; it is kind of you to take so much interest," he was saying with frigid politeness.

They were silent after that, and Marion said she was sure they must have crowds to talk about, and she would go upstairs and ask her mother about Lady Suffolk's drawing-room meeting; and they both made perfectly futile efforts to keep her in the room, and were ashamed of having made them when she had gone, and they were left to face the situation alone.

The Making of a Prig

"I suppose," said Paul, with an effort, "that your holidays will soon be beginning?"

"They have begun to-day," said Katharine. "This is the first day — of my last holidays."

"Your — last holidays?" She felt, without seeing, that he had looked up sharply at her.

"I don't suppose it will interest you," she went on, rousing herself to be more explicit; "but I am giving up my work in London, and going home for good."

There was the slightest perceptible pause before he spoke.

"Would you care to tell me why?"

"Because," said Katharine slowly, "I happened to find out, through a friend, that I was a prig; and I am going home to try and learn not to be a prig any more." She was looking straight at him as she finished speaking. His face was quite incomprehensible just then.

"Was that a true friend?" he asked.

"People who tell us unpleasant things about ourselves are always said to be our true friends, are they not?" she said, evasively.

"That is not an answer to my question; I was not dealing in generalities when I asked it. But of course, you have every right to withhold the answer, if it pleases you — "

"I don't think I know the answer," said

The Making of a Prig

Katharine. "I have always found your questions too difficult to answer; and as to this one,—I wish I could be sure that it was a friend at all." He moved his chair, involuntarily, a little nearer hers.

"Can I do anything to make you feel more sure?" he asked.

She shook her head, and he moved away again. "Of course, you are the best judge in the matter," he resumed, more naturally; "but it is rather a serious step to take at the outset of your career, is it not?"

"Perhaps," she said, indifferently; "but then, I am not a man, you see. There is no career possible for a woman, because her feelings are always more important to her than all the ambition in the world. A man only draws on his feelings for his recreation; but a woman makes them the whole business of her life, and that is why she never gets on. I don't suppose you can realise this, because it is so different for you. Everybody expects a man to get on; it is made comparatively easy for him, and nobody ever disputes his way of doing it. A man can have as much fun as he likes, as long as he is n't found out,—and it's easy for a man not to be found out," she added, with a sigh.

The Making of a Prig

"Easier than for a woman?" He spoke in the bantering tone that was so familiar to her.

"Oh, a woman is dogged by detectives from her cradle, mostly drawn from the ranks of her own sex. It is a compliment we pay ourselves, in one sense. We dare not inquire into the private life of a man, because of the iniquities he is supposed to practise; but there is so little scandal attached to a woman's name, that we are anxious not to miss any of it." She laughed at her small attempt to be frivolous, and Paul brightened considerably. He could understand her when she was in this mood, and his peace of mind was undisturbed by it.

"I suppose the man is still unborn who will take the trouble to champion his sex, and explain that men are not all profligates before they are married," he observed. "I wonder why women always think of us as cads, and then take us for husbands. I can't think why they want to marry us at all, though."

"And we can't think what reason there is for you to offer *us* marriage, unless you do it for position or something like that," retorted Katharine, and then bit her lip and stopped short, as she realised what she had said. In the embarrassing pause that followed, Marion came back into the room.

The Making of a Prig

"Well, you two don't look as though you'd had much conversation," she remarked.

"We haven't," said Katharine, getting up to leave. "Mr. Wilton's conversation, you see, is all bespoken already."

"Miss Austen is a little hard on me," said Paul. "I have had so little practice in conversation with brilliant and learned young lecturers, that —"

"That I will leave you to a less dismal companion," interrupted Katharine, a little abruptly.

"Will you allow me to suggest," he went on, as he held her hand for a moment, "that you should try and think more kindly of the particular friend who was so unpleasantly frank to you?"

"If I thought that the friend in question were likely to be affected by my opinion of him, perhaps I might," she said, as she turned away.

When she had gone, Marion asked him what he had meant.

"Merely a passing reflection on something she had been telling me," was his reply.

"Oh," said Marion, "did she tell you about her love affair?"

"My dear girl, Miss Austen is not likely to favour me with these interesting disclosures, is

The Making of a Prig

she? I did n't know she had a love affair, as you rather frankly express it."

"She is n't a bit the sort, is she? I only found it out this afternoon; he's an awful beast, I should think,—led her on, and treated her villainously, poor old Kitty! Is n't it a shame?"

"Did she tell you all that?"

"Don't look so surprised! Of course she did; at least, I guessed, because she looked so miserable. I always know; I 've had so much experience, you see. But it 's much worse for Kitty, don't you know, because she takes things so seriously. It 's a mistake, is n't it? I would give a good lot to meet the man who has ill treated her, though!"

"Yes? What would you do to him?"

"I would tell him he was a horrid little bounder, and that Kitty was well rid of him."

"In which case there is no occasion to pity her, is there?"

"Oh, how unsympathetic you are! Of course it 's just as bad, whatever the man is like. It 's always the saints like Kitty who break their hearts for the most worthless men. I 'm not made like that; I should soon console myself with some one else, and make the first one mad. But then, I 'm not clever."

The Making of a Prig

"Your cousin is a most interesting psychological study," said Paul vaguely.

"What do you mean? She is a very nice girl indeed," cried Marion indignantly; and Paul silently condemned the whole sex, without reservation.

It was a particularly bright and sunny evening when Katharine returned to her home, — a failure. She felt that, to be appropriate, it should have been dull and dreary; but it was on the contrary quite at variance with her feelings, and she grew unaccountably happier in spite of herself, as the train sped past the familiar landmarks on the way and brought her nearer every minute to the home of her childhood. For there was a sneaking consideration for herself in her sudden desire to serve others; she had felt out of tune with the world since it had been the means of revealing her deficiencies to herself, and she longed for the panacea of home sympathy, which was still connected in her mind with the days when she had been supreme in a small circle, a circle that believed in her if it did not precisely understand her. She had found something wanting in the sympathies and interests which had absorbed her for the last two years, and she turned instinctively to those earlier ones which may have

The Making of a Prig

offered her no great allurements at the time, but which at least contained no rude awakenings. She forgot the petty discomforts and frequent annoyances of her life at home, in her present desire for rest and peace; she was tired of fighting hard for her happiness and gaining nothing but a moiety of pleasure in return; and the weary condition of mind and body in which she found herself at the end of it all, probably helped her to exaggerate the advantages of that former existence of hers, and to mistake its monotony for restfulness.

She had her first disillusionment as she hastened out of the station. It was no one's fault that the Rector had been obliged to attend a meeting of the archæological society, and that Miss Esther had been detained in the village; but they had never omitted to meet her before, and that they should have done so on this particular occasion which was of so much import to her, appeared in the light of a bad omen, and she set it down sadly as another penalty that she was to pay for having neglected her real duty so long. But she had yet to learn that her ardent desire to sacrifice herself for somebody did not bring with it the necessary opportunity, and it was not encouraging to discover that no one was particularly anxious to be the recipient of her good works, and that her effort at well-doing was more resented by those in authority than her previous and undisguised course of self-indulgence. Even Miss Esther mistrusted her enthusiasm, and evidently looked upon it as another freak on the part of her capricious niece, which would probably prove as transient as the last; and Katharine felt that she was touching the extreme limits of her endurance in the first few days she spent at the Rectory.

"It is very hard," she complained to herself when she had been home about a week, "that they should make it so much easier for me to be bad than good. All the same," she added, with a touch of her old defiant spirit, "I am going to be good, whether they like it or not!"

CHAPTER XVII

IVINGDON was one of those villages, common to the chalk district, that cease to possess any charm in the wet weather. The small ranges of round-topped hills which formed the only feature in the flat green stretches of country entirely lost the few characteristics they possessed, in the absence of sunshine, and presented neither charm nor majesty in the heavy grey atmosphere that surrounded them. The landscape appeared even less inspiring than usual to Katharine, on a rainy day in the late autumn, as she plodded through the most squalid part of the village, and prepared to walk home through a kind of mist that had none of the exhilarating qualities of the stormy rain that always appealed to her. After four months of dull and virtuous renunciation, such a day as this was likely to hasten the reaction that had become inevitable. It was tea time when she reached the Rectory; and the aspect of the precisely arranged table, with its rigid erec-

The Making of a Prig

tion of double dahlias in the middle, and the starched figure of Miss Esther at the head of it, completed the feeling of revulsion in her mind.

"My dear," said her aunt, as Katharine flung herself into a chair, "have you no intention of making yourself tidy before we begin?"

"My only intention is that of having tea as speedily as possible," replied Katharine. "If Peter Bunce, or any other depressing personage is likely to turn up, he may as well see me in my wet weather hat as in anything else. Besides, I rather like myself in my wet weather hat, in spite of the disapproval it has excited among the gods of the neighbourhood."

She waited instinctively for the reproof that usually came as an accompaniment to her criticism of the neighbourhood; but Miss Esther for once was preoccupied, and allowed her to go on undisturbed. "Mrs. Jones has got another baby," continued Katharine. "That's the seventh. And Farmer Rickard seems to have seized the opportunity to turn her husband off for the winter. There positively isn't another scrap of news,—so may I have some tea?"

"Talking of babies," observed the Rector,

The Making of a Prig

looking up from his book, "I heard this morning that some one was going to be married. Now, whoever could it have been, I wonder!"

"I didn't know," said Katharine, "that any one was left to be married in this village, above the age of sixteen."

"Ah, to be sure," continued the Rector, smiling at his unusual effort of memory, "it was your cousin Marion. You remember Alicia Keeley, do you not, Esther? Well, this is her daughter; they both came to stay with us some years ago, if you remember; and she is to be married to a barrister, whose name — my child, that is the third time I have passed you the butter, and you have already helped yourself twice — whose name is Paul Wilton. It's very odd," he added, with his nervous laugh, "but, although the name is perfectly familiar to me, I do not seem to recollect the man in the least. The only Wilton I can recall with certainty is the exceedingly able and scholarly author of our best work on copper tokens; but —"

"Well, this is his son, of course, Cyril," interrupted Miss Esther impatiently. "I should not have thought it required much effort to remember the man who enjoyed your

The Making of a Prig

hospitality for at least two months. A very nice young man he was, too,—of an excellent family, and with a delicate regard for propriety which was most fortunate considering the embarrassing circumstances in which we were placed at the time. So he is going to marry into the family? What a coincidence! I don't remember much about Marion, she was so young when she stayed here; but if she has grown up at all like that terribly advanced mother of hers, poor Mr. Wilton will have his hands full. How did he meet her, I wonder? Did you ever see him in Curzon street, Katharine?"

"Sometimes; they were engaged early in the summer. But it is n't a bit important, is it?" said Katharine.

"You knew they were engaged, and you have kept it to yourself all this time?" exclaimed her aunt. "I really think you are the most exasperating girl, Katharine!"

"Why? I suppose it is rather cruel, though, to rob any one of the smallest piece of gossip, in a place like this," observed Katharine sarcastically.

"To be sure! to be sure! I remember him perfectly," the Rector was chuckling gleefully. "A delightful young fellow, with some knowledge of Oriental china. We must send them

The Making of a Prig

a little present, my dear, — something he would be able to appreciate. There is a delightful Elizabethan chest at Walker's — "

"I see no necessity for a wedding present at all," interrupted Miss Esther. "We only know him very slightly, and we have n't seen the Keeleys for years. If Katharine likes to send her cousin a little remembrance, that is her own affair and she can do as she likes," she added, with a princely condescension. "I really wonder, Cyril, that you can make such an extravagant suggestion, with the poor crying out at your very doors!"

The Rector reflected on the beauty of the old oak chest he had coveted for weeks, and sighed deeply. Katharine roused herself, and laughed in a distinctly forced manner.

"Send them your blessing, auntie," she said; "and congratulate Mr. Wilton on his good fortune in entering our particular family. I am sure it must be an alliance he has coveted ever since he first made our acquaintance! It will only cost a penny stamp, and I am sure the poor of the village will not grudge that for such a laudable object. Hey-day, do let us talk about something else! Do you know the Grange is put up for sale?"

"You don't say so!" exclaimed Miss Esther,

The Making of a Prig

who was as easily diverted as a child. "Dear me! and poor Mrs. Morton hardly laid to her last rest! The want of feeling that that young Edward has shown throughout is almost incredible. To requite the lifelong devotion of his mother by selling her old home a month after her death! Ah, well, I suppose we have all done our work here, and it is time for us to follow her!"

"What rubbish!" cried Katharine hotly. "Why should he pretend to be fond of his mother just because she is dead? She was never a bit fond of him, when she was alive, and he wanted her affection badly enough then. Besides, it can't matter to her whether the house is sold or not, and I expect he wants the money."

"Money? Why, she has left him every penny she had,—so what more can he want? I know she did, for a fact, because the housekeeper told me so."

"I shouldn't dream of disputing such an excellent authority, but I do know her generosity was purely accidental, and that she would have made another will if she had not been taken ill so suddenly," said Katharine, getting up and walking to the window. The view outside, with the sodden lawn and the drip-

The Making of a Prig

ping trees, was as cheerless as the conversation within.

"The house ought not to be allowed to stand," said the Rector, with an indignation that he never bestowed on the human imperfections so bitterly deplored by his sister. "A wretched modern thing, belonging to the very worst period of domestic art!"

"They are doing it up," said Katharine from the window. "I wonder," she added softly to the sodden lawn and the dripping trees, "if he knows that they have mended the gap in the hedge?" Perhaps it was only the dulness of the weather that was depressing her, but her eyes, as she laid her cheek against the window-pane, were full of tears. Miss Esther continued her speculations unconsciously.

"I suppose he will travel," she said. "It amounts to seven hundred a year, the housekeeper told me; and I'm sure it's seven hundred more than he deserves, the unfeeling fellow!"

"It isn't his fault that he didn't get on with his mother," said Katharine. "People can't choose their relations, can they? And I'm sure, under the present system, every obstacle is put in the way of our hitting it off with our own people."

The Making of a Prig

She was almost surprised at her own vehemence in Ted's defence. She had never seen him since the day he had called on her in Queen's Crescent and rejected the affection she so tardily offered him, and the smart of that rejection was still present with her, gently as he had expressed it; but she could no more suppress her old instinct of protection for him than she could control her thoughts.

"I find it quite impossible to understand you, when you are in these heartless moods," said her aunt crossly.

"Am I heartless?" said Katharine, with her eyes still full of tears. "I suppose that must be it; I wondered what was the matter with me this afternoon. Of course I am in one of my heartless moods. Oh, dear, how stupid it all is!" She sighed desperately, and turned away from the dreary outlook. "I'm sorry I didn't gather any more news in my excursion to the village," she went on presently, with an obvious effort to be agreeable. "Oh, I forgot, — I met the doctor."

"Yes? What had he to say for himself?" asked Miss Esther, whose dignity was always subject to her curiosity.

"He asked me to marry him, and I refused," answered Katharine; and she broke

The Making of a Prig

into a peal of laughter at the immediate effect of her words.

"What? Really, Katharine, you are perfectly incorrigible," said Miss Esther, in a tone that was expressive rather of incredulity than of disapproval.

"It's very odd," observed Katharine, "that one has only to tell the truth to be disbelieved. And I'm sure I was very sorry to be obliged to refuse him, because I felt there was no one else in the place he could possibly ask. Poor doctor!"

Miss Esther said a rapid grace to show how outraged she felt, and walked out of the room without another word. Katharine sighed once more and looked across at her father, who was apparently absorbed in his book and oblivious of what had been passing. But Katharine's acquaintance with the world, short as it had been, had considerably widened her vision, and she knew somehow as she looked at him that he was not reading at that moment.

"Daddy, dear daddy!" she cried, impetuously, "I couldn't help it this afternoon, I couldn't, really! I believe I have a devil in me some days, and this is one of them. Daddy, forgive me for being so selfish and horrid; I hate myself for my abominable tem-

The Making of a Prig

per, I do indeed. I think I have never been so miserable in my whole life before!"

"My child, what is it? I don't think I quite understand," said the Rector gently. She came and sat on the arm of his chair, and he stroked her hair mechanically.

"Of course you don't,—how should you?" she exclaimed, half laughing to hide the shake in her voice. "But I wish I knew why I have these bad fits; I would do just anything to get better, but *I can't!* When I don't feel wretched I feel absurd, and that's ever so much worse. Why is it that I feel like this, daddy?"

"Shall we send for the doctor?" asked the Rector innocently; and he wondered why she seemed amused.

"I don't fancy he would care to come just yet," she said, demurely. They were silent for a few moments. The Rector asked her presently if she would like to go away again.

"I don't know; I don't seem to want anything. Ivingdon is intolerable; but I said I would endure it for your sake, and it seems so feeble merely to have failed again. After all, I haven't done the least atom of good by giving up my work and coming home, have I?"

The Making of a Prig

The Rector remembered many incidents in the last four months, and did not contradict her; but his silence was so habitual to him that she hardly noticed it.

"Self-sacrifice is all very well in theory," she went on disconsolately, "but if nobody wants you to sacrifice yourself, what's the good of it? I don't believe there is a single Christian virtue that works properly, when you come to practise it; and I've wasted four good months in finding it out. Oh, dear, what a mortal idiot I've been! I wish you understood, daddy," she added wistfully.

"I'm not sure that I don't, Kitty," he said tentatively, and waited to be contradicted.

"I believe you do; I believe you always have understood!" she cried. "But I always expect too much from people, and I never can take any one on trust. How I can be so unlike you is a mystery to me."

"You are like your dear mother, bless her," said the Rector with unconscious humour; and they became silent again.

"Do you know," she went on presently, "if you'd promise not to mind, daddy, I half think I'd like to go away again, for a while. I've still got some money, you know, and I might try Paris, or some new place. It

The Making of a Prig

seems hopeless to stay on here, and worry Aunt Esther by everything I do or say; I know she considers me the cross she has to bear, but it seems a waste of Christian resignation, doesn't it?"

"Paris?" said the Rector with animation. "By all means go to Paris, — the most delightful place in the world! When I was a boy in Paris — Dear, dear, how it all comes back to me! That was before I was ordained, to be sure; ah, those were days to be remembered! I can give you an introduction to a friend of mine in Paris, Monsieur — Monsieur — Ah, it's gone now. But I can tell you the names of all his books. A charming fellow; knew everything and did everything; there was nothing too daring for him in those days. You'll get on with him, Kitty; the most delightful companion a man could have, in fact!" The old Rector was laughing like a schoolboy at his reminiscences.

"That's all very well," said Katharine rather cruelly; "but what will Aunt Esther say?"

"Ah," said the Rector, looking about him apprehensively, "there is certainly Esther to be considered."

"Yes, there is!" sighed Katharine. And

The Making of a Prig.

she added impetuously, "Poor daddy! what a saint you must have been all these years! I wonder why I never realised it before?"

"Oh, no," said the Rector, smiling. "I'm nothing but an old fool, who was never fit to have a daughter at all. Your mother ought to have left me to vegetate among my books, bless her heart!"

Katharine looked at him reflectively.

"I am beginning to understand," she said, in her quaint, thoughtful manner. "It has puzzled me all these months, but you have made it come quite clear at last. I see now what they meant by calling me a prig: it is because I have none of the qualities that would prevent you from ever becoming one."

"A prig?" said her father inquiringly.

"Ah," said Katharine, "it is something of too modern a growth to have come within your ken." She slipped off her seat, and began pacing restlessly up and down the room.

"A prig," she continued, more to herself than to her father, who was watching her narrowly nevertheless, "a prig is one who tries to break what the ordinary person is pleased to call the law of Nature, and to substitute the law of his own reason instead. It doesn't matter that this is what we are brought up to

The Making of a Prig

do, for the ordinary person insists on our forgetting that we are intelligent beings, and only wants us to run in the same rut as himself. And the ordinary person is very happy, so perhaps he is right. Education makes us all prigs, and we have to sit and wait for the particular experience that is to undo the effects of our education. It is great waste of time to be educated, is n't it? We are told that it is priggish to have ideals, and that is why being young is generally equivalent to being priggish. The world won't tolerate ideals; it sneers at us for trying to find out new ways of being good, and it likes to see us for ever grubbing among the same old ways of being bad. Did you know all this before, daddy? But you never told me, did you? Do parents ever tell their children anything useful, I wonder? Oh, I don't think so; we just have to go on until we find it all out, and break our hearts over it, most likely!" She paused to give a little bitter laugh. The Rector had an intent look on his face that was foreign to it. "I should like to know," she went on, more gently, "if it is n't possible to be brave, or steadfast, or true, without being a prig; it simply means that we have got to go on trying to be better than we are, and pretending that

The Making of a Prig

we don't know it all the while. It is such an anomalous position for a thinking person, isn't it? And yet, if we are honest about it we proclaim ourselves prigs at once. *I* am a prig, daddy. Did you know that too? I have gloried all my life in being above the ordinary littlenesses of womanhood; and then, when my hour came, I just learned that I was the same old woman after all. I was proud of knowing so much, and all the time I did not know what every ignorant woman in the world could have told me. Oh, the world is right, after all; I know it! But it has such uncomfortable ways of convincing us, hasn't it? I'm not bothering you, daddy, am I?" She stopped, and looked at him anxiously. The Rector did not speak. "Nothing will ever make you a prig," continued Katharine as she resumed her restless walk, "or Ted either, or Marion Keeley. Lovable people are never priggish, are they? Oh, I am never going to try to be anything, again. I shall become as much like the ordinary person as I can; I will let boys like Monty make love to me, and pretend that I like it; I will let myself go, and hide away my old feelings which were real ones, and invent a whole set of new ones for everyday use. Oh, dear, how

The Making of a Prig

absurd it all is! To make one's life a long course of deception, in order to prove to the world that we are real! And yet, that is the only way to avoid being called a prig. It is ridiculous to pretend that we care for what the big people think of us. We don't. It is the little, commonplace, ordinary folk, with the commonplace minds and the commonplace views, who make up our audience; and we acknowledge it all our lives by being afraid of their criticism. We play to them, and to them only, from the moment we begin to think for ourselves, until Providence is good enough to ring down the curtain. We make a wretched compromise with our real selves, in order to get through life without being laughed at for taking it seriously. And the end of it all is that we have to suffer our own contempt, instead of the commonplace person's. But everybody does the same, so it must be right, must n't it? Daddy," she added suddenly, as she came to a standstill before him, " daddy, do you think, if I don't try to be good any more, that I shall ever become just an ordinary pleasant person, — some one whom people will care to fall in love with? It would be so comforting to feel that people cared to fall in love with me. I am so tired of being thought

The Making of a Prig

clever and nothing else; cleverness seems like a kind of blight that helps one to miss the biggest thing in life. At least, I have missed it, and everybody says I am clever. Why don't you answer me, daddy? Why, daddy! I — I do believe you 're crying!"

"No, my child, you are mistaken," said Cyril Austen hastily. "I have been overworking my eyes lately, that is all. You must n't talk like that, little girl; it — it makes me unhappy. I should never have allowed you to go away by yourself, should I? I'm a useless old — But there, it is too late now. Let us talk about this Paris plan of yours. What if I were to come too, eh?"

"It would be beautiful!" cried Katharine. "But there is still Aunt Esther, is n't there?"

"Ah, yes!" said the Rector ruefully. "So stupid of me to forget!"

They made themselves very happy for a day or two over the Paris plan. They met like guilty conspirators when Miss Esther was out of the way, and amused themselves by arranging a scheme which they knew quite well she would never allow them to carry out. Katharine's spirits recovered something of their old vigour; and Miss Esther felt more bewildered than ever when she suddenly ap-

The Making of a Prig

peared in this new mood, and refused to have anything more to do with the parish.

"I am tired of good works," she announced vigorously. "They don't answer, and they destroy one's self-respect. Some people are cut out for that sort of thing, but I am not, and I am going to leave it to those who are. I am never again going to make myself uncomfortable by visiting people in their unpleasant homes. I don't want to go, for one thing; and it isn't good for them to be patronised, for another. Besides, they can't refuse to see me in any case, and I don't like forcing myself upon people in that uninvited manner. I am going to be happy in my own way, and that will give them a much fairer chance of being happy in theirs. I've done with the whole thing." And she returned cheerfully to the map of Paris.

But her new-found contentment was not to be allowed a long duration. A letter came for her a few days later, which altered the whole aspect of affairs, and finally quenched the Paris plan. The writing was unfamiliar to her, and she had to turn to the end of the closely written pages to discover who had sent it to her.

"Dear Miss Austen," it ran:—

The Making of a Prig

"It may be a matter of great surprise to you to hear from me in this unexpected manner. Nothing but the deep interest I feel in one who is, I have reason to believe, as great a friend of yours as of mine would give me the courage to take up my pen and write to you. I have for some time past been observing Ted's career with distress, if not with the deepest concern. You probably know that he gave up his work in the city on the death of Mrs. Morton, so I will not trouble you with more details than necessity compels you to hear. Of course you will understand the diffidence with which I approach you on so delicate a matter; but my great friendship, or what I might call our *mutual* friendship, for Ted Morton has given me the requisite courage. I do not know the reason for what I am about to break to you; in fact, to be explicit, I have not the slightest idea of what led him to take such a step, but I have my own conjectures about the matter, and these I will lay before you as briefly as the occasion demands. For some time past, indeed, I may say for months, he has been very depressed, and has tried to drown his trouble, whatever it might be, in distractions of various kinds. Do not for one moment suppose that I am making any insinuation detrimental to Ted's reputation; far from it! But there is no doubt that he has grown somewhat reckless in disposition, owing possibly to this same mysterious trouble of his, and this has hurried on the crisis which it is now my business to communicate to you. But to avoid unnecessary details, let me at once tell you in plain language what has

The Making of a Prig

happened to him. Three days ago I met him in the Strand about seven o'clock, and asked him to come and dine with me. He refused, with none of the punctilious courtesy that usually characterises him, and I left him thinking, strange as it might seem, that he preferred to be alone. But on going to look him up at his chambers last night, I found him in the condition which it has become my obvious duty to describe to you. Fortunately, the ingenuous disposition, which has made him feel his trouble much longer than most men, has also saved him from this last and worst step of all; for, in his ignorance, he took too large a dose of laudanum, and the effect has mercifully been injurious instead of fatal. He is now —"

Katharine read no more. Nothing further could be of importance after she had learnt so much. Ted had tried to destroy himself, and it was on her account.

"Whatever is the matter, Katharine? I have asked you the same question three times," Miss Esther was saying crossly. Katharine stared at her in reply, with large, terrified eyes. Her aunt repeated her question, and tried to possess herself of the letter. Katharine came to herself with a start, and snatched it back again, and thrust it into her father's hand.

"Read it, daddy," she tried to say, but no sound came; she seemed possessed of a great

The Making of a Prig

horror that robbed her of every faculty. The Rector smoothed out the letter silently, glanced at the florid signature, "Barrington Montague," and began to read it without waiting to put on his glasses. Miss Esther looked from one to the other, and was divided between her curiosity and her annoyance.

"Really, Katharine, you are quite devoid of manners. Am I not to have the right to ask a simple question in my own house? Who is the letter from, and what is it all about?"

Dorcas lingered by the door as long as she dared, under pretence of being wanted; but Miss Esther, who never relaxed her vigilance even in a crisis, detected the subterfuge and ordered her sharply out of the room. The accustomed tone of reproof helped Katharine to recover herself. She drew a deep breath, and made an effort to speak.

"Ted is dying," she said. "They are afraid to tell me, but I know it is so. And it is I who have killed him, *I!* I am going to him at once."

The Rector was blinking his eyes as he finished reading the letter. Miss Esther held out her hand again.

"I insist upon your giving me that letter, Cyril," she said in her discordant voice.

The Making of a Prig

Katharine struck down her hand fiercely. Her numbness was giving way to a kind of passionate frenzy.

"Leave it alone, Aunt Esther!" she cried vehemently. "It is no business of yours; you don't understand; nobody understands. I have made Ted take his life. I am going to him *now*."

The last sentence was the only one that reached Miss Esther's comprehension; she at once took up her usual attitude of disapproval.

"Indeed, Katharine, you will do nothing of the kind," she exclaimed querulously. "What are we coming to next, I wonder? I sincerely trust, Cyril, that you will point out to your daughter that it is quite impossible for her to visit a young man in his chambers. I really wish that tiresome young Edward would emigrate, or marry, or do something that would put him out of the way. What has he been doing now, I wonder?"

Katharine paid no heed; her eyes were fixed feverishly on her father's face.

"Ted is ill, and he wants me. You will let me go, daddy, won't you?" she said imploringly.

"I beg you to assert your authority, Cyril, by forbidding such a mad piece of folly," cried

The Making of a Prig

the shrill tones of Miss Esther. Katharine turned upon her furiously.

"*You*, what can *you* know about it? You have never known what it is to want to protect some one; you don't know the awful emptiness of having no one to care for. Daddy! you understand, don't you? I may go, mayn't I?"

The Rector glanced from one to the other. He had not put on his glasses, but he did not seem to want them just then. Slowly the tyranny of twenty years was losing its terrors for him; he even forgot to laugh nervously as the two women stood awaiting his answer; and although there was a smile on his face as he looked at them, it had only been called there by a reflection on his folly in the past. He marvelled at himself, as his eyes rested on the glowing features of his daughter, for ever having hesitated to support her.

"The child is in the right, Esther," he said, mildly. "I — I am fond of the dear boy myself, and he must not be left in the hour of his need. We will go together, eh, Kitty?"

Miss Esther stared at him dumbly. She had never heard him speak like that before. After all, nothing is so convincing as the sudden assumption of power by the oppressed;

The Making of a Prig

and few things are more complete than the humiliation of the oppressor.

"Let me see," continued the Rector: "we cannot catch anything before the 1.28. That will give us time for an early lunch, if you will kindly see to it, Esther. Kitty, my child, do not fret over the boy; we will soon put him to rights, eh?"

Katharine remained immovable, with Monty's letter crunched in her hand. "Ted has tried to kill himself— for *me*," were the words that ran remorselessly in her mind.

Cyril Austen walked out of the room with a firm step. Miss Esther rattled her keys, muttered something to herself, and followed him almost immediately.

She was dethroned at last.

CHAPTER XVIII

THE landlady had gone out of the room and closed the door. Katharine stepped softly to the side of the bed, and looked at the sleeping face. It was just the same as she had always known it, rounded and beardless, without a line or a wrinkle, and with the hair as loose and rumpled as it had been in the days before manhood had claimed its submission. "Dear old Ted," she murmured to herself with a half smile, "I don't believe he *could* look ill, however much he tried." She stole about the room, putting flowers in the vases, and lightening some of its London dinginess, until the sound of her name brought her back again to the bedside.

"Dear old man, don't look so scared," she laughed. "We heard you were ill, and we came up to look after you, daddy and I. Daddy is still downstairs; he discovered an old print in the hall, and he has n't got any further yet. There are a lot of old prints in the hall, so I suppose it will be ever so long

The Making of a Prig

before he does get any further. Isn't it like daddy?"

She smoothed his hair gently, and he laughed contentedly in reply. He did not seem at all surprised to see her; Kitty always had turned up, all his life, when he had got himself into a scrape; and it did not occur to him at the moment that she was more or less answerable for his present scrape.

"Just see how hit up I am!" he said. "So poor, isn't it?"

Her face clouded.

"Oh, Ted, how could you do it? Ought I to have stayed in London and looked after you?" she said reproachfully; and he saw that it was useless to try to conceal anything from her.

"It's all right, Kit," he hastened to explain in his humble manner. "Don't swear, old chum! I couldn't help it, on my honour I couldn't. I got so sick, and I just had to. And after all I played so poorly, you see, that it didn't come off."

Except for the subject of their conversation, they might have been back again in the lanes at Ivingdon. They had dropped naturally into their old boy and girl attitude, and hers was as before the stronger personality. But

The Making of a Prig

there was a subtle difference in their relations which she was the first to feel.

"I — I am glad it did n't come off, Ted," she said, trying to speak lightly. Ted gripped her hand for a moment, and then let it go again, as though he were half ashamed of his momentary show of sentiment.

"You see," he went on, in a very gruff voice, "that was the only part I left to Providence, and Providence muffed it. I'm such a rotten ass, — I always was, don't you know? If it had been you, now, you wouldn't have bungled it at all, would you?"

"Providence never has any sense of humour," said Katharine; and she got up hurriedly, so that he should not see her face. She poured out some medicine, and brought it to him.

"I say, it's awfully ripping to have you to look after me like this," he observed. "What did Miss Esther say?"

"She seemed upset," said Katharine, smiling slightly. "But you can always square Aunt Esther, when it's a question of illness; there are such a lot of texts in the Bible about illness, don't you know? By the way, when did you last have something to eat?"

Ted had no idea, beyond a vague notion that some one had brought him something on

The Making of a Prig

a tray in the morning, which he had not looked at. So she left him to interview the landlady, whom she found in the middle of a long history of the print in the hall and of the part it had played in the history of her own family as well, to which the Rector was listening patiently though with obvious inattention. Katharine managed to procure what she wanted, and returned with it to the sick room. The invalid was looking more flourishing than ever.

"You see," he explained, between the spoonfuls with which she fed him, "he's such an awfully snide doctor. He won't let me get up, and of course, I'm as right as rain, really. So cheap of him, isn't it?"

In spite of his assertion, however, he was very glad to play the invalid when she brought him some warm water, and proceeded to bathe his hands and face. It was pleasant, after the desolation of his life for the past six months, to lie back in a lazy attitude without feeling particularly ill, and allow the girl he liked best in the world to do things for him.

"It's so rum," he remarked, "that our hands never wear out with being washed so often. I can't think why they don't want soling and heeling after a time, like boots."

The Making of a Prig

"I think you are right, and that your doctor *is* rather 'snide,'" was all Katharine said, as she carried away the basin, and looked for his hair brushes. Ted's toilet table was characterised by a luxurious confusion, and she lingered for a moment to arrange the silver-topped bottles in some kind of order. "You never used to care for this sort of thing," she remarked, holding up a bottle of *eau de toilette*; "I remember how you teased me once, when I told you I put lavender water in my cold bath."

"Oh, well, of course it's beastly rot and all that," owned Ted; "but it's the thing to do, and one must, don't you know? Hullo, what are you playing at now?"

"I wish you would not be quite so languid," retorted Katharine. "How am I to brush your hair if you persist in behaving as though you were dying? I believe you are putting it on."

"It's not my fault if I'm not so beastly energetic as you," grumbled Ted. "Don't play about any more, Kit; come over here and talk. And you needn't fold up those towels; they're not used to it, really."

"I shouldn't think they were, from the look of them. Well, what have I got to talk about?"

The Making of a Prig

She came and sat down on the chair by his side, and he shifted his position so that he could see her face. She could have laughed aloud at his expression of utter contentment.

"Oh, some rot; anything you like. You've always got lots to gas about, haven't you? How is Ivingdon, and the Grange; and does Peter Bunce still come in on Sunday afternoons; and has the doctor got any new dogs? Fire ahead, Kit! you've been down there doing nothing all this time, and you must know all there is to know, unless you're as half alive as you used to be. Hasn't anything happened to the old place?"

"Yes," said Katharine, smiling back at him frankly. "They have mended the gap in the hedge."

"The devil they have!" cried Ted. "We'll have it broken open again at once, won't we? Why didn't you stop them? You knew I wasn't there to tell them myself. Just like their confounded impertinence!"

"Hush," interrupted Katharine. "You mustn't get excited, old man; it isn't good for you."

She smoothed his pillows and arranged his coverlet with nervous rapidity, and Ted, submitting happily to her services, wondered in-

The Making of a Prig

nocently what she was blushing about. But he did not trouble himself to find out.

"I am beastly glad I poisoned myself," he murmured, with lazy satisfaction.

She was glad of the diversion when the Rector arrived at last, and she was allowed to escape into the next room.

"Well, my boy, and how has the world gone with you?" she heard her father say in his genial tones.

"It's a beastly jolly world, and I'm the jolliest brute in it," was Ted's reply.

They took rooms in the next street, and came in every day to look after him; and when neither the conscience of the "snide" doctor, nor the desire of the invalid to be nursed proved sufficient to preserve the farce of his illness any longer, they still lingered on under pretence of being wanted, and sent carefully worded letters to Miss Esther from which she was forced to conclude that their presence in town was urgently required, much as they would have wished it otherwise. What really happened was, that Ted and Katharine regularly conducted the old Rector to the British Museum every morning, and passed the day alone together until it was time to fetch him away again in the afternoon. And in

The Making of a Prig

the evenings they initiated him into the joys of a music hall, or introduced him to a new comedian; and the Rector was happier than he had ever been since the well-remembered days in Paris. As for Katharine, her feelings defied her own powers of description; she only knew that she had the sensation of waking up from a long, bad dream. Perhaps Ted felt the same. "You've cured the biggest hump I ever had in my life," was the way he expressed it.

Looking back on the even tenor of those few weeks, afterwards, Katharine was at a loss to remember what she had talked about to Ted in the many hours they had spent together. Perhaps they had not talked at all; at the time it never seemed to matter whether they did or not; at all events, their conversation usually lacked the personal element that alone makes conversation distinctive. There was nothing surprising to Katharine in this: as long as she could remember Ted had been the one person in the world to whom it was impossible to talk about one's self; and his sympathy for her was as completely superficial as her love for him was mainly protective.

Once or twice she was led inadvertently into making a confidant of him.

The Making of a Prig

"I wonder why I never seem to feel things acutely now," she said to him one day as they were strolling along the Embankment. "I don't seem to care a bit what happens next, except that I have a sort of conviction it is going to be pleasant. I seem to want waking up again. Do you know what I mean, Ted?"

"Oh, it's nothing; you're feeling played, that's all," answered Ted, reassuringly. "My experience is that you're either played, or you're not played; and when you are, you'd better have a drink to buck you up. We'll have a cab, and lunch somewhere. Where shall we go to-day?"

And Katharine laughed at his practical view of things, and wondered why she had expected him to understand. Another time, it was Ted himself who gave the conversation a personal turn.

"Humps are deuced odd things," he observed, rather suddenly. It was a dull, warm afternoon in December, and they had been sitting idly for some minutes on one of the benches in the park, overlooking the Serpentine. "You feel that everything is awfully decent, and bills be hanged, and all that; and you curse your tailor and have a good time,

The Making of a Prig

and it doesn't matter if it snows. And then, when it's rather a bore to be under an obligation to a rotten little tradesman, or you want a new coat or something, and you pay up and feel awfully virtuous and don't owe a blessed halfpenny in the world, except for shirts and things that never expect to be paid for,—*then*, you go and get the very deuce of a hump."

"Whole books might be written on the psychological aspect of the hump," murmured Katharine.

"Look at those bounders, now," said Ted, who had not heard her. "It doesn't matter to *them* that rowing on the Serpentine on Saturday afternoon isn't the thing to do, especially in frock coats and bowlers. It makes one quite sorry for them, to see how little they know; they don't even know they are bounders, poor devils! But *they* never get the hump, confound them!"

"All the same," said Katharine, "it is a big price to pay for an immunity from humps, isn't it?"

"Life must be awfully easy, if you're a bounder," continued Ted. "You haven't got to be in good form, and you can walk about with any sort of girl you please, and you

The Making of a Prig

needn't worry about the shape of your hat, and it doesn't matter if you are seen on a green Brixton 'bus. It saves so much thinking, doesn't it?"

"Yes," said Katharine. "But you have to be a bounder all the same, and you know you can't even contemplate such a possibility, or impossibility, without shuddering. By the way, is all this intended to convey that you have got the hump this afternoon?"

"Oh, no," said Ted, with restored cheerfulness. "I ought never to have been born, of course; but that's quite another matter."

Late that evening the Rector proposed returning to Ivingdon. They had just been to the theatre, and Ted had asked them in to supper afterwards. Every trace of his mood of that afternoon had disappeared, and he was wrangling with Katharine over the strength of the Rector's toddy with all the energy of which his languid nature was capable. Katharine put down the tumbler she was holding and looked swiftly round at her father.

"Oh, daddy, not yet!" she cried impetuously. "I am happy now; don't let us spoil it all by going home. I feel as though something horrible would happen if we went home now.

The Making of a Prig

Can't we wait a little longer? I have never been happy like this before."

The Rector murmured something about its being three weeks to Christmas, but his sense of duty was obviously a perfunctory one, and he soon found he was not being listened to. And Ted's hand closed over her fingers as he took the hot glass from her, and his face shone with pleasure and his voice trembled, as he whispered, "Thank you for that, dear."

She did not shrink from him as she had done once before when he had looked at her with that same eager expression in his eyes.

"I don't know a bit whether I love him in the real way," she told her mirror that night. "I don't know anything about myself at all. I believe the prig is inborn in me, after all, and that it would suit me far better to fight for a living in the world, than to stay at home and just make Ted happy. But all the same, if he asks me again I shall marry him. It has been so peaceful lately, and I have felt so happy, and marriage with Ted will mean peace if it does n't mean anything more thrilling than that. Dear old Ted; why is n't he my brother, or my son, or some one I could just mother, and go on living my own life the while? Ah, well, he is going to be my hus-

The Making of a Prig

band; how strange it sounds! I wonder if women like me are ever allowed to be happy in their own way, gloriously and completely happy as I know I could be? But I suppose it is only the prig in me that thinks so. And Ted shall never know that I want more than he can possibly give me. Oh, Ted, old chum, I do love you so for loving me!"

A visit to Queen's Crescent slightly unsettled her. She took her father with her and introduced him to Phyllis Hyam, and tried to convince herself that she was glad she was not coming back any more; but in spite of the unfamiliarity of being there as a visitor, and the difficulty of finding topics of conversation for the Rector and Miss Jennings, who obviously misunderstood each other's attempts to be friendly, the sight of the dingy little hall and of Phyllis's round, good-humoured face, brought enough reminiscences to her mind to make her a little regretful as well.

"Do you still have bread and treacle, and is Polly Newland glad I have gone, and does any one ever talk about me?" she asked with interest. Even Phyllis looked strange, as though her best dress had been thrown on hurriedly and the distinction of being admitted to "Jenny's" room were rather too much for

The Making of a Prig

her; but there was a familiarity about her style of conversation that was consoling.

"Oh, yes," she replied in her off-hand way; "when we have a new one put into our room we always remember how blue you looked the first night you came. We have n't had a 'permanent' in our room since you left; and there have been some cheerful specimens, too! One was a nurse, who made the place smell eternally of disinfectants; and another kept bits of food in her drawer, and encouraged mice; and a third insisted on having the window shut. The curtains have n't been washed, either, since you made that row about them. I say, when are you coming back again?"

"You don't offer much inducement," laughed Katharine. "But I am not coming back, in any case."

"Going to get married?" asked Phyllis sharply. Katharine smiled, and did not contradict her. It was not an insinuation that one would be anxious to contradict in a place like Queen's Crescent, however diffident one might feel about it elsewhere. Phyllis shrugged her shoulders. "Well, don't go and make a hash of it," she said. "You're not the sort to be happy with any one, especially if it's made too easy for you. Well off? Of course; and

The Making of a Prig

worships the ground you tread on, I suppose! Oh, well, it's none of my business, and I only hope you haven't made a mistake. It's a risky thing at the best; and you were very happy here most of the time, and you've got to better that, you know. I wish you luck, I'm sure, but it takes a woman to understand any one like you, and I should like to see the man who thinks he does it as well."

"I hope you will some day," said Katharine, politely. But Phyllis did not respond with any warmth, and Katharine was glad to return to the masculine indifference of Ted. It was difficult to worry about the future in Ted's company; even the fact that he had not yet formally proposed to her did not seem to cause him any anxiety. It certainly made no difference in the freedom of their intercourse; and, as long as there was no immediate necessity for action, Ted was not the one to take the initiative. "I believe I shall have to propose to him myself," was the thought that sometimes crossed her mind as she studied his placid, good-looking face. But after her visit to Queen's Crescent, she began to wish he would not be quite so casual about it; for, without allowing even to herself that Phyllis's want of encouragement had in any way affected

The Making of a Prig

her decision, she had a lingering feeling that the present state of things could not go on for ever, and that it would be better for her, at all events, to have the matter definitely settled. So she made a kind of attempt, a day or two later, to rouse his apprehensions.

"Phyllis was wondering if I was ever coming back again to my work," she said to him abruptly.

"Oh, was she? Rather a nice girl, Phyllis, if she didn't dress so badly," observed Ted unconsciously. They were at a Wagner concert in the Queen's Hall, and the Siegfried Idyll had just drawn to a close. It seemed to her an auspicious moment.

"I said I was never coming back," pursued Katharine, studying his profile critically.

"Of course not," said Ted, humming the refrain they had just heard.

For once, Katharine felt faintly annoyed with him for his want of proper sentiment.

"I don't believe you care whether I do or not," she said in a piqued tone.

"Eh, what?" said Ted, staring round at her in blank amazement. "Ought I to have said anything else? But you settled that long ago, Kit, didn't you? There is nothing more to be said about it, is there?"

The Making of a Prig

"Oh, no, of course not," said Katharine, in what seemed to him a most unreasonable manner; "but all the same, I'm not at all sure that I sha'n't go back when the term begins again."

Ted stared more than ever.

"Oh, rats!" he exclaimed, heartily. "What's wrong, Kitty? Have you been hit up to-day, or anything? I'm such a rotten ass, I never know. Of course you're never going to grind any more; what an idea!"

"Why not?" asked Katharine, with uncomfortable persistence. Ted began to make fresh assertions, but paused in the middle and hesitated. He suddenly realised that there was only one answer to her question, and that he would have to make it now. He looked down and made havoc with his programme, and stammered hopelessly until Katharine took pity on him and came to his assistance with a laugh.

"It's all right, old man; I am never going back, of course," she said; and Ted brightened up again when he found that he need not propose to her yet, and was obviously relieved at the establishment of their old relations. She did nothing more to change them, and the only result of her abortive attempt was, that Ted was more attentive to her than before, and constantly made little plans for taking her to some unfrequented museum or picture gallery, evidently with some design in his mind which he had not the courage to carry out.

"Poor old Ted," she thought to herself, after they had spent a dull and silent afternoon at the Royal Institute among the colonial produce; "I wonder if he will ever get it out!"

Curiously enough, through all the weeks she spent in town, the thought of Paul Wilton rarely crossed her mind; and when it did she felt that it referred to some former life of hers, with which this present calm existence had no connection. Sometimes she wondered idly whether he were married yet, and if so, whether he ever gave a thought to her; but she could think of Marion as his wife without a regret, and she was glad to find that she had no desire whatever to see him again. The impression he seemed to have left in her mind, after all these months, was that of a disturbing element which had brought the greatest unhappiness into her life she had ever been forced to endure. It was inconsequent, perhaps, that, thinking thus, she should have been emphatic in her refusal to go and see the Keeleys; but although she was incapable of explaining why

The Making of a Prig

she felt so strongly about such a small matter, she was at least genuine in her belief that he had no further place in her thoughts.

And then, two days before they left town, she met him at last.

It was in Bury Street, late on a foggy afternoon, as she was on her way to the Museum with Ted. She had stopped with an exclamation of delight in front of an old book shop, and the owner, who was talking to an intending purchaser inside, came out good-naturedly and offered to light the gas jet over the tray of dusty volumes. "I shall have to stop now," whispered Katharine; "supposing you go on for daddy and bring him back here?"

The light flared up, and made a bright semicircle in the gloom that was fast closing up round the shop. The customer who was inside concluded his purchase, and came out just as Ted was strolling off. Apparently they did not see each other, and the fog soon swallowed up the retreating form; but Katharine turned round at this moment from the book she was examining, and met the stranger face to face.

"Ah," he said, quietly; "at last!"

"Yes," she repeated; "at last!"

It did not strike her until afterwards that it was not at all the mode of address with

The Making of a Prig

which she would have greeted him had she been more prepared; but at the time it came quite naturally to her lips. He still held her hand as he went on speaking.

"And Ted? Where have you sent him? Will he be long?"

She resented the implication in his words.

"I have not sent him anywhere. He has gone to fetch my father from the Museum; they will be back directly. Do you mean to say you recognised Ted in that instant?"

"Why, surely! Did you not recognise me, although I was standing back there in the shadow?"

"Of course I didn't," cried Katharine hotly, as she pulled away her hand. "I never saw you until you came out into the light. I should have stopped Ted if I had."

"Oh, to be sure; pardon my mistake. Of course you would have detained Ted in that case." And he smiled as though he were faintly amused at something.

She had noticed his glad look of recognition, and she hated him for it. What right had he to be glad to see her? And now that he was laughing at her and making insinuations about Ted, true insinuations moreover, she hated him still more for his acuteness.

The Making of a Prig

"So you are back in town?" he was saying, with what appeared to be meant for a kindly interest. "I am not surprised, though. I always knew you would have to come back."

"What do you mean?" she asked, feeling more annoyed than ever. It was so like him to know everything about her without being told, and then to put a complexion upon it that he gave her no opportunity of contradicting. "We came up, daddy and I, because Ted was ill; and we are going back again on Wednesday."

"Really? My mistake again. It is difficult to imagine Ted except in the complete enjoyment of his health. Not seriously ill, I hope?"

"Oh, no," she said, with an uncomfortable conviction that she was being made to expose herself in all her weakness; "but there was no one to nurse him, so I came. He is all right now."

"So I should judge from the brief glimpse I had of him just now. Lucky fellow, Ted! He looked very jolly, I thought; no doubt he has good cause for his happiness. You are looking well too, if I may say so. It is very delightful to be young, is it not?"

She felt a wild rage against him for detecting

The Making of a Prig

the situation so absolutely, and for making it merely a subject for his raillery. She did not know how she would have wished him to take it, but she hated him all the same for so calmly accepting it.

"I don't understand you," she said, speaking rapidly. "It isn't a bit delightful; you know it isn't. You know I hate you; you know I am the most miserable person in the whole world. You know everything there is to know about me; and I hate you! Why did you come back to spoil it all, when I was trying so hard to be happy?"

Her own words amazed her. She knew they were true as she spoke them; but she had not known it ten minutes ago.

"I'm sorry," he said, gravely. "Shall I go?"

He had completely dropped his jesting tone, but she hated him for his pity even more than she had hated him for his ridicule; she tried to speak, but her anger choked her utterance.

"When will you be at Ivingdon again?" he asked. "Did you say Wednesday? And you are going to leave Ted in town?"

She asked herself why he did not go, instead of standing there and making conversation by inventing questions to which he could not pos-

The Making of a Prig

sibly want to know the answers. But she mechanically made a gesture in the affirmative to both of them; and he repeated his former inquiry with gentle insistence.

"Shall I go now?"

"Yes, go!" she cried fiercely, and ignored the hand he proffered her, and let him go without another word.

The fog swallowed him up, and she stood and gazed at the place where he had stood, and wondered vaguely if he had been there at all or if she had not dreamt the whole incident. For one moment the wild impulse seized her to rush after him into the fog and the darkness, and to implore him to take her with him anywhere, so long as she might be with him. And then a smile flickered across her face as the bookseller came out and spoke to her; and she paid for the first volume she picked up; and the Rector and Ted emerged from the fog into the semicircle of light, and life resumed its ordinary aspect again.

"Has he gone?" asked Ted.

"Who? Mr. Wilton? I did not know you saw him. Oh, yes; he went some time ago. Isn't this a jolly little thing I have picked up?" said Katharine lightly; and Ted apparently thought no more about it.

The Making of a Prig

That evening she was almost feverishly gay. The Rector sat and smiled happily as she turned everything that occurred into ridicule, and made every passer-by a subject for her wit. They did not go to a theatre, on account of the bad weather; and when Monty dropped in to coffee later on, she kept him in a perpetual condition of adoring approval until the fact of Ted's gloomy silence was gradually forced upon her, and she blamed herself hotly for her stupidity. She was very cool to Monty after she had realised her blunder; and the poor fellow, who was quite ignorant of his offence, took the first opportunity to depart. Even then, in spite of her efforts to be kind to him, Ted did not wholly recover his spirits; and she sighed inwardly as she reflected that she could not even be sure of accomplishing the one task she had set herself to perform.

And the next day her old restlessness possessed her again. All the work of the past six weeks seemed to have been suddenly undone; nothing brought her any happiness, she reflected bitterly; she was incapable of happiness and it was absurd of her to have expected to find it. All the same, perhaps if Ted were to say something to her—but Ted still said

The Making of a Prig

nothing, and went about making plans for her enjoyment on this her last day in town, as though their coming separation were of no matter at all; and he seemed as unconscious of her change of mood as he had been all along of her unusual contentment. The day was not a success; their little improvised amusements had been far more satisfactory than the carefully planned ones of to-day, and Ted's silence on the one subject of interest grew more marked as the time wore on, and ended in raising an uncomfortable barrier between them. Once she felt sure that he would have spoken if the Rector had not come in unexpectedly; and once, he startled her by suddenly taking both her hands in his and looking into her eyes for a full minute, while she waited passively for him to speak. But he turned very red instead, and called himself a fool and hurried out of the room, and left her half amused and half regretful. She felt very tender towards him after that; and the old desire to mother him was very strong within her when they stood together at last on the platform at Euston, and had only a few moments left in which to say what was in their minds.

"God bless you, dear! I shall see you again

soon?" was all she could bring herself to say in that last moment.

"No — yes — perhaps. I am going to write to you quite soon. I'm a rotten ass, as you know, but — you will try and understand, won't you, Kitty?"

The train went on, and she leaned out of the window and laughed.

"I am sure I shall understand," she said.

CHAPTER XIX

She waited in vain during the next two days for Ted's letter. His parting words to her, however, seemed to have again restored her peace of mind; and the virtuous mood in which she returned to Ivingdon was so unprecedented as to rouse surprise rather than the admiration it deserved. The climax was reached when Miss Esther insisted on giving her a tonic.

"It is very ridiculous," she remonstrated, "that one is never allowed to drop one's characteristic attitude for a moment. If I had come home and behaved as childishly as I usually do, you would have been quite satisfied; but just because I am inclined to be civilised for a change, you choose to resent it. One would think you had taken out a patent for all the virtues."

"My dear, that is doubtless very clever, but I wish you would drink up this and not keep me standing," returned her aunt, who was, as ever, occupied with actions and not

The Making of a Prig

with theories about them; and Katharine had to seek consolation for her temporary discomfort in the absurdity of the situation.

She wondered slightly why Ted had not written to her at once, but after the vacillation he had already shown she was not unprepared for a further delay; it was more than likely that he found the complexities of writing what he could not speak to be greater than he supposed, and it amused her to conjecture that he would probably end in coming to her for the help he had learnt to expect from her in all the crises of his life. Meanwhile, there was a whole lifetime before them in which they could work out the effects of their action, and in her present mood she saw no satisfactory reason for hurrying it; she did not realise how persistently she was recalling every instance of Ted's kindness to her, as if to strengthen her resolution, and she was unconscious of the doggedness with which she avoided dwelling on a certain episode in the London visit which she had never even mentioned to her father. She had cheated herself, by degrees, into a complacency that she mistook for resignation.

At last, by the mid-day post on Saturday morning, she received her letter. It came

The Making of a Prig

with another one, written in a hand that brought association without distinct recollection to her mind; and she opened the latter first, principally because it was the one that interested her least. The first page revealed its identity; it was from Mrs. Downing, and was characteristically full of underlined words and barely legible interpolations, and she was obliged to read it through twice before she was able to grasp its meaning. The drift of it was that the enterprising lady principal was about to open a branch of her school in Paris, where everything was to be French, "*quite* French, you know, my dear Miss Austen,—staff, conversation, cooking, games, *everything*; a place to which I can send on the dear children from here when they want finishing. The French are such *delicious* people, are they not? *So* unique, and *so* French!" The morals, however, were to be English; so, in spite of the unique French element in the French character, there was to be an English head to the establishment, and it was this position that she proceeded in a maze of extravagant compliments to offer to her former junior mistress. "Not a duenna, of *course*, for that will be supplied in the person of the excellent Miss Smithson, who will act nomi-

The Making of a Prig

nally as housekeeper, and make an *exquisite* background to the whole. There are always some of those dear foolish mammas who will insist on placing propriety before education,—so benighted, is it not? But Miss Smithson was intended by Nature, I am sure, to propitiate that kind of mamma; while *you*, my dear Miss Austen, I intend to be something more than a background. I look to you to give a *tone* to the school, to manage the working of it all,—the amusements, the lectures, indeed, the whole *régime;* to be responsible for the dear children's happiness, and to see that they write happy letters home every week,—to take *my* place, in fact. I could tell you *all* in two minutes, etc., etc."

Katharine laid down the letter with an involuntary sigh; the position it offered was full of attractions to her, and the salary would have been more than she had ever hoped to demand. "I wish she had asked me six weeks ago," she said aloud, and then accused herself fiercely of disloyalty and picked up Ted's letter, and studied the boyish handwriting on the envelope as though to give herself courage to open it. She had wanted to be alone with his letter, and had carefully watched her father out of the house before shutting herself into

The Making of a Prig

the study; so the sound of a footstep on the gravel path outside brought a frown to her face, and she remained purposely with her back to the window so that the intruder, whoever he was, should see that she did not mean to be disturbed. But the voice in which she heard her name spoken through the open window arrested her attention.

She dropped the unopened letter on the table, and turned slowly round to face the speaker. The strangeness of his coming, when she had been obstinately putting him out of her thoughts since last Monday, had a paralysing effect upon her nerves; and Paul swung himself over the low window seat, and reached her side in time to save her from falling. She recovered herself immediately, however, and shrank back from his touch.

"I do not understand why you are here," she found herself saying with difficulty.

"That is what I have come to explain," he replied. "I could hardly expect you to understand."

His tone was curiously gentle. It struck her, as she looked at him again, that he was very much altered. She had not noticed his appearance much as he stood outside the book shop, with the dark fog at his back; but now, as the light from the window behind fell full on his head she saw the fresh streaks of white in the black hair, and the sight affected her strangely. Perhaps, while she in her arrogance had believed him to be living in an ill-gotten contentment, he, too, had had something to suffer.

"Won't you sit down?" she said, and took a chair herself, and waited for him to begin. The one idea in her mind was that he should not suspect her of nervousness.

"You were kind enough, when we last met in the summer," began Paul, "to congratulate me on my engagement to your cousin. I am going to ask you to extend your kindness now, and to congratulate us both on being released from that engagement."

Katharine looked wonderingly at him. But there was nothing to be gathered from his face. She smiled rather sadly.

"Poor Marion!" she said, softly. "Isn't anybody to be allowed to remain happy?"

"You mistake me," he corrected her carefully. "Your cousin took the initiative in the matter; she is obviously the one to be congratulated."

"And you?"

"I? Oh, I suppose I have only my own

The Making of a Prig

ignorance to blame. If I had had more knowledge of women, I should have known better what was expected of me. As it is, my engagement has proved a complete failure."

There was a pause, till Katharine roused herself to speak in a lifeless kind of voice that did not seem to belong to her.

"I am sorry if it has made you unhappy," she said. Paul looked at her critically.

"Are you sure?" he asked, smiling.

Katharine folded and unfolded her hands uneasily, and wished he would go away and remove his disquieting presence from her life for ever.

"Oh, yes," she said. "One is always sorry when people are unhappy, of course."

"Only that?" His voice had a touch of disappointment in it, and she began to tremble for her composure. He got up and walked to the window and looked across the lawn, where the wintry sun was struggling through the bare branches of the elm trees and making faint intricate patterns on the whitened grass below. "This is where I first met you, three years ago," he went on as though he were talking to himself. "You were only a child then, and you interested me. I used to won-

The Making of a Prig

der what there was about you that interested me so much, a mere child like you! You were very sweet to me in those days, Katharine."

"I — I wish you would n't," said Katharine. But he did not seem to hear her.

"Most men would have behaved differently, I suppose," he went on, still looking away from her. "It is very fatal to admit the possibility, even to ourselves, of making a new system for an effete civilisation like ours; and I was a fool to suppose that women could be dealt with by any but the obvious methods. It is my own fault, of course, that in my anxiety to keep your respect I managed to destroy your affection."

She wanted to vindicate herself, to protest against what seemed to her his confident self-righteousness; but the old influence was creeping over her again, and it numbed her.

"I wish you would not say those things," she said, weakly. The unopened letter lying on the red table-cloth seemed like a protest against the futility of the scene that was passing, and she found herself controlling a desire to laugh at the mockery of it all.

He turned round again with a half-suppressed sigh, and took out his watch.

"Just twelve," he said, reflectively. "I

The Making of a Prig

must be off if I mean to walk to the station. You will forgive me for having worried you with all this? I had a sort of feeling that I should like to tell you about it myself; our old friendship seemed to demand that little amount of frankness, though I suppose you will think I have no right to talk about friendship any longer. I acknowledge that I have given you every reason to be vexed with me; if I can ever do anything to remove the disagreeable impression from your mind, I hope you will let me know. Good-bye."

"You — you are not going?" She had risen too, and was standing between him and the door. She did not know why she wished to keep him, but she knew she could not let him go.

"Unless you can show me a satisfactory reason for remaining," was his reply. She was trembling violently from head to foot.

"I cannot bear that you should leave me like this," she said in a low voice.

"It rests with you to say whether I am to go or not," said Paul in the same tone. She was looking straight into his eyes; but what she saw, for all that, was the unopened letter on the red table-cloth. She put out her hands as if to push him away from her, but he mis-

The Making of a Prig

took her movement and grasped them both in his own.

"Don't, oh, don't!" she cried, struggling feebly to release herself. "I want you to go away, please. I thought it was all over and that I should never see you again, and I was beginning to feel happy, just a little happy; and now you have come back, and you want it to begin all over again, and I can't let it, — I am not strong enough! Oh, won't you go, please?"

"If you send me, I will go," said Paul, and waited for her answer. But none came, and he laughed out triumphantly. She had never heard him laugh so thoroughly before.

"I knew you couldn't, you proud little person," he said, with a sudden tenderness in his smile. "The woman in you is so strong, is it not, Katharine? Ah, I know far more about you than you know yourself; but you don't believe that, do you? Shall I tell you why I came to you to-day? It was just to say to you that I could not live without you any longer. Isn't that strange? I have been brutally frank with you to-day, Katharine, there is not another woman in the world who would have taken it as you have done. I knew you would, before I came to you; and

The Making of a Prig

the knowledge gives me courage to tell you one thing more. You know the failure of my attempt to marry for ambition; will you, in your sweetness, help me to marry for love?"

He dropped her hands and moved away from her. The delicacy of his action, slight though it was, appealed to her strongly. She turned her back to the table to avoid seeing the white letter on the red table-cloth.

"I cannot marry you," she said, hurriedly. "I would have been your slave a few months ago, but I cannot be your wife now."

Except for a tightening of his lips, he did not move a feature.

"That is not true; I cannot believe it," he said shortly.

"Why not?" she asked in a tired voice. She hoped he would not guess how near she was to submission.

"Because it is not possible. You are not the kind of woman who changes. You must love me now, because you loved me then. You cannot deny that you loved me then?"

"No," said Katharine, "I cannot deny it."

"Then why do you pretend that you do not love me still? I do not believe it is because of my engagement to your cousin. You are made of finer clay than others, and —"

The Making of a Prig

"Oh, no; that is not the reason," she said, interrupting him impatiently.

"Will you not tell me why it is?" he asked, approaching her again. There was no mistaking the tenderness in his tone now, and she cast about in her mind for some excuse to dismiss him before she completely lost her power of resistance. "Have I made you so angry that you will never forgive me?"

"No, no; you never made me angry," she protested. "But you made me feel absurd, and that is ever so much worse. I cannot be sure, now, that you are not merely laughing at me. Have you forgotten that you once thought me a prig? I have not altered; I am still a prig. How can you want to marry me when you have that image of me in your mind? It is hopeless to think of our marrying, — you with a secret contempt for me, and I with a perpetual fear of you!"

The man in him alone spoke when he answered her.

"Surely, it is enough that we love each other?"

She shook her head.

"Ah, you know it is not," she replied, with the strange little smile that had so often baffled him. "I — I do so wish you would un-

The Making of a Prig

derstand — and go. Or shall I find my father and tell him that you are here?"

He laid his hand against her cheek, and watched her closely.

"Is it all over, — our friendship, your love for me, everything?" he whispered. "Do you remember how sweetly you nursed me three years ago? Have you forgotten the jolly talks we had together in the Temple? And all the fun we had together in London? Is it all to come to an end like this?"

"I can't marry you; I don't love you enough for that," she said, moving restively under his touch. He stroked her cheek gently.

"Then why do you thrill when I touch you?" he asked. "Why do you not send me away?" It was his last move, and he watched its effect anxiously. She looked at him helplessly.

"I — I do send you away," she said faintly, and he made her join feebly in the laugh against herself. There was something contemptible in her surrender, she felt, as he folded her in his arms and looked down at her with a manly air of possession.

"If this is not love what is it, you solemn little Puritan?" he murmured.

The Making of a Prig

"I don't know," said Katharine dully. She submitted passively to his embrace, and allowed him to kiss her more than once.

"Of course you don't know," he smiled. "What a woman you are, and how I love you for it! Don't be so serious, sweetheart; tell me what you are thinking about so deeply?"

It was pity for him, her old genuine love for him reawakening, that made her at last rouse herself to tell him the truth.

"Will you please let me go, Paul?" she asked submissively. And as he loosened his arms and allowed her to go, she took one of his hands and led him with feverish haste round to the table, where Ted's letter still lay like a silent witness against herself. They stood side by side and looked at it, the white envelope on the red table-cloth, and it was quite a minute before the silence was broken. Then Katharine pulled him away again and covered up the letter with her hand and looked up in his face.

"Do you know what is in that letter?" she asked, and without waiting for a reply went on almost immediately. "It is from Ted, to ask me to be his wife."

"And you are going to say —"

"Yes."

The Making of a Prig

Paul smiled incredulously.

"It is impossible," he said. "I decline to believe what you say now, after what you said to me on Monday afternoon."

"Ah," she cried, "I was mad then. You always make me mad when I am with you. You must not talk any more of Monday afternoon; you must forget what I said to you then, and what I have said to you to-day; you must forget that I have allowed you to kiss me—"

"Forget?" interrupted Paul. "Are *you* going to forget all this?"

She turned away with a little cry.

"You make it so hard for me, Paul; and it seemed so easy before you came!"

"Then it does n't seem so easy now?"

She evaded his question. "I know I am right, because I thought it all out when you were not here," she went on piteously. "I cannot trust myself even to think properly when you are there; you make me quite unlike myself. That is why I am going to marry Ted. Ted is the sanest person I know; he leaves me my individuality; he does n't paralyse me as you do; and I am simply myself when I am with him."

"Simply yourself!" echoed Paul. "My

The Making of a Prig

dear little girl, whatever in heaven or earth has allowed such a misapprehension to creep into your head?"

"I know what you mean," she said. "I have thought that out, too. You know more about me than anybody in the whole world; Ted will never know as much as you know, although I am going to be his wife. You are the only person I could ever talk to about myself; you are the only person who understands. I know all that. But one does not want that in a husband; one wants some one who will be content with half of one's self, and allow the other half to develop as it pleases. You would never be content with less than the whole, would you, Paul? Ah, that is why I loved you so madly! It is so queer, isn't it, that the very things that make us fall in love are the very things that make marriage impossible?"

He did not speak, and she put her arms round his neck impulsively and drew his head down to hers.

"Don't you understand, dear?" she said. "It is impossible to find everything we want in one person, so we have to be content with satisfying one side of ourselves, or accept the alternative and not marry at all. Ted wants

The Making of a Prig

me badly, or I would rather choose not to marry at all. But he must have some one to look after him,—he can't live alone like some men; and I have always looked after him all my life. He has come in my way again now, so I am going to look after him to the end. I am very fond of Ted, and we have learnt to be chums, so I don't think it will be a failure. Oh, do say you understand, Paul?"

"Do you love him?" asked Paul.

"Yes," she replied.

"As you loved me?"

"No," said Katharine, simply. "I could never love any one again like that. I wore myself out, I think, in my love for you. Oh, I know I am spoiled; I know I have only the second best of myself to give to Ted; but if he is content with that, ought I not to be glad to give it?"

"But *you*, your own happiness," he urged brokenly. "Have you no thought for your own happiness?"

"Happiness?" she said, smiling again. "Oh, I do not expect to find happiness. Women like me, who ask for more than life can possibly give them, have no right to expect the same happiness as the people who have found out that it is better to make a compromise and to take what they can get! Oh, I shall never be greatly happy, I know that. But I do not mind much; it is enough for me that I did once taste the real, glorious happiness, if it was only in snatches."

"Won't you taste it again?" he said, drawing her suddenly to him. "Won't you give up this impossible scheme of yours, and come to me? We will be married over there by your father, — now, — this very day. We will go abroad, travel, do what you will. Only come with me, Katharine. You belong to me, and to me only; you dare not deny it. Come with me, Katharine."

"No," she said, shaking her head. "I am not going to spoil your life, as you have spoilt mine. You will be a great man, Paul, if you do not marry me."

"Listen," he said, without heeding her. "This is the last time I shall ask you; this is the last time I shall hold you in my arms, — *so*. I shall go away after this, and you will never see me again, nor hear of me again. I shall never kiss you any more, nor ask you to come away with me, nor tell you I love you as I never loved another woman. If you come to me on your knees and beg me to love you again, I will not relent. Do you understand me? This is the last, the very last time. *Now* what have you to say? Will you come with me?"

She threw back her head and met his gaze as he bent over her.

"No," she said again. He covered her face with kisses.

"And now?"

"No," she repeated desperately; and she crept away from him at last, and took her letter from the table and tried to walk to the door.

A slippered footstep shuffled along the hall and stopped outside the library door. The next moment the Rector was in the room.

"Kitty, my child, have you seen my hat anywhere? I feel convinced I put it down somewhere, and for the life of me —"

He paused as he saw Paul, and held out his hand with a smile of welcome.

"Delighted to see you again, my dear sir, delighted! That is to say," added the old man, looking to Katharine for assistance, "I suppose I *have* seen you before, though for the moment I cannot quite recall your name. But my memory is getting a bad one for names, a very bad one, eh, Kitty? Anyhow, you will stop to lunch, of course; and meanwhile, if I can only find my hat —"

The Making of a Prig

"Daddy, it is Mr. Wilton," explained Katharine, making an effort to speak in her usual voice. Strange to say, it did not seem difficult to become usual again now that her father was in the room. "He stayed with us once, a long time ago; you remember Mr. Wilton, don't you?"

"To be sure, to be sure; of course I remember Mr. Wilton perfectly!" said the Rector, shaking hands with him again. "I can remember distinctly many of our little talks on archæology and so forth. Let me see, any relation to the great numismatist? Ah, now I know who you are quite well. There was an accident, or a calamity of some sort, if I recollect rightly. Kitty, my child, have you found my hat?"

"Will you stay to lunch?" Katharine was asking him.

"Of course he will stay to lunch," cried the Rector, without giving him time to reply. "I've picked up some fine specimens of old Sheffield plate that I should like to show you, Mr. Wilton. Stay to lunch? Why, of course. Dear me, I know I saw it somewhere— Got to catch the two-thirty? Oh, that's all right; we'll drive you to the station after lunch. That child will like a chat with you, eh, Kitty?

The Making of a Prig

You used to be great friends, and she has something — no, no, I've looked there twice — something of interest to tell you, something of very great interest, eh, Kitty? A nice young fellow he is, too," continued the old man, stopping for a moment in his fruitless search. "By the way, you know him, don't you? It's young — Ah, now I remember! I left it in the vestry; so stupid of me!"

Paul stopped him as he was hurrying out of the room.

"I must be off, thank you, sir. I am not going to catch the two-thirty at all. I think I will walk on somewhere and catch something else, if there happens to be anything. I am sure I wish Miss Katharine every happiness. Good-morning."

He went out by the window as he had come, and they watched him as he walked across the lawn, the neat figure crowned by the conventional felt hat. He had not shaken hands with Katharine nor looked at her again.

The Rector glanced after him and smoothed his hair thoughtfully.

"Curious man that," he remarked with his simple smile. "He always looks to me as though there were a tragedy in his life."

"Oh, I don't think so," said Katharine,

The Making of a Prig

coldly. "It is only his manner. He takes a joke tragically. Besides, he has never married unhappily, or anything like that."

"That may be," said Cyril Austen, with one of his occasional flashes of intuition; "but it means a tragedy to some men if they have n't got married at all, and I fancy that 's one of them. Ah, well, his father was one of our best—"

Miss Esther's voice came shrilly down the passage, and the Rector hastened out of the room without finishing his sentence.

"The annoyances of life," thought Katharine cynically, "are much more important than the tragedies."

She picked up her letter once more and tore it open. Even then she did not read it at once, but looked out of the window first and beyond the garden, where a man's felt hat was moving irregularly along the top of the hedge. She made an impatient gesture and turned her back to the light, and unfolded Ted's letter at last. And this is what it contained:—

"By the time you get this, I shall have cleared out. I may be an infernally rotten ass, but I won't let the best girl in the world marry me out of kindness, and that is all you were going to do. I tried to think you were a little keen on me a few weeks ago, but of

The Making of a Prig

course I was wrong. Don't mind me. I shall come up smiling again after a bit. It was just like my poorness to think I could ever marry any one so clever and spry as yourself. Of course you will buck up and marry some played-out literary chap, who will gas about books and things all day and make you happy. Good old Kit, it has been a mistake all along, has n't it? When I come back, we will be chums again, won't we? I am off to Melbourne in the morning and shall travel about for a year, I think. You might write to me — the jolly sort of letters you used to write. Monty knows all my movements.

Yours ever,
Ted."

The letter fell from her hand, and she turned and gazed blankly out of the window. The felt hat was no longer to be seen at the top of the hedge.

CHAPTER XX

High up in one of the houses on the shady side of the Rue Ruhmhorff, Katharine sat on her balcony and thought. Her reflections were of the desultory order begotten of early spring lethargy and early spring sunshine, relating to street cries innumerable and to the mingled scent of violets and asphalt in the air, to the children playing their perpetual game of hop-scotch on the white pavements, and to the artisan opposite who was mixing his salad by the open window with a naïve disregard for the public gaze. Her pupils were all in the Bois under the able supervision of the excellent Miss Smithson, and there was temporary calm in the three *étages* that formed Mrs. Downing's Parisian establishment for the daughters of gentlemen.

"Will he ever have done, I wonder?" speculated Katharine lazily. She was taking quite a languid interest in the progress of the salad, and smiled to herself when the man took off his blue blouse and attacked it afresh in

The Making of a Prig

his shirt sleeves. His wife joined him after a while, evidently, to judge from her emphatic gestures, with critical intent. But the man received her volley of suggestions with an expressive shrug of the shoulders, and they finally went off to their mid-day meal.

"What pitiable jargon we talk, all the world over, about the triumph of mind over matter," murmured Katharine, yawning as she spoke. "And all the while matter goes on triumphing over mind on every conceivable occasion! It even gets into the street cries," she added with another yawn, as a flower vender came along the street below and sent up his minor refrain in unvarying repetition. "Des violettes pour embaumer la chambre," he chanted, "du cresson pour la santé du corps!"

It was more than a year since she had accepted Mrs. Downing's offer and settled here in Paris; more than a year since Ted had gone abroad and Paul Wilton had bidden her farewell. But she never looked back on those days now, though not so much from design as from lack of incentive; for her life had strayed into another channel, and her days were full of the kind of occupation that leaves no room for the luxury of reminiscence. It never even occurred to her to wonder whether she was

The Making of a Prig

happy or not; she seemed to have completely lost her old trick of wanting a reason for everything she thought or felt, and for the time being she had become eminently practical. Even now, in spite of the enervating effect of the first spring weather, her thoughts returned to the business of the moment, and she wondered why the father of her newest pupil, who had made an appointment with her for eleven o'clock, was so late in coming. A ring at the electric bell seemed to answer her thought, and the maid came in almost immediately with a gentleman's card on a tray.

"British caution," was Katharine's criticism, as Julie explained that the English monsieur had not attempted to teach her his name. By the merest chance she glanced at the card before her visitor came in, and was spared the annoyance of betraying the surprise she must otherwise have felt. As it was, she had time to recover from her astonishment, even to remark how different the familiar name and address seemed to her when, for the first time as now, she saw them transcribed on a visiting card,—"Mr. Paul Wilton, Essex Court, Temple."

"I am so glad to see you," she exclaimed, with a look that did not contradict the wel-

The Making of a Prig

come in her voice. And Julie, who had never seen her mistress look so joyous before, went back to Marie in the kitchen with a highly coloured account of the meeting she had just witnessed, which explained to that frivolous but astute little person how it was that Madame always looked so leniently on her flirtations with the *charcutier* round the corner.

"I have never caught you idling before," said Paul, referring to the attitude in which he had seen her through the open door before she had turned round with that glad look in her eyes.

"I don't suppose you have," she said. "It isn't so very long since I learnt how to idle. Do you remember how bitterly you used to complain because I never wanted to lounge? I often lounge now; and my greatest joy is to think about nothing at all. Don't you know how restful it is to think about nothing at all?"

"You must have altered a good deal," he observed.

"Do you think I have, then?"

"Ask me that presently," he replied, with an answering smile. "I have got to hear all the news first,—how keeping school agrees with you, and everything there is to tell about yourself. So make haste and begin, please."

The Making of a Prig

"Oh, there is nothing to tell about myself; at least, nothing more than you can learn from the prospectus! Would you like to see one? You can read it and learn what an important person I am, while I go and leave a message for Miss Smithson."

When she came back, he regarded her with a look of amused interest.

"This is a very novel sensation," he remarked.

"I am glad it amuses you," said Katharine; "but I never knew before that the prospectus was funny."

"Oh, no; it isn't that," he explained. "The humour of a prospectus is the kind of grim joke that could only be expected to appeal to a parent. What I meant was the fact of your appearing to me for the first time in the character of hostess."

"I wondered how it was that I did not feel so awed by your presence as usual," she remarked. "Now I know it is because you, even you, are sensible to the chastening atmosphere of the home of the young idea. You had better come round the establishment at once, before the favourable impression begins to wear off."

"Oh, please!" he implored. "You will surely let me off? I haven't a daughter or a

The Making of a Prig

niece, or any kind of feminine relation who could be of the least commercial value to you. And I really don't feel equal to facing crowds of unsophisticated girls in short frocks, with pocket editions of their favourite poets in their hands. Girls of that age always expect you to be so well informed, and I haven't run a favourite poet for years."

"When you first met me," she said emphatically, "*I* was an unsophisticated girl in a short frock, with a whole list of favourite poets. And I distinctly remember one occasion on which I bored you for half an hour with my views on Browning."

"I am not here to deny it," said Paul. "It is only an additional reason for my wishing to stay and talk to you, now that you have ceased to have any views on any subject whatever. Besides, I exhausted the subject of unsophistication in short frocks when I first had the pleasure of meeting you, four years ago. And, interesting as I found it then, I have no particular wish to renew it now."

"All of which is an unpleasant reflection on the enormous age I seem to have acquired in four years," she cried. "They must have been singularly long years to you!"

"With the exception of the last one," said

The Making of a Prig

Paul, "they were much the same as any other years to me."

"Now, that's odd," she remarked; "because last year has seemed to go more quickly than any other year in my life. I wonder why it seemed so long to you?"

"It didn't," he replied promptly. "It was the other three that did that, because I spent them in learning wisdom."

"And the last one in forgetting it? How you must have wasted the other three! Ah, there are the girls at last," she added, springing to her feet. "That means déjeûner, and I am as hungry as two wolves. You will stop of course?"

"More developments," he murmured. "You used to scorn such mundane matters as meals, in the days when the poets were food enough for you. But please don't imagine for a moment that I am going to face that Anglo-French crowd out there; I would almost as soon listen to your opinion of Browning."

"Do you mean to say," she complained, "that you expect me to minister to your wants in here? What will Miss Smithson say, what will the dear children say in their weekly letters home? You don't really mean it?"

"On the contrary," he replied, placidly, "I

The Making of a Prig

am going to take you out to lunch in the most improper restaurant this improper city can produce. So go and put on that Parisian hat of yours, and be as quick as you like about it. I am rather hungry, too."

"You really seem to forget," she said, "that I am the respectable head of a high-class seminary for—"

"I only wish you would allow me to forget it," he interrupted. "It is just because you have been occupying yourself for a whole year, and with the most lamentable success, in growing elderly and respectable, that I intend to give you this opportunity of being regenerated. May I ask what you are waiting for, now?"

"I am waiting for some of the conventional dogma you used to preach to me in the days when *I* wanted to be improper," she retorted. "It would really save a great deal of trouble if our respective moral codes could be induced to coincide sometimes, would n't it?"

"It would save a great deal of trouble if you were to do as you are told, without talking quite so much about it. It is now half-past—"

"I tell you it is impossible," she protested. "You must have your déjeûner here, with unsophistication twenty-five strong — and Miss

The Making of a Prig

Smithson. What is the use of my having acquired a position of importance if I deliberately throw it away again by behaving like an improper schoolgirl?"

"What is the use of a position at all," replied Paul, "if it does n't enable you to be improper when you choose? Don't you think we might consider the argument at an end? I am quite willing to concede to Miss Smithson, or to any other person in authority, that you have made all the objections necessary to the foolish possessor of a conscience, if you will only go and tell her that you do not intend to be in to lunch."

"I have told her," said Katharine inadvertently, and then laughed frankly at her own admission. "I always spoil all my deceptions by being truthful again too soon," she added plaintively.

"Women alway spoil their vices by incompletion," observed Paul. "They have reduced virtue to an art, but there is a crudity about their vice that always gives them away sooner or later. That is why they are so easily found out; it is not because they are worse than men, but because they are better. They repent too soon, and your sins always find you out when you begin to repent."

The Making of a Prig

"That's perfectly true," said Katharine, half jestingly. "You would never have discovered that I was a prig if I had not become partly conscious of it first."

"That," said Paul deliberately, "is a personal application of my remarks which I should never have dreamed of making myself; but, since you are good enough to allow it, I must say that the way you have bungled the only vice you possess is quite singular. If you had been a man no one would have detected your priggishness at all; at its worst it would have been called personality. It is the same with everything. When a woman writes an improper book she funks the crisis, and gets called immoral for her pains; a man goes the whole hog, and we call it art."

"According to that," objected Katharine, "it is impossible to tell whether a man is good or bad. In fact, the better he appears to be the worse he must be in reality; because it only means that he is cleverer at concealing it."

"None of us are either good or bad," replied Paul. "It is all a question of brains. Goodness is only badness done well, and morality is mostly goodness done badly. I should

The Making of a Prig

like to know what I have said to make you smile?"

"It isn't what you have said," laughed Katharine; "it is the way you said it. There is something so familiar in the way you are inventing a whole new ethical system on the spur of the moment, and delivering it just as weightily as if you had been evolving it for a lifetime. Do go on; it has such an additional charm after one has had a holiday for more than a year!"

"When you have done being brilliant and realised the unimportance of being conscientious, perhaps you will kindly go and get ready," said Paul severely. And she laughed again at nothing in particular, and raised no further objection to following what was distinctly her inclination.

When they had had déjeûner and were strolling through the Palais Royal, he alluded for the first time to their parting at Ivingdon more than a year ago. She gave a little start and reddened.

"Oh, don't let us talk about that; I am so ashamed of myself whenever I think of it," she said hastily.

"I am sorry," he replied with composure, "because I particularly wish to talk about it

The Making of a Prig

just now. You must remember that, until I met Ted in town last week, I had no idea you were not married."

She turned and stared at him suddenly.

"I never thought of that," she said, slowly.

"Of course you did n't. In fact, all your proceedings immediately following that particular day in December seem to have been characterised by the same lack of reflection. You might have known that there was no one who could tell me of your erratic actions. And how was I to guess that you would go flying off to Paris just when everything was made easy for you to stop in England? I was naturally forced to conclude, as I neither saw nor heard from you again, that you had carried out your absurdly heroic purpose of marrying Ted. I must say, Katharine, you have a wonderful faculty for complicating matters."

"Nothing of the sort," she said indignantly. "And your memory is no better than mine, for you seem to forget that it was you who made our parting final. You were so tragic that of course I thought you meant it."

"Before we criticise my own action in the matter," said Paul, "I should rather like to know why you did come and bury yourself here, without telling anybody?"

The Making of a Prig

"Oh, it is easy for you to smile and be sarcastic! I had to come, of course; it was the only thing to be done. Nature had made me a prig, and everything was forcing me to continue to be a prig, and all my attempts at being anything else didn't come off. What chance is there for any one with priggish tendencies in a world like ours? It simply bristles with opportunities for behaving in a superior way, unless you resolutely make up your mind to skim over the surface of it and never to think deeply at all. What was I to do? Ted had gone abroad to escape from my overbearing superiority, and you had left in disgust because marrying for love wasn't good enough for me; and then I had Mrs. Downing's letter, and she persisted in thinking that I was the only person in the world who could manage the mothers of her fashionable pupils. It seemed as though I were destined to remain a superior person to the end of my days, and I wasn't going to fight against my natural tendencies any longer. I determined that if I had got to be a prig at all, I would at least make as good a prig as possible. Now do you understand why I came?"

"Before I attempt to do that, do you mind mentioning where you are going to take me?"

The Making of a Prig

said Paul casually. She looked round quickly and found that they had wandered down to the Seine and were close to the landing-stage of the boats that went to St. Cloud; and an importunate proprietor was representing to them in broken English the charms of a trip down the river.

"Oh, let us go!" she cried impulsively. "It would be so beautiful! Miss Smithson will never respect me again, but I don't feel as though I *could* go back to all those girls just yet. Oh, don't be so musty! It *won't* be chilly, and you are not a bit too old, and you have just got to come. Oh, don't I remember those moods of yours when everything was too youthful for you! I never knew any one with such a plastic age as yours."

He smiled perfunctorily, and gave in; and they were soon journeying down the Seine. Katharine was in a mood to appreciate everything, and she leaned over the side of the boat and made a running commentary on the beauty of the scene as they glided along between the banks. Paul tried two or three seats in succession, and finally chose one with an air of resignation and felt for his tobacco pouch.

"There is a smell of oil," he said. "And the chestnuts at Bushey are far finer."

The Making of a Prig

"Can't you lower your standard just for this one afternoon?" she suggested mockingly. "It would be so pleasant if you were to allow that Nature, for once, was almost good enough for you. I am so glad it is always good enough for me; it gives one's critical faculty such a rest."

"Or proves the non-existence of one," added Paul.

"It is surprising," she continued in the same tone, "how you always manage to spoil the light side of life by treating it seriously. Do you ever allow yourself a happy, irresponsible moment?"

"Perhaps I haven't seen as much of the light side as you have," he returned, quite unmoved. "And it is always easier to play our tragedy than our comedy; the *mise en scène* is better adapted to begin with. That is why the mediocre writer generally ends his book badly; he gets his effect much more easily than by ending it well."

"What has made you so cynical, I wonder?" she asked lazily.

"Principally, the happiness of the vulgar," returned Paul promptly. "It is not our own unhappiness that makes us cynical, but the badly done happiness of others. Quite an

The Making of a Prig

ordinary person may be able to bear misfortune more or less nobly, but it takes a dash of genius to be happy without being aggressive over it."

"I can't imagine your taking the trouble to be aggressive over anything," observed Katharine. "That is probably why you prefer to remain sombre, whether the occasion demands it or not. It is very prosaic to have to acknowledge that a man's most characteristic pose is merely due to his laziness. On the whole, I am rather glad I am quite an ordinary person; I would much sooner be happy, even if it does make me vulgar."

"Happiness is like wine," said Paul, without heeding her. "It demoralises you at the time, and it leaves you flat afterwards. The most difficult thing in life is to know how to take our happiness when it comes."

"It is more difficult," murmured Katharine, "to know how to do without it when it does n't come."

They landed at St. Cloud, and walked up through the little village and into the park where the ruins of the palace were. They had strayed away from their fellow passengers by this time, and the complete solitude of the place and its atmosphere of decay affected them

The Making of a Prig

both in the same way, and they gradually dropped into silence. He was the first to break the pause.

"Don't you think it is time we brought this farce to an end?" he asked with a carelessness of manner that was obviously assumed.

"Who is being farcical?" she returned just as lightly.

"You did that admirably, but it hasn't deceived me," said Paul serenely. "You know as well as I do that it is futile to go on any longer like this. We have tried it for a year, and I for one don't think very much of it. Your experiences have doubtless been happier than mine; but if you mean to tell me that they have taught you to prefer solitude to companionship, then you are as thorough a prig as you came over here to become. And that I don't believe for a moment, for at your worst you were always inconsistent, and inconsistency is the saving grace of the prig."

"I appreciate the honour of your approval," replied Katharine with exaggerated solemnity; "but, for all that, I still think that living with unsophistication in short petticoats is likely to be less tiring, on the whole, than living with some one for whom nothing in heaven or earth has yet been brought to perfection."

The Making of a Prig

She ended with a peal of laughter. Paul strolled on at the same measured pace as before.

"Besides," she added, "I thought we had both done with the matter a year ago. What is the use of dragging it up again?"

"I thought," added Paul, "that we had also done with taking ourselves seriously, a year ago. But you seem to wish the process to be renewed. Very well, then; let us begin at the beginning. The initial difficulty, if I remember rightly, was the fact that we were very much in love with each other."

"I know *I* was n't," said Katharine hotly. "I never hated any one so much in my life, and—"

"Which gets over the initial difficulty, does it not? Secondly then, you determined in the most unselfish manner possible that a wife would inevitably cripple what you were kind enough to call my career. I need hardly say how touched I felt by your charming consideration, but I should like to point out—"

"It is perfectly detestable of you to have come all this way on purpose to laugh at me," cried Katharine.

"I should like to point out," repeated Paul,

"that I feel quite capable of pursuing my career without any suggestions from my wife at all, and that, engrossing as her presence would undoubtedly prove—"

"It seems to me," interrupted Katharine, "that you don't want a wife at all; you only want an audience."

"I don't think," said Paul, smiling indulgently, "that we need quarrel about terms, need we? Well, as I was saying, my career would probably continue to take care of itself, even if there were two of us to be asked out to dinner, instead of one. And that disposes of the second obstacle, doesn't it? The third and last—"

"Last? There are millions of others!"

"The third and last," resumed Paul, "was, I think, the trifling fact that I had once presumed to call you a prig, in consequence of which you chose to pretend you were afraid of me. Wasn't that so?"

"Afraid of you? What a ridiculous idea!" she exclaimed. "Why, I was never afraid of you in my life!"

"Which disposes of the third and last difficulty," said Paul promptly.

Katharine stamped her foot and walked on in front of him.

The Making of a Prig

"You don't seem to think," she said, "that I might not *want* to marry you."

"Oh, no," said Paul; "I don't."

She said no more, but continued to walk a little way in front of him so that he could not see her face. She only spoke once again on their way down to the boat.

"How was Ted looking when you saw him?" she asked abruptly. "Perhaps you didn't notice, though?"

"Oh, yes," said Paul, blandly. "I've never seen him looking better; he seemed to have had a splendid time out there. He asked after you, by the way, and seemed rather surprised that I hadn't heard from you."

She made no comment, and they reached the boat in silence.

"You will come back to tea with me?" she said, as they stood waiting for it to start.

"With you,—or with unsophistication?"

"Oh, with me of course! Don't you think you have been funny enough for one afternoon?"

"Our best jokes are always our unconscious ones," murmured Paul. "Seriously, though, I think I won't bother you any more. I shall only be in the way if I stay any longer."

"Now what have I done," she demanded

The Making of a Prig

indignantly, "to make you think you are in the way?"

"Oh, of course — nothing. So foolish of me!" said Paul humbly. "I shall be delighted to return with you; there are still so many things we want to say to each other, are there not?"

However, they did not say them on the way home, for Katharine soon became thoughtful again, and he made no further attempt to draw her out but remained studiously at the other end of the boat until they landed; and after that, the noise of the cab in which they drove across Paris was sufficient excuse for refraining from anything like conversation. At the top of the stairs, as they stayed for a moment outside her *appartement* to recover their breath, she suddenly turned to him with one of her unaccountable smiles.

"Well?" he said.

"You know I did n't mean to be cross, don't you?" she asked him in a hurried undertone.

"You absurd little silly!" was all he said.

They sat for a long time over tea, and neither of them felt inclined to talk. But the silence was not embarrassing. And the early spring day drew to a close and the room grew dark with shadows; and still they sat there,

The Making of a Prig

and it did not occur to either of them to make conversation. At last, Katharine stirred in her seat at the end of the sofa and looked towards the dim outline of his figure against the window, and finished her reflections out loud.

"After all," she said thoughtfully, "the great thing is to be sane. Nothing else matters much if one can only be sane about things. There are heaps of reasons why you and I should not marry, if we were to begin hunting them up; but why bother about it? You know and I know that we have simply got to try the experiment, and chance the rest. One must risk something. And it can't be much worse than going on alone like this."

"No," said Paul, "it can't be worse than that."

He came and sat on the sofa, too, and there was silence once more. He put out his hand to find hers, and she gave it him and laughed softly.

"I have an idea," she said irrelevantly. "We must marry Ted to Marion."

"We?" said Paul, smiling. And she laughed again.

"Isn't it ridiculous," she said, "after all our views about marriage and so on,—to end

The Making of a Prig

in behaving just like any one else who never had any views at all?"

"Yes," agreed Paul. "We haven't even stuck to our priggishness.'

"*We?*" exclaimed Katharine.

But there is always a limit to a man's confessions, and Paul's was never finished.

BY THE SAME AUTHOR.

AT THE RELTON ARMS.

Miss Evelyn Sharp is to be congratulated on having, through the mouth of one of her characters, said one of the wisest words yet spoken on what is rather absurdly called "The Marriage Question" (page 132). It is an interesting and well-written story, with some smart characterisation and quite a sufficiency of humour. — *Daily Chronicle.*

A delightful story. The most genuine piece of humour in a book that is nowhere devoid of it, is that scene in the inn parlour where Digby finds himself engaged to two young women within five minutes; while the two brief colloquies of the landlady and her cronies make one suspect that the author could produce an admirable study of village humour. — *Athenæum.*

A distinctly clever book, of a fresh conventionality. — *Academy.*

WYMPS: FAIRY TALES.

With 8 coloured Illustrations and decorated cover by
Mabel Dearmer.

Of the stories it is impossible to speak too highly; they are true fairy literature, and the most exigent taste will be satisfied with them. — *Truth (London).*

A FLY-LEAF POEM.

(*To a little girl with a story-book, —*
"*Wymps*," *by* EVELYN SHARP).

Here, in this book, the wise may find
A world exactly to their mind.
From fairy kings to talking fish,
There's everything such people wish.

Sweeter little maid than you
Never read a story through.
Through a sweeter little book
Little maid shall never look.
    MR. WILLIAM WATSON
        in The Academy.

The simple brilliancy of the cover alone reveals something of the hidden delights of these charming new stories. — *Punch.*

Quite the most gorgeously coloured book of the season. In a red, green, and yellow cover that puts to the fade even a French poster, and with most marvellous pictures, excelling even the cover, the volume must take a literally blazing place on a child's book-shelf. "Wymps" has other attractions, — six, *original* fairy stories. Now, originality is a rare thing in fairy stories, so that altogether we find the book unique.
        Literary World (Boston).

List of Books
IN
BELLES LETTRES
Published by John Lane
The Bodley Head
VIGO STREET, LONDON, W.

Adams (Francis).
ESSAYS IN MODERNITY. Crown 8vo. 5s. net. [*Shortly.*
A CHILD OF THE AGE. Crown 8vo. 3s. 6d. net.

A. E.
HOMEWARD: SONGS BY THE WAY. Sq. 16mo, wrappers, 1s. 6d. net. [*Second Edition.*
THE EARTH BREATH, AND OTHER POEMS. Sq. 16mo. 3s. 6d. net.

Aldrich (T. B.).
LATER LYRICS. Sm. fcap. 8vo. 2s. 6d. net.

Allen (Grant).
THE LOWER SLOPES: A Volume of Verse. Crown 8vo. 5s. net.
THE WOMAN WHO DID. Crown 8vo. 3s. 6d. net. [*Twenty-third Edition.*
THE BRITISH BARBARIANS. Crown 8vo. 3s. 6d. net. [*Second Edition.*

Atherton (Gertrude).
PATIENCE SPARHAWK AND HER TIMES. Crown 8vo. 6s. [*Third Edition.*

Bailey (John C.).
ENGLISH ELEGIES. Crown 8vo. 5s. net. [*In preparation.*

Balfour (Marie Clothilde).
MARIS STELLA. Crown 8vo. 3s. 6d. net.

Beeching (Rev. H. C.).
IN A GARDEN: Poems. Crown 8vo. 5s. net.
ST. AUGUSTINE AT OSTIA. Crown 8vo, wrappers. 1s. net.

Beerbohm (Max).
THE WORKS OF MAX BEERBOHM. With a Bibliography by JOHN LANE. Sq. 16mo. 4s. 6d. net.
THE HAPPY HYPOCRITE. Sq. 16mo. 1s. net.

Bennett (E. A.).
A MAN FROM THE NORTH. Crown 8vo. 3s. 6d. [*In preparation.*

Benson (Arthur Christopher).
LYRICS. Fcap. 8vo, buckram. 5s. net.
LORD VYET AND OTHER POEMS. Fcap. 8vo. 3s. 6d. net.

Bridges (Robert).
SUPPRESSED CHAPTERS AND OTHER BOOKISHNESS. Crown 8vo. 3s. 6d. net. [*Second Edition.*

Brotherton (Mary).
ROSEMARY FOR REMEMBRANCE. Fcap. 8vo. 3s. 6d. net.

Brown (Vincent)
MY BROTHER. Sq. 16mo. 2s. net.
ORDEAL BY COMPASSION. Crown 8vo. 6s. [*In preparation.*
TWO IN CAPTIVITY. Crown 8vo. 3s. 6d. [*In preparation.*

THE PUBLICATIONS OF

Buchan (John).
SCHOLAR GIPSIES. With 7 full-page Etchings by D. Y. CAMERON. Crown 8vo. 5s. net.
MUSA PISCATRIX. With 6 Etchings by E. PHILIP PIMLOTT. Crown 8vo. 5s. net.
GREY WEATHER. Crown 8vo. 5s. [*In preparation*.
JOHN BURNET OF BARNS. A Romance. Crown 8vo. 6s. [*In preparation*.

Campbell (Gerald).
THE JONESES AND THE ASTERISKS. A Story in Monologue. 6 Illustrations by F. H. TOWNSEND. Fcap. 8vo, 3s. 6d. net. [*Second Edition*.

Case (Robert H.).
ENGLISH EPITHALAMIES. Crown 8vo, 5s. net.

Castle (Mrs. Egerton).
MY LITTLE LADY ANNE. Sq. 16mo, 2s. net.

Chapman (Elizabeth Rachel)
MARRIAGE QUESTIONS IN MODERN FICTION. Crown 8vo, 3s. 6d. net.

Charles (Joseph F.).
THE DUKE OF LINDEN. Crown 8vo, 5s. [*In preparation*.

Cobb (Thomas).
CARPET COURTSHIP. Crown 8vo, 3s. 6d. [*In preparation*.
MR. PASSINGHAM. Crown 8vo, 3s. 6d. [*In preparation*.

Crane (Walter).
TOY BOOKS. Re-issue of. 2s.
THIS LITTLE PIG'S PICTURE BOOK, containing:
  I. THIS LITTLE PIG.
  II. THE FAIRY SHIP.
  III. KING LUCKIEBOY'S PARTY.
MOTHER HUBBARD'S PICTURE-BOOK, containing:
  IV. MOTHER HUBBARD.
  V. THE THREE BEARS.
  VI. THE ABSURD A. B. C.

Crane (Walter)—*continued.*
CINDERELLA'S PICTURE BOOK, containing:
  VII. CINDERELLA.
  VIII. PUSS IN BOOTS.
  IX. VALENTINE AND ORSON.
Each Picture-Book containing three Toy Books, complete with end papers and covers, together with collective titles, end-papers, decorative cloth cover, and newly written Preface by WALTER CRANE, 4s. 6d. The Nine Parts as above may be had separately at 1s. each.

Crackanthorpe (Hubert).
VIGNETTES. A Miniature Journal of Whim and Sentiment. Fcap. 8vo, boards. 2s. 6d. net.

Craig (R. Manifold).
THE SACRIFICE OF FOOLS. Crown 8vo, 6s.

Crosse (Victoria).
THE WOMAN WHO DIDN'T. Crown 8vo, 3s. 6d. net. [*Third Edition*.

Custance (Olive).
OPALS: Poems. Fcap. 8vo. 3s. 6d. net.

Croskey (Julian).
MAX. Crown 8vo. 6s.

Dalmon (C. W.).
SONG FAVOURS. Sq. 16mo. 3s. 6d. net.

D'Arcy (Ella).
MONOCHROMES. Crown 8vo. 3s. 6d. net.
POOR HUMAN NATURE. Crown 8vo. 3s. 6d. [*In preparation*.

Dawe (W. Carlton).
YELLOW AND WHITE. Crown 8vo. 3s. 6d. net.
KAKEMONOS. Crown 8vo. 3s. 6d. net.

Dawson (A. J.)
MERE SENTIMENT. Crown 8vo. 3s. 6d. net.
MIDDLE GREYNESS. Crown 8vo. 6s.

Davidson (John).
PLAYS: An Unhistorical Pastoral; A Romantic Farce; Bruce, a Chronicle Play; Smith, a Tragic Farce; Scaramouch in Naxos, a Pantomime. Small 4to. 7s. 6d. net.

Davidson (John)—*continued.*
FLEET STREET ECLOGUES. Fcap. 8vo, buckram. 4s. 6d. net.
[*Third Edition.*
FLEET STREET ECLOGUES. 2nd Series. Fcap. 8vo, buckram. 4s. 6d. net. [*Second Edition.*
A RANDOM ITINERARY. Fcap. 8vo, 5s. net.
BALLADS AND SONGS. Fcap. 8vo, 5s. net. [*Fourth Edition.*
NEW BALLADS. Fcap. 8vo, 4s. 6d. net. [*Second Edition.*

De Lyrienne (Richard).
THE QUEST OF THE GILT-EDGED GIRL. Sq. 16mo. 1s. net.

De Tabley (Lord).
POEMS, DRAMATIC AND LYRICAL. By JOHN LEICESTER WARREN (Lord de Tabley). Five Illustrations and Cover by C. S. RICKETTS. Crown 8vo. 7s. 6d. net. [*Third Edition.*
POEMS, DRAMATIC AND LYRICAL. Second Series. Crown 8vo. 5s. net.

Devereux (Roy).
THE ASCENT OF WOMAN. Crown 8vo. 3s. 6d. net.

Dick (Chas. Hill).
ENGLISH SATIRES. Crown 8vo. 5s. net. [*In preparation.*

Dix (Gertrude).
THE GIRL FROM THE FARM. Crown 8vo. 3s. 6d. net.
[*Second Edition.*

Dostoievsky (F.).
POOR FOLK. Translated from the Russian by LENA MILMAN. With a Preface by GEORGE MOORE. Crown 8vo. 3s. 6d. net.

Dowie (Menie Muriel).
SOME WHIMS OF FATE. Post 8vo. 2s. 6d. net.

Duer (Caroline, and Alice).
POEMS. Fcap. 8vo. 3s. 6d. net.

Egerton (George)
KEYNOTES. Crown 8vo. 3s. 6d. net.
[*Eighth Edition.*
DISCORDS. Crown 8vo. 3s. 6d. net.
[*Fifth Edition.*
SYMPHONIES. Crown 8vo. 6s.
[*Second Edition.*
FANTASIAS. Crown 8vo. 3s. 6d.
THE HAZARD OF THE HILL. Crown 8vo. 6s. [*In preparation.*

Eglinton (John).
TWO ESSAYS ON THE REMNANT. Post 8vo, wrappers. 1s. 6d. net.
[*Second Edition.*

Farr (Florence).
THE DANCING FAUN. Crown 8vo. 3s. 6d. net.

Fea (Allan).
THE FLIGHT OF THE KING: A full, true, and particular account of the escape of His Most Sacred Majesty King Charles II. after the Battle of Worcester, with Sixteen Portraits in Photogravure and over 100 other Illustrations. Demy 8vo. 21s. net.

Field (Eugene).
THE LOVE AFFAIRS OF A BIBLIOMANIAC. Post 8vo. 3s. 6d. net.
LULLABY LAND: Poems for Children. Edited, with Introduction, by KENNETH GRAHAME. With 200 Illustrations by CHAS. ROBINSON. Uncut or gilt edges. Crown 8vo. 6s.

Fifth (George).
THE MARTYR'S BIBLE. Crown 8vo. 6s. [*In preparation.*

Fleming (George).
FOR PLAIN WOMEN ONLY. Fcap. 8vo. 3s. 6d. net.

Flowerdew (Herbert).
A CELIBATE'S WIFE. Crown 8vo. 6s. [*In preparation.*

Fletcher (J. S.).
THE WONDERFUL WAPENTAKE. By "A SON OF THE SOIL." With 18 Full-page Illustrations by J. A. SYMINGTON. Crown 8vo. 5s. 6d. net.
LIFE IN ARCADIA. With 20 Illustrations by PATTEN WILSON. Crown 8vo. 5s. net.
GOD'S FAILURES. Crown 8vo. 3s. 6d. net.
BALLADS OF REVOLT. Sq. 32mo. 2s. 6d. net.
THE MAKING OF MATTHIAS. With 40 Illustrations and Decorations by LUCY KEMP-WELCH. Crown 8vo. 6s.

Ford, (James L.).
THE LITERARY SHOP, AND OTHER TALES. Fcap. 8vo. 3s. 6d. net.

Frederic (Harold).
MARCH HARES. Crown 8vo. 3s. 6d. net. [*Third Edition.*
MRS. ALBERT GRUNDY: OBSERVATIONS IN PHILISTIA. Fcap. 8vo. 3s. 6d. net. [*Second Edition.*

Fuller (H. B.).
THE PUPPET BOOTH. Twelve Plays. Crown 8vo. 4s. 6d. net.

Gale (Norman).
ORCHARD SONGS. Fcap. 8vo. 5s. net.

Garnett (Richard).
POEMS. Crown 8vo. 5s. net.
DANTE, PETRARCH, CAMOENS, cxxiv Sonnets, rendered in English. Crown 8vo. 5s. net.

Geary (Sir Nevill).
A LAWYER'S WIFE. Crown 8vo. 6s. [*Second Edition.*

Gibson (Charles Dana).
DRAWINGS: Eighty-Five Large Cartoons. Oblong Folio. 20s.
PICTURES OF PEOPLE. Eighty-Five Large Cartoons. Oblong folio. 20s.
LONDON: AS SEEN BY C. D. GIBSON. Text and Illustrations. Large folio, 12 × 18 inches. 20s.
[*In preparation.*
THE PEOPLE OF DICKENS. Six Large Photogravures. Proof Impressions from Plates, in a Portfolio. 20s.

Gilliat-Smith (E.).
THE HYMNS OF PRUDENTIUS. In the Rhythm of the Original. Pott 4to. 5s. net.

Gleig (Charles)
WHEN ALL MEN STARVE. Crown 8vo. 3s. 6d.
THE EDGE OF HONESTY. Crown 8vo. 6s. [*In preparation.*

Gosse (Edmund).
THE LETTERS OF THOMAS LOVELL BEDDOES. Now first edited. Pott 8vo. 5s. net.

Grahame (Kenneth).
PAGAN PAPERS. Fcap. 8vo. 5s. net.
[*Out of Print at present.*
THE GOLDEN AGE. Crown 8vo. 3s. 6d. net. [*Seventh Edition.*
See EUGENE FIELD'S LULLABY LAND.

Greene (G. A.).
ITALIAN LYRISTS OF TO-DAY. Translations in the original metres from about thirty-five living Italian poets, with bibliographical and biographical notes. Crown 8vo. 5s. net.

Greenwood (Frederick).
IMAGINATION IN DREAMS. Crown 8vo. 5s. net.

Grimshaw (Beatrice Ethel).
BROKEN AWAY. Crown 8vo. 3s. 6d. net.

Hake (T. Gordon).
A SELECTION FROM HIS POEMS. Edited by Mrs. MEYNELL. With a Portrait after D. G. ROSSETTI. Crown 8vo. 5s. net.

Hansson (Laura M.).
MODERN WOMEN. An English rendering of "DAS BUCH DER FRAUEN" by HERMIONE RAMSDEN. Subjects: Sonia Kovalevsky, George Egerton, Eleanora Duse, Amalie Skram, Marie Bashkirtseff, A. Ch. Edgren Leffler. Crown 8vo. 3s. 6d. net.

Hansson (Ola).
YOUNG OFEG'S DITTIES. A Translation from the Swedish. By GEORGE EGERTON. Crown 8vo. 3s. 6d. net.

Harland (Henry).
GREY ROSES. Crown 8vo, 3s. 6d. net.

Hay (Colonel John).
POEMS INCLUDING "THE PIKE COUNTY BALLADS" (Author's Edition), with Portrait of the Author. Crown 8vo. 4s. 6d. net.
CASTILIAN DAYS. Crown 8vo. 4s. 6d. net.
SPEECH AT THE UNVEILING OF THE BUST OF SIR WALTER SCOTT IN WESTMINSTER ABBEY. With a Drawing of the Bust. Sq. 16mo. 1s. net.

Hayes (Alfred).
THE VALE OF ARDEN AND OTHER POEMS. Fcap. 8vo. 3s. 6d. net.

Hazlitt (William).
LIBER AMORIS; OR, THE NEW PYGMALION. Edited, with an Introduction, by RICHARD LE GALLIENNE. To which is added an exact transcript of the original MS., Mrs. Hazlitt's Diary in Scotland, and letters never before published. Portrait after BEWICK, and facsimile letters. 400 Copies only. 4to, 364 pp., buckram. 21s. net.

Heinemann (William).
THE FIRST STEP; A Dramatic Moment. Small 4to. 3s. 6d. net.

Henniker (Florence).
IN SCARLET AND GREY. (With THE SPECTRE OF THE REAL by FLORENCE HENNIKER and THOMAS HARDY.) Crown 8vo. 3s. 6d. net. [Second Edition.

Hickson (Mrs. Murray).
SHADOWS OF LIFE. Post 8vo. 3s. 6d. [In preparation.

Hopper (Nora).
BALLADS IN PROSE. Sm. 4to. 6s.
UNDER QUICKEN BOUGHS. Crown 8vo. 5s. net.

Housman (Clemence).
THE WERE WOLF. With 6 Illustrations by LAURENCE HOUSMAN. Sq. 16mo. 3s. 6d. net.

Housman (Laurence).
GREEN ARRAS: Poems. With 6 Illustrations, Title-page, Cover Design, and End Papers by the Author. Crown 8vo. 5s. net.
GODS AND THEIR MAKERS. Crown 8vo, 3s. 6d. net.

Irving (Laurence).
GODEFROI AND YOLANDE: A Play. Sm. 4to. 3s. 6d. net.
[In preparation.

Jalland (G. H.)
THE SPORTING ADVENTURES OF MR. POPPLE. Coloured Plates. Oblong 4to, 14 × 10 inches. 6s.
[In preparation.

James (W. P.)
ROMANTIC PROFESSIONS: A Volume of Essays. Crown 8vo. 5s. net.

Johnson (Lionel).
THE ART OF THOMAS HARDY: Six Essays. With Etched Portrait by WM. STRANG, and Bibliography by JOHN LANE. Crown 8vo. 5s. 6d. net. [Second Edition.

Johnson (Pauline).
WHITE WAMPUM: Poems. Crown 8vo. 5s. net.

Johnstone (C. E.).
BALLADS OF BOY AND BEAK. Sq. 32mo. 2s. net.

Kemble (E. W.)
KEMBLE'S COONS. 30 Drawings of Coloured Children and Southern Scenes. Oblong 4to. 6s.

King (K. Douglas).
THE CHILD WHO WILL NEVER GROW OLD. Crown 8vo. 5s.

King (Maud Egerton).
ROUND ABOUT A BRIGHTON COACH OFFICE. With over 30 Illustrations by LUCY KEMP-WELCH. Crown 8vo. 5s. net.

Lander (Harry).
WEIGHED IN THE BALANCE. Crown 8vo. 6s.

The Lark.
BOOK THE FIRST. Containing Nos. 1 to 12. With numerous Illustrations by GELETT BURGESS and Others. Small 4to. 6s.
BOOK THE SECOND. Containing Nos. 13 to 24. With numerous Illustrations by GELETT BURGESS and Others. Small 4to. 6s.
[All published.

Leather (R. K.).
VERSES. 250 copies. Fcap. 8vo. 3s. net.

Lefroy (Edward Cracroft.)
POEMS. With a Memoir by W. A. GILL, and a reprint of Mr. J. A. SYMONDS' Critical Essay on "Echoes from Theocritus." Cr. 8vo. Photogravure Portrait. 5s. net.

Le Gallienne (Richard).
PROSE FANCIES. With Portrait of the Author by WILSON STEER. Crown 8vo. 5s. net.
[Fourth Edition.
THE BOOK BILLS OF NARCISSUS. An Account rendered by RICHARD LE GALLIENNE. With a Frontispiece. Crown 8vo. 3s. 6d. net.
[Third Edition.
ROBERT LOUIS STEVENSON, AN ELEGY, AND OTHER POEMS, MAINLY PERSONAL. Crown 8vo. 4s. 6d. net.

Le Gallienne (Richard)—continued.

ENGLISH POEMS. Crown 8vo. 4s. 6d. net.
[*Fourth Edition, revised.*
GEORGE MEREDITH: Some Characteristics. With a Bibliography (much enlarged) by JOHN LANE, portrait, &c. Crown 8vo. 5s. 6d. net. [*Fourth Edition.*
THE RELIGION OF A LITERARY MAN. Crown 8vo. 3s. 6d. net.
[*Fifth Thousand.*
RETROSPECTIVE REVIEWS, A LITERARY LOG, 1891-1895. 2 vols. Crown 8vo. 9s. net.
PROSE FANCIES. (Second Series). Crown 8vo. 5s. net.
THE QUEST OF THE GOLDEN GIRL. Crown 8vo. 6s. [*Fifth Edition.*
LOVE IN LONDON: Poems. Crown 8vo. 4s. 6d. net. [*In preparation.*
See also HAZLITT, WALTON and COTTON.

Legge (A. E. J.).
THREADBARE SOULS. Crown 8vo. 6s. [*In preparation.*

Linden (Annie).
GOLD. A Dutch Indian story. Crown 8vo. 3s. 6d. net.

Lipsett (Caldwell).
WHERE THE ATLANTIC MEETS THE LAND. Crown 8vo. 3s. 6d. net.

Locke (W. J.).
DERELICTS. Crown 8vo. 6s.

Lowry (H. D.).
MAKE BELIEVE. Illustrated by CHARLES ROBINSON. Crown 8vo, gilt edges or uncut. 6s.
WOMEN'S TRAGEDIES. Crown 8vo. 3s. 6d. net.
THE HAPPY EXILE. With 6 Etchings by E. PHILIP PIMLOTT. (Arcady Library, Vol. V.) Crown 8vo. 6s.

Lucas (Winifred).
UNITS: Poems. Fcap. 8vo. 3s. 6d. net.

Lynch (Hannah).
THE GREAT GALEOTO AND FOLLY OR SAINTLINESS. Two Plays, from the Spanish of JOSÉ ECHEGARAY, with an Introduction. Small 4to. 5s. 6d. net.

McChesney (Dora Greenwell).
BEATRIX INFELIX. A Summer Tragedy in Rome. Crown 8vo. 3s. 6d. [*In preparation.*

Macgregor (Barrington).
KING LONGBEARD. With nearly 100 Illustrations by CHARLES ROBINSON. Small 4to. 6s.

Machen (Arthur).
THE GREAT GOD PAN AND THE INMOST LIGHT. Crown 8vo. 3s. 6d. net. [*Second Edition.*
THE THREE IMPOSTORS. Crown 8vo. 3s. 6d. net.

Macleod (Fiona).
THE MOUNTAIN LOVERS. Crown 8vo. 3s. 6d. net.

Makower (Stanley V.).
THE MIRROR OF MUSIC. Crown 8vo. 3s. 6d. net.
CECILIA. Crown 8vo. 5s.

Mangan (James Clarence).
SELECTED POEMS. With a Biographical and Critical Preface by LOUISE IMOGEN GUINEY. Crown 8vo. 5s. net.

Mathew (Frank).
THE WOOD OF THE BRAMBLES. Crown 8vo. 6s.
A CHILD IN THE TEMPLE. Crown 8vo. 3s. 6d.
THE SPANISH WINE. Crown 8vo. 3s. 6d. [*In preparation.*
AT THE RISING OF THE MOON. Crown 8vo. 3s. 6d.

Marzials (Theo.).
THE GALLERY OF PIGEONS AND OTHER POEMS. Post 8vo. 4s. 6d. net.

Meredith (George).
THE FIRST PUBLISHED PORTRAIT OF THIS AUTHOR, engraved on the wood by W. BISCOMBE GARDNER, after the painting by G. F. WATTS. Proof copies on Japanese vellum, signed by painter and engraver. £1 1s. net.

Meynell (Mrs.).
POEMS. Fcap. 8vo. 3s. 6d. net.
[*Fifth Edition.*
THE RHYTHM OF LIFE AND OTHER ESSAYS. Fcap. 8vo. 3s. 6d. net.
[*Fifth Edition.*

Meynell (Mrs.)—*continued.*
THE COLOUR OF LIFE AND OTHER ESSAYS. Fcap. 8vo. 3s. 6d. net. [*Fifth Edition.*
THE CHILDREN. Fcap. 8vo. 3s. 6d. net. [*Second Edition.*

Miller (Joaquin).
THE BUILDING OF THE CITY BEAUTIFUL. Fcap. 8vo. With a Decorated Cover. 5s. net.

Milman (Helen).
IN THE GARDEN OF PEACE. With 24 Illustrations by EDMUND H. NEW. Crown 8vo. 5s. net.

Money-Coutts (F. B.).
POEMS. Crown 8vo. 3s. 6d. net.

Monkhouse (Allan).
BOOKS AND PLAYS: A Volume of Essays on Meredith, Borrow, Ibsen, and others. Crown 8vo. 5s. net.
A DELIVERANCE. Crown 8vo. 5s. [*In preparation.*

Nesbit (E.).
A POMANDER OF VERSE. Crown 8vo. 5s. net.
IN HOMESPUN. Crown 8vo. 3s. 6d. net.

Nettleship (J. T.).
ROBERT BROWNING: Essays and Thoughts. Portrait. Crown 8vo. 5s. 6d. net. [*Third Edition.*

Nicholson (Claud).
UGLY IDOL. Crown 8vo. 3s. 6d. net.

Noble (Jas. Ashcroft).
THE SONNET IN ENGLAND AND OTHER ESSAYS. Crown 8vo. 5s. net.

Oppenheim (M.).
A HISTORY OF THE ADMINISTRATION OF THE ROYAL NAVY, and of Merchant Shipping in relation to the Navy from MDIX to MDCLX, with an introduction treating of the earlier period. With Illustrations. Demy 8vo. 15s. net.

Orred (Meta).
GLAMOUR. Crown 8vo. 6s.

O'Shaughnessy (Arthur).
HIS LIFE AND HIS WORK. With Selections from his Poems. By LOUISE CHANDLER MOULTON. Portrait and Cover Design. Fcap. 8vo. 5s. net.

Oxford Characters.
A series of lithographed portraits by WILL ROTHENSTEIN, with text by F. YORK POWELL and others. 200 copies only, folio. £3 3s. net.

Pennell (Elizabeth Robins).
THE FEASTS OF AUTOLYCUS: THE DIARY OF A GREEDY WOMAN. Fcap. 8vo. 3s. 6d. net.

Peters (Wm. Theodore).
POSIES OUT OF RINGS. Sq. 16mo. 2s. 6d. net.

Phillips (Stephen)
THE WOMAN WITH A DEAD SOUL, AND OTHER POEMS. Crown 8vo. 4s. 6d. net.

Plarr (Victor).
IN THE DORIAN MOOD: Poems. Crown 8vo. 5s. net.

Posters in Miniature: over 250 reproductions of French, English and American Posters with Introduction by EDWARD PENFIELD. Large crown 8vo. 5s. net.

Price (A. T. G.).
SIMPLICITY. Sq. 16mo. 2s. net.

Radford (Dollie).
SONGS AND OTHER VERSES. Fcap. 8vo. 4s. 6d. net.

Risley (R. V.).
THE SENTIMENTAL VIKINGS. Post 8vo. 2s. 6d. net.

Rhys (Ernest).
A LONDON ROSE AND OTHER RHYMES. Crown 8vo. 5s. net.

Robertson (John M.).
NEW ESSAYS TOWARDS A CRITICAL METHOD. Crown 8vo. 6s. net.

St. Cyres (Lord).
THE LITTLE FLOWERS OF ST. FRANCIS: A new rendering into English of the Fioretti di San Francesco. Crown 8vo. 5s. net. [*In preparation.*

Seaman (Owen).
THE BATTLE OF THE BAYS. Fcap. 8vo. 3s. 6d. net. [*Third Edition.*
HORACE AT CAMBRIDGE. Crown 8vo. 3s. 6d. net.

Sedgwick (Jane Minot).
SONGS FROM THE GREEK. Fcap. 8vo. 3s. 6d. net.

Setoun (Gabriel).
THE CHILD WORLD: Poems. With over 200 Illustrations by CHARLES ROBINSON. Crown 8vo, gilt edges or uncut. 6s.

Sharp (Evelyn).
WYMPS: Fairy Tales. With Coloured Illustrations by Mrs. PERCY DEARMER. Small 4to, decorated cover. 6s.
AT THE RELTON ARMS. Crown 8vo. 3s. 6d. net.
THE MAKING OF A PRIG. Crown 8vo. 6s.
ALL THE WAY TO FAIRY LAND. With Coloured Illustrations by Mrs. PERCY DEARMER. Small 4to, decorated cover. 6s.

Shiel (M. P.).
PRINCE ZALESKI. Crown 8vo. 3s. 6d. net.
SHAPES IN THE FIRE. Crown 8vo. 3s. 6d. net.

Shore (Louisa).
POEMS. With an appreciation by FREDERIC HARRISON and a Portrait. Fcap. 8vo. 5s. net.

Shorter (Mrs. Clement) (Dora Sigerson).
THE FAIRY CHANGELING, AND OTHER POEMS. Crown 8vo. 3s. 6d. net.

Smith (John).
PLATONIC AFFECTIONS. Crown 8vo. 3s. 6d. net.

Stacpoole (H. de Vere).
PIERROT. Sq. 16to. 2s. net.
DEATH, THE KNIGHT, AND THE LADY. Crown 8vo. 3s. 6d.

Stevenson (Robert Louis).
PRINCE OTTO. A Rendering in French by EGERTON CASTLE. Crown 8vo. 7s. 6d. net.
A CHILD'S GARDEN OF VERSES. With over 150 Illustrations by CHARLES ROBINSON. Crown 8vo. 5s. net. [*Third Edition.*

Stimson (F. J.)
KING NOANETT. A Romance of Devonshire Settlers in New England. With 12 Illustrations by HENRY SANDHAM. Crown 8vo. 6s.

Stoddart (Thos. Tod).
THE DEATH WAKE. With an Introduction by ANDREW LANG. Fcap. 8vo. 5s. net.

Street (G. S.).
EPISODES. Post 8vo. 3s. net.
MINIATURES AND MOODS. Fcap. 8vo. 3s. net.
QUALES EGO: A FEW REMARKS, IN PARTICULAR AND AT LARGE. Fcap. 8vo. 3s. 6d. net.
THE AUTOBIOGRAPHY OF A BOY. Fcap. 8vo. 3s. 6d. net.
THE WISE AND THE WAYWARD. Crown 8vo. 6s.

Sudermann (H.).
THE SINS OF THE FATHERS. A Translation of DER KATZENSTEG. By BEATRICE MARSHALL. Crown 8vo. 6s. [*In preparation.*

Swettenham (Sir F. A.).
MALAY SKETCHES. Crown 8vo. 5s. net. [*Second Edition.*

Syrett (Netta).
NOBODY'S FAULT. Crown 8vo. 3s. 6d. net. [*Second Edition.*
THE TREE OF LIFE. Crown 8vo. 6s.

Tabb (John B.).
POEMS. Sq. 32mo. 4s. 6d. net.
LYRICS. Sq. 32mo. 4s. 6d. net.

Taylor (Una),
NETS FOR THE WIND. Crown 8vo. 3s. 6d. net.

Tennyson (Frederick).
POEMS OF THE DAY AND YEAR. Crown 8vo. 5s. net.

Thimm (Carl A.).

A COMPLETE BIBLIOGRAPHY OF FENCING AND DUELLING, AS PRACTISED BY ALL EUROPEAN NATIONS FROM THE MIDDLE AGES TO THE PRESENT DAY. With a Classified Index, arranged Chronologically according to Languages. Illustrated with numerous Portraits of Ancient and Modern Masters of the Art. Title-pages and Frontispieces of some of the earliest works. Portrait of the Author by WILSON STEER. 4to. 21s. net.

Thompson (Francis)

POEMS. With Frontispiece by LAURENCE HOUSMAN. Pott 4to. 5s. net. [*Fourth Edition.*

SISTER-SONGS: An Offering to Two Sisters. With Frontispiece by LAURENCE HOUSMAN. Pott 4to. 5s. net.

Thoreau (Henry David).

POEMS OF NATURE. Selected and edited by HENRY S. SALT and FRANK B. SANBORN. Fcap. 8vo. 4s. 6d. net.

Traill (H. D.).

THE BARBAROUS BRITISHERS: A Tip-top Novel. Crown 8vo, wrapper. 1s. net.

FROM CAIRO TO THE SOUDAN FRONTIER. Crown 8vo. 5s. net.

Tynan Hinkson (Katharine).

CUCKOO SONGS. Fcap. 8vo. 5s. net.

MIRACLE PLAYS. OUR LORD'S COMING AND CHILDHOOD. With 6 Illustrations by PATTEN WILSON. Fcap. 8vo. 4s. 6d. net.

Wells (H. G.)

SELECT CONVERSATIONS WITH AN UNCLE, NOW EXTINCT. Fcap. 8vo. 3s. 6d. net.

Walton and Cotton.

THE COMPLEAT ANGLER. Edited by RICHARD LE GALLIENNE. With over 250 Illustrations by EDMUND H. NEW. Fcap. 4to, decorated cover. 15s. net.
Also to be had in thirteen 1s. parts.

Warden (Gertrude).

THE SENTIMENTAL SEX. Crown 8vo. 3s. 6d. net.

Watson (H. B. Marriott).

AT THE FIRST CORNER AND OTHER STORIES. Crown 8vo. 3s. 6d. net.

GALLOPING DICK. Crown 8vo. 6s.

THE HEART OF MIRANDA. Crown 8vo. 5s.

Watson (Rosamund Marriott).

VESPERTILIA AND OTHER POEMS. Fcap. 8vo. 4s. 6d. net.

A SUMMER NIGHT AND OTHER POEMS. New Edition. Fcap. 8vo. 3s. net.

Watson (William).

THE FATHER OF THE FOREST AND OTHER POEMS. With New Photogravure Portrait of the Author. Fcap. 8vo. 3s. 6d. net.
[*Fifth Edition.*

ODES AND OTHER POEMS. Fcap. 8vo. 4s. 6d. net.
[*Fourth Edition.*

THE ELOPING ANGELS: A Caprice. Square 16mo. 3s. 6d. net.
[*Second Edition.*

EXCURSIONS IN CRITICISM: being some Prose Recreations of a Rhymer. Crown 8vo. 5s. net.
[*Second Edition.*

THE PRINCE'S QUEST AND OTHER POEMS. Fcap. 8vo. 4s. 6d. net.
[*Third Edition.*

THE PURPLE EAST: A Series of Sonnets on England's Desertion of Armenia. With a Frontispiece after G. F. WATTS, R.A. Fcap. 8vo, wrappers. 1s. net.
[*Third Edition.*

Watson (William)—*cont.*
  THE YEAR OF SHAME. With an Introduction by the BISHOP OF HEREFORD. Fcap. 8vo. 2s. 6d. net. [*Second Edition.*
  POEMS. A New Volume. Ready for Christmas. Fcap. 8vo. 4s. 6d. net.
  A Large Paper Edition at 12s. 6d. net.

Watt (Francis).
  THE LAW'S LUMBER ROOM. Fcap. 8vo. 3s. 6d. net. [*Second Edition.*
  FATHER ANTIC, THE LAW. Crown 8vo. 5s. net. [*In preparation.*

Watts-Dunton (Theodore).
  JUBILEE GREETING AT SPITHEAD TO THE MEN OF GREATER BRITAIN. Crown 8vo. 1s. net.
  THE COMING OF LOVE AND OTHER POEMS. Crown 8vo. 5s. net.

Wenzell (A. B.)
  IN VANITY FAIR. 70 Drawings. Oblong folio. 20s.

Wharton (H. T.)
  SAPPHO. Memoir, Text, Selected Renderings, and a Literal Translation by HENRY THORNTON WHARTON. With 3 Illustrations in Photogravure, and a Cover designed by AUBREY BEARDSLEY. With a Memoir of Mr. Wharton. Fcap. 8vo. 6s. net. [*Fourth Edition.*

Wotton (Mabel E.).
  DAY BOOKS. Crown 8vo. 3s. 6d. net.

Xenopoulos (Gregory).
  THE STEPMOTHER: A TALE OF MODERN ATHENS. Translated by MRS. EDMONDS. Crown 8vo. 2s. 6d. net.

THE YELLOW BOOK

An Illustrated Quarterly.

Pott 4to. 5s. net.

I. April 1894, 272 pp., 15 Illustrations. [*Out of print.*
II. July 1894, 364 pp., 23 Illustrations.
III. October 1894, 280 pp., 15 Illustrations.
IV. January 1895, 285 pp., 16 Illustrations.
V. April 1895, 317 pp., 14 Illustrations.
VI. July 1895, 335 pp., 16 Illustrations.
VII. October 1895, 320 pp., 20 Illustrations.
VIII. January 1896, 406 pp., 26 Illustrations.
IX. April 1896, 256 pp., 17 Illustrations.
X. July 1896, 340 pp., 13 Illustrations.
XI. October 1896, 342 pp., 12 Illustrations.
XII. January 1897, 350 pp., 14 Illustrations.
XIII. April 1897, 316 pp., 18 Illustrations.

BALLANTYNE PRESS

www.ingramcontent.com/pod-product-compliance
Lightning Source LLC
Chambersburg PA
CBHW030543300426
44111CB00009B/842